THE PHILOSOPHY OF JÑĀNADEVA

THE PHILOSOPHY

OF

JÑĀNADEVA

As Gleaned from the Amṛtānubhava

B.P. BAHIRAT

MOTILAL BANARSIDASS PUBLISHERS
PRIVATE LIMITED • DELHI

First Edition: Bombay, 1956
Reprint: Delhi, 1984, 1998

ISBN: 81-208-1574-2

MOTILAL BANARSIDASS

41 U.A. Bungalow Road, Jawahar Nagar, Delhi 110 007
8 Mahalaxmi Chamber, Warden Road, Mumbai 400 026
120 Royapettah High Road, Mylapore, Chennai 600 004
Sanas Plaza, Subhash Nagar, Pune 411 002
16 St. Mark's Road, Bangalore 560 001
8 Camac Street, Calcutta 700 017
Ashok Rajpath, Patna 800 004
Chowk, Varanasi 221 001

PRINTED IN INDIA

BY JAINENDRA PRAKASH JAIN AT SHRI JAINENDRA PRESS,
A-45 NARAINA INDUSTRIAL AREA, PHASE I, NEW DELHI 110 028
AND PUBLISHED BY NARENDRA PRAKASH JAIN FOR
MOTILAL BANARSIDASS PUBLISHERS PRIVATE LIMITED,
BUNGALOW ROAD, DELHI 110 007

TO

SHRI DADA MAHARAJA

WITH VENERATION, LOVE AND GRATITUDE.

दुरिताचें तिमिर जावो । विश्व स्वधर्मसूर्यें पाहो ।
जो जें वांछील तो तें लाहो । प्राणिजात ॥

– ज्ञानेश्वरी, १८–१७९६.

MAY THE DARKNESS OF SIN DISAPPEAR, AND THE SUN OF TRUE RELIGION SHINE UPON THE WORLD. MAY ALL THE DESIRES OF ALL LIVING BEINGS BE FULFILLED.

— Jnaneshwari, XVIII-1796.

CONTENTS

PREFACE TO THE THIRD EDITION

I have taken the opportunity to include in the present edition the text of the Amritanubhava's Sanskrit versification by Shri Prahlad Maharaj Badve of Pandharpur. He lived in the 17th century A.D. He was a great saint, scholar as well as an ardent devotee of Jñānadeva. His style is simple and conveys clearly the import of the original.

I have also added to the bibliography the names of some important works published during the last twenty years.

Shri N. P. Jain of Motilal Banarsidass has laid me under deep obligation by taking the responsibility of publishing this new edition.

B. P. BAHIRAT

PREFACE TO THE SECOND EDITION

It is gratifying to note that a second edition of this work is called for within a short period of its first edition. It indicates a sympathetic understanding and appreciation on the part of the readers, of the philosophy of the greatest and beloved saint of Maharashtra.

I have taken the opportunity of making some verbal improvements and adding the Appendix. It includes a free translation of some passages from Jnaneshwari and Abhangas. They are given as illustrative of the religious and ethical implications of Jnanadeva's Philosophy of Chidvilas.

I express my heartfelt gratitude to Shri Ramadas Bhatkal of Popular Book Depot - Bombay, for undertaking the publication of this second edition.

B. P. BAHIRAT.

Pandharpur 7-9-1961.

PREFACE TO THE FIRST EDITION

JNANADEVA was a great genius of Maharashtra in whom we find a rare combination of poetry, philosophy and deep religious experience. As a saint he is held in high respect among religious sects. As a poet he is appreciated among literary circles. His contribution to the solution of the persistent problems of philosophy has not been however, fully recognized. As a matter of fact this contribution is his great gift not only to Maharashtra but to all mankind for whose welfare his heart yearned day and night. He has written all his works in his mother tongue—Marathi. It was but natural on the part of the eastern or western scholars not acquainted with Marathi language, to have neglected them. Some Marathi scholars have tried to explain his philosophical view point. But some of them have neglected his peculiar contribution while others have not brought forth its full significance. An attempt has, therefore, been made in this work to present in English the philosophy of Jnanadeva in a systematic form and to convey a clear impression of his lofty and integral idealism

The chief works of Jnanadeva are *Jnaneshwari, Amritanubhava* and *Abhangas* or religious lyrics. *Jnaneshwari* is his famous commentary on the Bhagawad Gita. This classical work is selected by the famous world-organization UNESCO for translation into English, French and Spanish languages for international propagation. The Abhangas or religious lyrics of Jnanadeva are mainly the outpourings of his devotional heart though they also contain his religious and moral teachings as well as descriptions of his ycgic experiences. *Amritanubhava,* however, occupies a unique position. It is an independent work that sets forth clearly his philosophical point of view. The present work is mainly based upon *Amritanubhava.* The other works of Jnanadeva have also been taken into consideration and they yield a more consistent world view when seen in the light of *Amritanubhava.*

Jnanadeva's original contribution to idealistic thought in Indian philosophy is his theory of *Chidvilas* or the play of the Pure Intelligent *Atman.* The main target of his criticism is the theory of ignorance advocated by Shamkar. Though other thinkers like Ramanuja have criticised it before him, Jnanadeva does it in his own way, He stands on the same *Advaitic* ground as Shamkar and points out the discrepancies in the conception of *ajnana* or ignorance and also shows the lines of its consistent developments. The rejection of the conception of ignorance results in the transformation of the conceptions of God, the individual self and the world. God is not the phenomenal appearance of the Absolute as Shamkar believes. He is the very Absolute and contains within Himself the principle and the explanation of plurality. The world is not caused by *Maya* or the mystery of ignorance but it is the expression of infinite Divine love and joy. So Shamkar's attitude leads to asceticism while Jnanadeva's angle of vision leads to the path of loving devotion and self-less activism.

According to Jnanadeva it is not the *Maya* but the power of the Lord that is responsible for the appearance of the world. This doctrine resembles to that of Kashmir Shaivism. But Jnanadeva does not stop here. He analyses the conception of this power and comes to the conclusion that the power is the power of love. So the love of God becomes the central reality of which His power and wisdom are but aspects. Love is not the quality of God, but God Himself, out of which all creation flows spontaneously. This infinite love is the deepest fact of the universe. There is a tender divine benediction over all things. So Jnanadeva says that God and his Love are the only two inmates of the home of the universe and not even a blade of grass is created without their mutual help. (Amt. I, 12-13).

To appreciate and fully realize in life this spring of Divine Love is *Bhakti* or the supreme devotion. It is called by Jnanadeva "*Akritrim Bhakti*" or natural devotion. As the temple, the deity and the worshippers can be hewn out of the same mountain-rock, so there can be the process of devotion even in the state of union with God. (Amt. IX, 41) As the Ganges united with the ocean plays upon its bosom, so the devotee united with God experiences the sweet flavour of devotion (*Jnaneshwari*, XVIII, 1138) "It is in love, and in nothing else that we find not only the supreme value of life but also the supreme reality of life and indeed of the universe" these words of McTaggart (quoted by Dr. T. M. Forsyth, M.A., D.PHIL., in his "*God and The World*" p. 146) will represent the view of Jnanadeva if we understand love to mean not merely a personal love felt by one individual for another, but its very spring that wells up in the heart of Divinity. So Jnanadeva called his work '*Anubhavamrita*" which means "The sweet Nectar of Experience".

Indian idealism proceeding from the Upanishadic philosopher Yajnyavalkya finds its maturest expression in the writings of Jnanadeva. As such it deserves a place of honour in the history of Indian philosophy. His philosophic view point leads to activism in addition to supplying a sound theoretic foundation to the *Bhakti* cult in Maharashtra. Such luminaries as Namdeva, Ekanath and Tukarama drew their inspiration from this great spiritual fountainhead. Jnanadeva's philosophy of the Spirit has considerable historical importance but there are elements in it that have lasting and living universal significance. Hence the importance of its study cannot be overemphasised.

Dr. R. D. Ranade, M.A., D.Litt. kindly allowed me to make use of the English renderings of some verses of the Amritanubhava in his "Mysticism in Maharashtra".

Dr. V. A. Sukhatankar, M.A., PH.D., who happened to visit Pandharpur, expressed his deep sympathy for my work and encouraged me to publish it. Both of them have laid me under deep obligation for which I express my heartfelt gratitude.

I offer my thanks to my friend Mr. M. Gopalacharya, M.A., for discussing with me Janadeva's criticism of *Ajnanvada* and helping me by clarifying some difficult points.

I cannot express in words what I owe to my revered spiritual teacher to whose memory this work is dedicated as my humble offering.

Pandharpur
21-2-1956

B. P. BAHIRAT

श्रीज्ञानदेवकृतमंगलाचरणम्

यदक्षरमनाख्येयमानन्दमजमव्ययम् ।
श्रीमन्निवृत्तिनाथेति ख्यातं दैवतमाश्रये ॥१॥

गुरुरित्याख्यया लोके साक्षाद्विद्याहि शांकरी ।
जयत्याज्ञा नमस्तस्यै दयार्द्रायै निरंतरम् ॥२॥

सार्द्धं केन न कस्यार्द्धं शिवयोः समरूपिणोः ।
ज्ञातुं न शक्यते लग्नमिति द्वैतच्छलान्मुहुः ॥३॥

अद्वैतमात्मनस्तत्त्वं दर्शयन्तौ मिथस्तराम् ।
तौ वन्दे जगतामाद्यौ तयोस्तत्त्वाभिपत्तये ॥४॥

मूलायाग्राय मध्याय मूलमध्याग्रमूर्तये ।
क्षीणाग्रमूलमध्याय नमः पूर्णाय शंभवे ॥५॥

CHAPTER I

THE AGE OF JNANADEVA

Political condition

JNANADEVA lived in the latter half of the thirteenth century A.D. Jnaneshwari was written in Shaka 1212 (1290 A.D.). The fact that the completion of the work took place in 1290 A.D. is undisputed as it is mentioned at the end of the work itself.[1] Similarly Jnanadeva mentions the name of 'Shri Ramachandra' i.e. King Ramadevarava of Yadava dynasty as 'a just ruler who supported all arts and sciences'.[2] Devagiri — the present Daulatabada — was the capital of the Yadava Kings. King Bhillama (1187-1191 A.D.) was the first sovereign of this Yadava dynasty. He put an end to the Chalukya rule and founded Devagiri. His son Jaitrapal, it is said, had Mukundaraja -- the author of Paramamrita and Vivekasindhu — as his spiritual teacher. Jaitrapal's son Singhan was a valorous king who conquered Malwa, Gujarath and Southern Maharashtra and annexed them to his kingdom. The town Shinganapur was founded by him and so is named after him. 'Sangit Ratnakar,' an authoritative Sanskrit work on Indian Music, was written by Sharangadhar during his reign. King Ramadevarava was the great-grandson of this Singhan. He ruled from 1271 to 1309 A.D. The famous Hemadri, the towering personality of the times, was his chief minister or Shrikaranadhipa. He was a great administrator as well as an able organizer. He compiled the encyclopaedic work named 'Chaturvarga Chintamani' which stands foremost among his other minor religious works. He is said to have built many temples in a peculiar style called Hemadapanti after his name and invented the Modi script in Marathi. Bopadeva, the famous grammarian, was a friend of Hemadri. The Yadava period was really a golden period in the history of Maharashtra and "Devagiri formed a centre of learning, art and culture in the midst of Maharashtra attracting men of great attainments and scholarship from all parts of India. Astronomy, Astrology, Mathematics, Theology, Medicine and Statecraft received encouragement from the Yadavas."[3]

King Ramadevarava was a just ruler, a great patron of learning and a devotee of the God of Pandharpur whose shrine he visited with reverence. His name stands in the inscription of Pandharpur temple where a list of those persons who endowed sums of money for the purpose of building, is found.[4] Ramadevarava, however, does not seem to be a brave king because in his reign Allauddin Khilji invaded his capital, defeated him and made him his subsidary who had to pay a yearly tribute. But during Jnanadeva's life time Maharashtra was unmolested by foreign invasions and was enjoying all prosperity.

Literary Condition

If we look to the literary condition we see that it is Jnanadeva who has written the first original philosophical work in Marathi language. Mukundaraja, the author of Paramamrit and Viveksindhu, is called the first poet of Maharashtra. But his priority to Jnanadeva is doubtful. Writers like Ajagaonkar have tried to prove that he lived after Jnanadeva.[5] Then again his works lack originality. Mukundaraja himself tells that he has followed Shamkara in his work.[6] So his works are in the main expository of Shamkara's philosophy. There is also Mahanubhava literature, but it is poetic and religious more than philosophical. It has no original philosophical point of view. It contains only a gross pluralism. Jnanadeva was a great poet as well as a great philosopher and his work is the first of its kind in Marathi literature.

Religious Condition

Though Maharashtra was enjoying secular prosperity its religious condition was far from satisfactory. There was, as it were, a religious fermentation. Five centuries ago Shamkaracharya had attacked Vedic ritualism and advocated the doctrine of renunciation. Ramanuja had tried to reconcile both, but his influence was not felt so much in Maharashtra. The ritualism was fast disappearing and its place was being taken by the worship of various deities. The inferior deities were also offered animal sacrifices. Jnanadeva describes a person worshipping inferior deities as the very incarnation of ignorance. He observes: "Like the foolish farmer giving up his old business and beginning something new every day, the man overpowered by ignorance installs new images of gods often and again, and worships them with the same intensity. He becomes the disciple of a Guru (a spiritual teacher) who is surrounded by worldly pomp, gets himself initiated by him and is unwilling to see any other person who has got real spiritual dignity. He is cruel to every being, worships various stone images and has no consistency of heart. Leaving the image of god in his house, he wanders among the so-called holy places performing the rites of several deities on various occasions. On the eleventh day of the month he worships Krishna and on the fourth he worships Ganesha. On the fifth he performs the rites of serpents and on the fourteenth those of goddess Durga. In the first half of the month of Ashwin he worships goddess Chandi. On Sunday he visits Bhairava, and on Monday he runs with Bela leaves in his hand to Mahadeva. He does not keep quiet even for a moment and is like a prostitute whose residence is open to all, his mind is open to all kinds of worship and hence he is the very incarnation of ignorance."[7]

Besides these deity-worships there were too many religious performances current amongst the different strata of society. Hemadri has described various such religious performances numbering about two thousand. He prescribes five to ten performances for each day and gives details about the deities to be propitiated. He gives a list of various dishes to be prepared and offered to the priests for gaining their favour. He also gives various authoritative quotations from Shrutis, Smritis and Puranas.[8]

Besides this degenerated form of Vedic Religion, there were various sects like Jain, Lingayata and Mahanubhava trying to get supremacy. Jnanadeva has criticised different views of Ahimsa. Besides criticising Mimamsakas and Ayurvedics he has also criticised Jainas. "Some people" he says, "drink water filtered through a piece of cloth as their religious duty. But many germs are destroyed in the very process of filtering. Some again eat uncooked food because they are afraid of injuring the germs. But in the very act of eating uncooked food, they do injury to themselves. A non-injury is not a non-injury at all. It is like cutting the boughs of a tree for making a fence around it or like cutting one's hands to satisfy one's hunger. It is like putting down a temple in order to build a wall around it or like burning one's quilts to get warmth."[9] Lingayata religion was promulgated by Basava in the 12th century A.D. and it was attacking Jainism. The Mahanubhava sect worshipped Krishna and Dattatraya. But it closely guarded its doctrines. Its works were written in a cryptic language not easy to decipher. Asceticism was its ideal and like Buddhism it advocated renunciation not for men alone but for women also Because of its secrecy and extreme ascetic tendency the Mahanubhava cult did not find favour with the saints of Maharashtra and we find its criticism in the works of Ekanatha and Tukarama.

The Spiritual Lineage of Jnanadeva

The spiritual lineage of Jnanadeva can be traced to the two sources; the Nath cult and the Warakari or Bhakti cult of Pandharpur. The Nath lineage is described at the close of Jnaneshwari as follows, Shiva-Shakti-Matsyendra-Gorakha-Gahini-Nivritti and Jnanadeva.[10] Tryambakpant, the great grandfather of Jnanadeva, was initiated by Gorakhanath. Gorakhanath's disciple Gahininath initiated both Govindpant and Nirai, the grandfather and grandmother of Jnanadeva.[11] He also initiated Jnanadeva's brother Nivrittinath who in his turn was the initiator of Jnanadeva. Before Jnanadeva this spiritual wealth was a great secret known only to the teacher and his disciple. Jnanadeva wanted to disseminate it among all. So we find his request to his master to this effect in the closing words of Jnaneshwari. The history of these Nathas before Gorakhanath is not yet explored. These Nathas were a wandering sect of persons gifted with great yogic powers. Their regular place of residence is not known. Both Bengal and Maharashtra claim their residence. The hill named Matsyendragad and a tamarind tree called Gorakh-chincha are in the district of Satara. These are shown as sacred to Matsyendranath and Gorakhanath respectively. Nivrittinath was initiated by Gahininath at Brahmagiri near Nasik. He describes his master thus — "His heart was parched by renunciation but was cooled by Divine Love. He was wandering without being affected by pleasure or pain, without being attached to any worldly object and the Divine Bliss made his heart its constant abode. By his grace my family has become sanctified."[12] Nivrittinath and his sister

Muktabai had also the fortune of meeting Gorakhanath.[13] Historical evidence about the existence of Matsyendranath is not available,[14] but Gorakhanath has written some works that are published and hence we see that he was a great organizer of the Nath cult which has played an important role in the creation and consolidation of Neo-Hinduism after the decline of Buddhism. Siddhsiddhant-Paddhati is his imporant and authoritative work that deals with philosophical problems such as the nature of Ultimate Reality, its relation with individual souls and the world. This work is written in Sanskrit, partly in the form of aphorisms and partly in the form of verses, and it must have greatly influenced the philosophy of Jnanadeva.

The Bhakti Cult of Pandharpur

The history of the Bhakti cult of Pandharpur is also uncertain. According to tradition, Pundalika was the first great high-priest of the God of Pandharpur. The Pandurangashtaka of Shamkaracharya mentions the name of Pundalika for whom God appeared on the bank of Bhima. If these verses are composed by the first Shamkaracharya, we can say that Pundalika must have lived before the eighth century A.D. But the authenticity of the verses is doubtful. Malu Sonar has written a work in Marathi called Malu-Taran in which he has given a history of Pandharpur, and, if his account is reliable, the date of Pundalika goes as far back as the first century A.D. But unfortunately, the writer of this work is not reliable. However, the inscription on the Samadhi of Krishnaswami together with the idols of Vithal and Rukmini found in Alandi dated 1209 A.D. and the inscription at Pandharpur dated 1237 and 1273 A.D. show that Pundalika and his God were enjoying a wide reputation nearly four or five centuries before Jnanadeva. Jnanadeva's father and grandfather were regular visitors to

Pandharpur. This fact and his coming in contact with the great devotee Namadeva were of prime importance in shaping his philosophy which became the foundation of the Bhakti cult in Maharashtra.

[1] *Jnaneshwari*, XVIII-1810.

[2] *Jnaneshwari*, XVIII-1804.

[3] Paper by V. K. Bhave, read at The All India History Congress (1938).

[4] The inscription is called Chauryansi inscription and its date is Shak 1195. (1273) A.D.) i.e. two years before Jnanadeva was born. It was first published by V. K. Rajwade 50 years ago. Dr. S. G. Tulpule of Poona University with the help of Pandharpur Samsodhan Mandal and Badve Committee has recently taken new prints of this inscription. He has found more than twentyfive prominent mistakes in Mr. Rajwade's reading. His article appears in the Journal of Poona University (I. 1).

[5] Ajagaokar J. R. — *Maharashtra Kavi Charitra* Part I. P. 14.

[6] *Viveksindhu* (VII-47). Though Jnanadeva has made a similar statement in his Jnaneshwari (XVIII-1723) and his difference from Shamkar is not quite explicit in that work, we clearly see in his original works like Amritanubhava and Changadeva Pasasthi how he has got his peculiar angle of vision.

[7] *Jnaneshwari*, XIII, 81-822.

[8] *Chaturvarga Chintamani*-Vritkhand..

[9] *Jnaneshwari* (XIII; 230-235).

[10] *Jnaneshwari* (XVIII; 1751-58).

[11] The Gatha of Namadeva (Avate Edition) p. 81. Abg. 834.

[12] The Gatha of Jnanadeva (Avate Edition) p. 17. Abg. 135.

[13] The Gatha of Jnanadeva (Avate Edition) p. 146. Abg. 1349.

वैराग्यें तापला सप्रेमें निवाला । ठेवा जो लाधला शांती सुख ॥

[14] Matsyendranath is regarded as the author of several works like *Kauljnannirnaya.* Those are found in the Nepal Darbar Pustakalaya. Dr. Bagchi has published some of them.

CHAPTER II

LIFE AND WORKS OF JNANADEVA

Sources of Jnanadeva's Biography

THE chief sources of Jnanadeva's biography are the writings of Nāmadeva, Satyamalanath and Sachchidananda Baba. Namdeva was his contemporary and his deep intimacy with Jnanadeva is weiknown. The other two were the disciples of Jnanadeva. The abhangas of Namadeva called Adi, Tirthavali and Samadhi contain the account of Jnanadeva's ancestry and his whole life, his travels and entering Samadhi. Pangarkar has given an account of the other two biographies but unfortunately both of them are yet unpublished.[1] Later biographers are Mahipati, Nabhaji and Niranjana Madhava.

Ancestors of Jnanadeva

Jnanadeva's ancestors were Kulkarnis of Apegaon, Apegaon is situated on the bank of the river Godavari. It is eight miles from Paithan which was then famous for its Sanskrit learning. Hariharpant was the grandfather of Jnanadeva's great-grand father Triambakpant. He was looking after the revenue affairs of Apegaon in Shaka 1060 (1138 A. D.) His grandson Trimbakpant was a great devotee. He obtained spiritual initiation at the hands of Gorakhanath. Triambakpant's son Govindpant was also a devotee of Shri Vithal of Pandharpur. Govindpant and his wife Nirabai were both initiated by Gahininath. The pious couple gave birth to a child in their old age. It was named Vithal after the name of their beloved deity.

Vithalpant

Vithalpant was a clever boy. He learnt the Sacred Vedas, Sanskrit grammar and poetry. After finishing his studies, he took the permission of his parents and went on a pilgrimage to sacred places like Dwaraka, Pindarak and Saptashringi. When he arrived at Bhimashamkar and saw the source of the river Bhima he was reminded of Pandharpur which is situated on the bank of the same river. He made up his mind to go there. On his way he halted at Alandi to see Siddheshwar. Alandi is situated on the bank of the river Indrayani. It is thirteen miles from Poona. Sidhopant, the then Kulkarni of Alandi, was glad to see the young scholar and gave his daughter Rukmini to him in marriage. After some days the married couple with Sidhopanta's family, visited Pandharpur and returned to Apegaon. Govindpant and Nirabai were glad to see them, but they, however, did not live long to enjoy this happiness. After passing some years at Apegaon, Vithalpant and Rukmini left the town and went to stay at Alandi, according to Sidhopant's advice.

Vithalpant's heart yearned for self-realization and he thought of giving up his householder's life. One day he left home, went to Banaras and became a disciple of a sanyasi. He renounced the world, became an ascetic and was named Chaitanyashrama.

His spiritual teacher Ramashrama

Tradition says that the sanyasi whom Vithalpant approached was Ramananda. This Ramananda cannot be identified with the Ramananda who was the follower of Ramanuja and the teacher of Kabir because he was not even a contemporary of Jnanadeva. In an unpublished manuscript of Namadeva's Abhangas the name of Vithalpant's initiator is given as Ramashrama.[2] It is told that Vithalpant, while staying at Banaras, heard the glory of renunciation in a discourse on the Gita delivered by Ramashrama and got himself initiated by him.[3] Niloba, in one of his Abhangas, says that the name of Vithalpant's teacher was Nrisimhashrama.[4] We get the names of Ramadvaya and Nrisimhashrama as the welknown writers on Advait Vedant, who wrote Vedant-Kaumudi and Bheda-dhikkar respectively. But one of them lived in the first half of the fourteenth century while the other in the sixteenth century A.D.[5]

Mahipati in his biography of Jnanadeva mentions the name of Ramashrama and not of Ramananda.[6] He is a later biographer and must have based his account on that of Namadeva. The importance of the name of Vithalpant's teacher lies in the fact that some writers want to show the relation of Jnanadeva with Ramanuja through the latter's disciple Ramananda. But for the following reasons we cannot identify Ramananda with the teacher of Vithalpant:-

(1) Namadeva's account of Jnanadeva should be taken to be the most reliable of all the accounts. He mentions the name of Ramashrama and not that of Ramananda.

(2) All the biographers agree to the name Chaitanyashrama which Vithal assumed on his entering the ascetic order. Among the disciples of Ramananda we find the names like Anantananda and Bhavananda. He would have also named his new disciple Chaitanyananda instead of Chaitanyashrama.

(3) Both Namadeva and Mahipati say that Vithalpant, while at Banaras, heard discourses on the Gita by a monk who emphasized the path of renunciation. Now the tenor

of the whole Shamkara Bhashya on the Gita is that of emphasizing Sannyas (the path of renunciation) and of Ramanuja-Bhashya is that of laying stress on Bhakti-yoga (the path of devotion).[7] So the monk who expounded the Gita must have been a follower of Shamkara and not of Ramanuja.

(4) Lastly, the period of Ramananda does not correspond to that of Vithalpant. According to Dr. Bhandarkar the period of Ramananda was about 1300 to 1411 A. D.[8]

Vithalpant's teacher was, therefore, Ramashrama and not Ramananda. Namadeva refers to him as a Shripad in his Abhangas of Adi. (i.e. Jnanadeva's ancestry).

Now this Shripad went on a pilgrimage and while on his way to Rameshwar visited Alandi. There he saw Vithalpant's wife Rukmini circumambulating an Ashwattha tree. Her heart was pining for her husband. Seeing the very image of piety, the Shripad's heart was filled with paternal love. When Rukmini saw him, she came near and bowed to him with great reverence. He gave her his blessings saying "let pious sons be born to you." No sooner did he utter these words, than the Shripad saw tears rolling down the eyes of Rukmini. He made inquiries and came to know the cause of her grief. She told him how her dear husband had forsaken her and gone away. The Shripada at once remembered his new disciple. His heart told him that the new sanyasi in his hermitage was no other than Rukmini's husband. He gave up the pilgrimage, returned to Banaras and after a pressing inquiry learnt that what his heart had told him was true. He ordered Chaitanyashrama to give up sanyasa and accept the life of a householder again. So Chaitanyashrama became Vithalpant once again. He returned to Alandi and led the life of a householder according to the command of his spiritual teacher who had advised him to give up all fear because God would help him.[9] Rukmini's joy knew no bounds but alas it lasted only for a few days.

The orthodox Brahmins of Alandi excommunicated Vithalpant. He was greatly harassed and even persecuted, but he did not utter a word against them. Twelve years elapsed and Rukmini gave birth to Nivrittinath in 1273 A.D. After two years Jnanadeva was born (1275 A.D.) Jnanadeva's younger brother Sopan was born in 1277 A. D. and Muktabai, the youngest of all, was born in 1279 A. D.

Though there is a difference of opinion as regards the birth dates, Pangarkar has given the Abhangas of Janabai Namadeva, Visoba Khechar and a passage from Sachchidanand Baba's Jnaneshwar-Vijaya which support the above dates.[10] Jnanadeva passed away in 1296 A.D. and the fact is told by Namadeva, Chokhoba, Visoba, and Janabai. Jnanadeva's age was twenty two at that time as we find it in one of his Abhangas " बाल छंदो बावीस जन्मे । तोडीली भवाब्धीची कर्मे. " This also supports the above dates.

His tragic end

Taking his children with him Vithalpant lived outside the town. All the four children were spiritual gems but the orthodox Brahmins of Alandi thought it a bad omen even to look at them. Dejected with these adverse circumstances Vithalpant, one day, decided to leave his home. He went to Triambakeshwar (a village near Nasik, situated in the vicinity of the source of the river Godavari) with his children. As they were going round Brahmagiri a mountain near Triambakeshwar—they met a tiger. Vithalpant hurried away with his children, but missed Nivrittinath who had entered a cave. In the same cave lived saint Gahininath who offered Nivrittinath his spiritual wealth. Thus misfortune was turned into a golden opportunity. Nivrittinath rejoined his father and young brothers. Returning to Alandi, Vithalpant asked the Brahmins about his atonement. They told him the remedy of giving up his life! For the sake of the happiness of his offspring Vithalpant left home one day, went to the sacred Ganges and ended his life by throwing himself in the holy river. A year after, his wife Rukmini leaving all her children under the protection of her eldest son, followed the example of her husband. Yet the orthodox Brahmins of Alandi were not appeased and did not consider Vithalpant's children as purified. They wanted a certificate of atonement from the Pandits of Paithan. Nivrittinath along with Jnanadeva and others went to Paithan accordingly. There, all of them were ridiculed for bearing names indicative of their spiritual dignity. In the assembly the learned Pandits laughed at them as children of a sanyasi. But when they saw that Jnanadeva caused a passing buffalo to recite Vedas, they were silenced and gave them a certificate of purification. When all of them returned the buffalo followed them.

Jnanadeva's Career

While returning to Alandi all of them halted at Newase—a small town on the bank of the river Pravara in the Ahamadnagar district. Jnaneshwari — the sweetest exposition of the Bhagavadgita — was written here.[11] The pillar still stands near which sat Jnanadeva in front of his dear master Nivrittinath. Nectar like words oozed out of his lips and were taken down by Sachchidananda Baba. After the completion of Jnaneshwari Nivrittinath told Jnanadeva to compose an independent work and the Amritanubhava was written accordingly.[12] While returning to Alandi the buffalo of Paithan gave up its life at Ale (in Poona District) where a tomb still stands and annually pilgrimage is held on the eleventh day of the latter half of the month of Chaitra.[13]

Changadeva, a great yogi, came to see Jnanadeva. He had attained some yogic powers and was proud of them. But when he met Jnanadeva he gave up all his pride and became his humble disciple. Jnanadeva advised him in sixty five verses that are known as Changadeva Pasasthi.

After passing some months in Alandi Jnanadeva, along with Nivrittinath and others, went to Pandharpur where he came in contact with the great devotee Namadeva. They became intimate friends. The great philosopher became a great devotee of God Vithal and the great apostle of the Warakari Cult. Jnanadeva took Namadeva with him and travelled up to Banaras visiting all the holy places in the Northern India and all the country resounded with their sweet kirtanas. They returned to Pandharpur and there was a great feast in which the contemporary saints like Goroba the potter, Sanvata the gardener, Chokhoba the untouchable, Parisa Bhagawat the Brahmin, and others took part. Then Jnanadeva expressed his wish to enter Samadhi and they all went to Alandi. There was a great religious festival. It was the eleventh day of the latter half of the month of Kartik. They all kept awake all night long singing the name of the Lord. Next day they all dined together. Then Nara, Vitha, Mahada, and Gonda—the four sons of Namadeva — swept clean the place of the Samadhi. Namadeva besmeared the body of Jnanadeva with the sandal-paste, marked his forehead with the pigment of musk, put on garlands of fragrant flowers, waved sacred lights and paid homage to the dearest of his heart. It was the thirteenth day of the second half of Kartik. Jnanadeva sat on the Asan. Jnaneshwari, his monumental work, was placed before him. He closed his eyes and while engrossed in Love Divine he entered Sanjivan Samadhi![14] The slab was placed on the door by Nivrittinath. With deep sorrow they remembered the sweet company of the great saint. Tears rolled down their eyes incessantly. The day is held sacred and thousands of pilgrims yearly visit Alandi to pay their respectful homage to Jnanadeva whom they regard as their spiritual father and mother.

The Works of Jnanadeva

The works of Jnanadeva so far available are—

1 Jnaneshwari or Bhavarth—Dipika
2 Amritanubhava
3 Changadeva-Pasashthi
4 Haripatha
5 Namana
6 Miscellaneous Abhangas.

There is unanimity of opinion regarding the authorship of all of these. There are also other works like the Yoga-vasishtha, Bhaktiraja, Panchikaran, Shukashtaka, Gayatri-tika, Uttargita, Prakritgita and Samas which are sometimes ascribed to Jnanadeva. But they do not appear to have come from the pen of the author of Jnaneshwari.

Jnaneshwari

Jnaneshwari is the *magnum opus* of Jnanadeva's brilliant career. It is his celebrated Marathi commentary on the Bhagavadgita. Jnaneshwari is also called Jnanadevi and Bhavartha-Dipika i.e. a torch enlightening the import of the original text. Jnanadeva himself does not use any title. He describes his work as an ornament to the Gita, in the form of the Marathi version.[15] The titles Jnaneshwari and Jnanadevi are used by Namadeva while Janabai suggests the other title i.e. Bhavartha-Dipika.[16]

Jnaneshwari was not written but delivered extempore, chapter by chapter by Jnanadeva when he was only a lad of fifteen and it is a wonderful miracle of his uncommon genius.

The ancient Indian scriptures were written in Sanskrit and were beyond the ken of the common people. Jnanadeva used Marathi language instead of Sanskrit. Out of a deep compassion he delivered the message of the Lord with his original interpretations, to the common masses in their own mother-tongue. There are seven hundred verses of the Gita while the number of the ovis in the Jnaneshwari is about nine thousand. In these he tries to bring out fully the spirit of loving devotion that pervades the Song of the Lord. Bhakti or loving devotion is the fruit of right knowledge and the spring of right actions. This is the message of the Gita and Jnanadeva proclaims it in words that are so sublime, so lucid and so enchanting. The object of the Jnaneshwari is to spread spiritual bliss, to eliminate the dearth of discrimination and to enable any aspirant to have the glimpse of Divine Knowledge.[17] Jnaneshwari is the first and the greatest work in the Marathi language both from the point of view of a high literary excellence and of an elevating philosophy of life.

Instead of adopting the traditional method of dividing the Gita into three compartments, each consisting of six chapters, Jnanadeva gives his original views about the divisions. The first three chapters, according to him, form the first division in which the way of action is described. Next eight chapters i.e., from 4 to 11 form the second division which describes the pathway of Bhakti or devotion. But it is devotion through action.[18] The third division consists of chapters 12 to 15 where the path of knowledge is described. Jnanadeva thinks that the Gita proper ends here.[19] The 16th chapter discusses the qualities which help or hinder the growth of knowledge. The last two chapters are devoted to answer some incidental questions of Arjuna. Besides these answers, the last chapter sums up the whole Gita. It is called by Jnanadeva 'Kalasadhyaya' i.e. the pinnacle of the temple of the Gita.

Jnanadeva adopts the theory of Chidvilas which maintains that the universe is the expression of the Absolute Reality.[20] His philosophy is the source of his exquisite poetry contained in Jnaneshwari. The Shanta Rasa or the "peaceful flavour" predominates the whole work.[21] In the case of Jnanadeva this Shanta Rasa does not mean merely a negative otherworldly sentiment. It is identical with Bhakti Rasa which is a positive feeling of deep devotion.

In describing a true devotee Jnanadeva says that he is united with God and yet serves Him.[22] So there is the union of Bhakta with his God and yet a separation from Him. This is the secret of Bhaktiyoga that is revealed in the Jnaneshwari. Prof. Patwardhan rightly says, "That the general drift of the teachings of Jnanadevi is to emphasize Upasana and Bhakti, service and love of God, not the identity of the Bhakta and his Lord, is to be inferred from the fact that Jnanadeva is at his best, his spirit in the full swing of its pinions and his soul in sympathetic raptures in those portions of Jnanadevi that deal with the Bhaktiyoga system which maintains that salvation is to be attained by means of Bhakti or is Bhakti"[23]

Jnaneshwari is the gospel of thousands of Warakaris i.e. the devotees of Vithal who regularly visit Pandharpur.

It forms the fountainhead at which the chief and more prominent exponents of Bhagawat Dharma in Maharashtra like Ekanatha and Tukarama have drunk deep and received the inspiration to compose great works like the Ekanathi Bhagavata and the Gathas of Abhangas.

Amritanubhava

Amritanubhava of Jnanadeva is the greatest philosophical work in Marathi literature. It is not based on any ancient authorities like the Upanishads or Vedanta Sutras. Jnanadeva relies upon his own religious experience and his original philosophical insight. He expounds his theory of Sphurtivada with a fine logical acumen as well as with a mastery and wealth of poetic imagery. He refutes the other theories like the dulism of Samkhya, the Subjective Idealism and the Nihilism of Baudhas and the Ajnanavada or the theory of ignorance supported by Shamkaracharya. The Ajnanavadi is his chief opponent. About one-third part of Amritanubhava is devoted to the refutation of the theory of ignorance. Amritanubhava ends in revealing the secret of Akritrima Bhakti or natural devotion and forms the philosophical basis of the religion of Bhakti in Maharashtra.

Changadeva Pasashthi

Changadeva Pasashthi of Jnanadeva contains only sixty-five verses. They are adressed to Changadeva who was a Hathayogi. When Changadeva came in contact with Jnanadeva he realized the futility of his yogic powers. He gave up his Hatha-yoga and became Jnanadeva's disciple. This small work gives a clear exposition of the philosophy of Jnanadeva within a short compass.

Haripatha

The word Haripatha means remembering the name of the Lord Hari with intense affection. Haripatha consists of twenty eight Abhangas. Jnanadeva describes in it the importance of the name of the Lord. The utterance of the name of God is the only royal road to meet Him. All the other means like yogic practices, performance of sacrifices, wandering from one holy place to another, and bathing in the sacred waters, are of no avail. The devotees of God feed upon the nectar of His name. There is neither time nor season for the utterance of God's name. The name of God is like a door of His temple. If any one stands for a moment at this door he goes beyond the four salvations. Haripatha is the outcome of the natural devotion described in Amritanubhava.

Namana

The Namana is a hymn in praise of the Lord of the universe. It contains one hundred and eight stanzas in the ovi metre. Describing the importance of prayer, Jnanadeva says, "Prayer is the supreme end. It is the precious secret. It is the Divine experience. Prayer is the faith in God nay. it is God Himself."[21]

Miscellaneous Abhangas

The Abhangas are religious lyrics. About nine hundred Abhangas of Jnanadeva are available. They deal with various subjects such as the description of the lovely form of God Vithal, the sweetness of the name of the Lord, advice to the aspirants, the greatness of the spiritual teacher, criticism of religious superstitions and hypocrisy, the futility of asceticism and the supremacy of the path of devotion. There are some Abhangas of Jnanadeva, called 'Virahini.' The Virahini is a woman experiencing viraha or the pangs of separation from her lover. In these Abhangas the Lord of the Universe is depicted as the lover and His devotee as His beloved. Divine love is infinite and the finite individual who has tasted its sweetness is never satisfied. He wants to experience it again and again and always pines for fresh draughts. This sweet and the highest experience of a devotee is expressed in the Virahini Abhangas. It is the culmination of the Haripatha or uttering the name of the Lord with intense love.

[1] Pangarkar, L. R. मराठी वाङ्मयाचा इतिहास Vol. I. pp. 499-501.

[2] Sen, Dr. K. M.—*Medieval Mysticism of India* p. 70. According to Dr. Sen Ramananda's period is from 1370 to 1440 A.D.

[3] Saraswati Mandir Library, Tanjore, Manuscript No. 1801 quoted by Mr. Subandha in the 'Namdeva' Magazine (Sept. 1943).

गीता व्याख्यानी संन्यास महिमा । ऐकोनी आश्रमा अतीत आला ॥ ८ ॥
विचारले मनी पुरे हा संसार । अनंत अपार दुःखराशी ॥ ९ ॥
मग श्रीरामाश्रमाशी गेला पै शरण । ...... ॥ १० ॥

[4] *Nilobacha Gatha* (Chitrashala Edition) p. 432. Abg. 1566.

[5] Dasgupta Dr. S. N.—*The History of Indian Philosophy*, Volume II, p. 216.

[6] *Bhakti-Vijaya*, VIII-118.

[7] गीताशास्त्रस्य संक्षेपतः प्रयोजनं परं निःश्रेयसं सहेतुकस्य संसारस्यात्यंतोपरमलक्षणम् ।

गीता शांकरभाष्य प्रस्तावना

परं ब्रह्म पुरुषोत्तमः ... पांडुतनययुद्धप्रोत्साहनव्याजेन परमपुरुषार्थलक्षणमोक्षसाधनतया वेदांतोदितं स्वविषयं ज्ञानकर्मानुगृहीतभक्तियोगमवतारयामास ।

गीता रामानुजभाष्य प्रस्तावना.

[8] Bhandarkar, Dr. R. G.—*Vaishnavism, Shaivism and Minor Religious Systems*, pp. 94-95.

9 "अविधिकर्माचें न धरावे भय । यासि आहे साह्य जगदीश ॥"
नामदेवाची गाथा Abg. 955

10 Pangarkar, L. R. —श्रीज्ञानेश्वर महाराज चरित्र आणि ग्रंथ विवेचन,
(Third Edition, p. 40)

11 ऐसें युगीं परी कळीं । आणि महाराष्ट्र मंडळीं ।
श्री गोदावरीच्या कूळीं । दक्षिणिलीं ॥
त्रिभुवनैकपवित्र । अनादि पंचक्रोश क्षेत्र ।
जेथ जगाचें जीवनसूत्र । श्रीमहालया असे ॥
तेथ महेशान्वय-संभूतें । श्रीनिवृत्तिनाथसुतें ।
केलें ज्ञानदेवें गीते । देशीकार लेणें ॥
Jnaneshwari, XVIII, 1802-5

12 निवृत्ती म्हणती ऐक ज्ञानदेवा । अनुभव करावा अमृताऐसा ॥
नामदेवाची गाथा (*Chitrashala Edition*, *Abg.* 964)

13 येउनी उतरली आळ्याचीये वनीं । पशु तये स्थानीं शांत झाला ॥
Ibid. Abg. 964

14 जाऊनी ज्ञानेश्वर बैसले आसनावरी । पुढे ज्ञानेश्वरी ठेवियेली ॥
तीन वेळा तेव्हां जोडिले करकमळ । झांकियेले डोळे ज्ञानदेवे ॥
Ibid, Abg. 127

15 तेथ महेशान्वयसंभूते । श्रीनिवृत्तीनाथ सुते ।
केलें ज्ञानदेवे गीते । देशीकार लेणे ॥
Jnaneshwari, XVIII, 1806

16 भाव अक्षरांची गाठी । ब्रह्मज्ञानानें गोमटी ॥
ते हे माय ज्ञानेश्वरी । संत जना माहेश्वरी ॥
— *Namadevachi Gatha* Abg. 2363

17 फिटो विवेकाची वाणी । हो काना मना जिणी ।
देखो आवडे तो खाणी । ब्रह्मविद्येची ॥
दिसो परतत्व डोळा । पाहो सुखाचा सोहळा ।
रिघो महाबोध सुकाळा– । माजी विश्व ॥
Jnaneshwari, XIII, 1162-63

18 तंव कर्में ईश भजावा । हें जें बोलिले ॥

Ibid. XVIII, 1414.

19 तरी अध्यायीं पंधरावा । श्रीकृष्णें तया पांडवा ॥
शास्त्रसिद्धांत आघवा । उगाणिला ॥
म्हणोनि इये अध्यायीं । निरुप्य नुरेचि कांहीं ॥

Ibid, XVI, 41,46.

20 हें आंतबाहेर मिया कोंदलें । जग निखिल माझेंचि वोतिलें ॥

Ibid, IX-302.

21 नुसधीच शांतिकथा । आणिजेल कीर वाक्पथा ।
जे शृंगाराच्या माथा । पाय ठेवी ॥

Ibid, XIII, 1157.

22 ऐसे मीचि होउनि पांडवा । करिती माझी सेवा ॥

Ibid, IX, 196.

23 Patwardhan, Prof. W. B. Wilson Philological Lectures, Lecture III.

24 नमन हेंचि परम । नमन हें सुवर्म ॥
नमन हाचि अनुभव । नमन हाचि मुख्य भाव ।
नमन हाचि पै देव । देवाधिदेव तू पावसी ॥

Namadevachi Gatha, p. 103.

Cf. "Prayer is not to inform God of what He does not know. It is an eye through which we see God."

— W. T. Grenfell

CHAPTER III

AMRITANUBHAVA AND ITS COMMENTATORS

The Date of its Composition

ACCORDING to Namadeva's account Amritanubhava was written as an independent work after the completion of Jnaneshwari. Prof. W. B. Patwardhan, however, has expressed another view in his Wilson Philological Lectures (1917). He thinks that Amritanubhava is chronologically earlier than Jnaneshwari. His main reasons are as follows:—

(1) Amritanubhava opens with Sanskrit verses invoking the writer's spiritual teacher and the deity. This is according to the custom of Sanskrit writers. There are no such verses in Jnaneshwari. Hence it seems that Jnanadeva was under the influence of Sanskrit writers while writing the Amritanubhava. Jnaneshwari was written later on when this influence had waned.

(2) From the second opening Sanskrit verse it is clear that Jnanadeva has written his work following the teachings of Shamkar. The work shows no acquaintance with the other systems of India Philosophy. In Jnaneshwari we find descriptions of other systems like Samkhya, Yoga, etc. Hence Amritanubhava was composed earlier.

(3) Reference to Shiva only and not to Hari or Vishnu is made in Amritanubhava but we find reference to all of them in Jnaneshwari, which shows that Jnaneshwari was written when the author had become more liberal.

(4) The language, the vocabulary and the imagery in Amritanubhava appears so scanty, poor and monotonous when compared with that of Jnaneshwari. It may thus safely be concluded that Amritanubhava preceded Jnaneshwari.

But these objections against the priority of Jnaneshwari to Amritanubhava, are not convincing and can be answered thus.—

(1) The opening Sanskrit verses do not indicate the imitation of Sanskrit authors by Jnanadeva. He himself has said that the work was based upon his own experience and not on other ancient works. The name of the work itself shows the same thing. Moreover one Sanskrit verse is also found at the beginning of one of the manuscripts of the Jnaneshwari.[1]

(2) The word "Shamkari Vidya" in the second verse has been misunderstood to denote the teaching of Shamkaracharya. "Shamkari Vidya" means knowledge revealed by Shiva who is regarded as the primal spiritual teacher by Jnanadeva. In Jnaneshwari the same knowledge is termed "Shambhavi Vidya"[2] i.e. the knowledge revealed by Shambhu or God Shiva. The word "Shamkari" would also mean "leading to spiritual wellbeing" and it is interpreted this way by Ekanatha in his commentary on this verse.[3]

The absence of reference to other systems does not show that the author was not acquainted with them while writing Amritanubhava. In fact he has criticised not only Ajnanvada but Shunyavada also.[4] As there are references in the Gita to various systems it was but natural that the commentator should also write upon these. There was no such necessity of expounding other systems while writing an independent work like Amritanubhava.

(3) Amritanubhava being a philosophical work it is but natural that the names of several deities are not mentioned in it.

(4) For the same reason, the style of the work is not as poetic or full of emotion as that of Jnaneshwari. Still Jnanadeva has tried his best to make the exposition as lucid as possible by using various similies. The style of the work does not show the immaturity of the author. On the contrary it expresses the philosophical depth of Jnanadeva's composition.

Dr. Ranade is also of the same opinion. Referring to Amritanubhava he says, "there is a direct reference in Amritanubhava to the treatment of certain problems in Jnaneshwari which makes Amritanubhava appear to come later than Jnaneshwari.[5]" He quotes in support of his statement the verse

वैकुंठाचेनि सुजाणें । ज्ञानापाशी सत्वगुणें । बांधिजे हें निरूपण । बहु केलें ॥
— अमृतानुभव ३–१७.

and shows how it has a direct reference to the same problem treated in Jnaneshwari when commenting upon the verses of the Bhagwadgita. सुखसंगेन बध्नाति ज्ञानसंगेन चानघ. अ. १४, ६.

The Title and the Number of the Verses

There are two current names for the work. They are — Anubhavamrita and Amritanubhava. The first title is mentioned in the work itself.[6] The second is popularly used. There is, however, a negligible difference between the two, and both denote the author's intention of expounding the "Nature of the Ultimate Experience."

As for the number of verses, Shivakalyan says that it is eight hundred.[7] But we find eight hundred and four verses in the Nirnayasagar edition with Shivakalyan's commentary edited by Mr. Kunte. (Shaka 1810). Dhavale's edition is a mere reprint of it (1944 A.D.). Hence there is no change in the number. The editions of Joga and Sakhare have 806 and 807 verses respectively. Mr. Chandorkar states that he has found in a munuscript 25 verses that are not found in any other edition.[8] Looking to the content of those additional verses we find that they come at the end of the work. They only describe its greatness and add nothing to its philosophy. No commentary of Shivakalyan upon these is found and the language is not so archaic as that of Amritanubhava proper. Hence we can safely conclude that they are later interpolations.

The Division of Chapters

Amritanubhava is divided into ten chapters. In some old manuscripts there are no divisions. Hence it is probable that it had no chapters in its original form and some later commentator might have introduced the division.[9] The third chapter begins with "Yayacheni", and the division between the 7th and the 8th chapters seems to be unnatural. These facts confirm the view that originally it had no chapter divisions.

The Commentators of Amritanubhava

Amritanubhava being a difficult work it was but natural that several writers should write commentaries on it. No other Marathi work has enjoyed this unique privilege. The chief commentators are —

(1) *Ekanatha* (1533 — 1599 A.D.) — The oldest of the commentators is Ekanath. Unfortunately his commentary is

not available as yet. But the evidence of its existence can be obtained from the quotations given in the commentary by Bhayya Kaka Kibe. Kibe's commentary called "Jyostsna" quotes the verses of Ekanatha commenting on the opening five Sanskrit verses of the Amritanubhava. Mr. Bhave has also mentioned about the existence of this commentary in his history of Marathi Literature, but he has given no evidence.[1c]

(2) *Shivakalyan:*— The commentary of Shivakalyan is called Nityanandaikya- Dipika and was written in Shaka 1557 (1635 A.D). Shivakalyan traces his spiritual lineage to Jnanadeva's younger sister Muktabai. At the end of his commentary he has given the list of his spiritual ancestors. Muktabai— Vateshwar—Chakrapani—Vimalanand—Changa Keshavdas — Janakraj — Nrisimha — Hridayanand — Vishweshwar — Keshavraj — Haridas — Paramanand — Nityanand — Shivakalyan. Shivakalyan is the thirteenth person in the list, and taking into consideration the period of three and a quarter centuries that passed between Muktabai (who passed away in 1297 A.D) and Shivakalyan, the list is not improbable. Besides Nityanandaikya—Dipika Shivakalyan has also written a Marathi commentary on the tenth chapter of the Shrimad-Bhagawata. Shivakalyan has tried to interpret the stand point of Amirtanubhava in the light of Samkshep-Sharirak (a work by the great advaitic philosopher Sarvajnatman). In his introduction he says that the Amritanubhava is written for those who have gone beyond the view points of Parinama (evolution) and Vivarta (illusion) and have attained the perfect vision.[11] The total number of Shivakalyan's own verses is 6294.

(3) *Pralhadbuwa Badve* (died 1718 A.D.):— Pralhadbuwa has written Sanskrit verses on Amritanubhava. These

verses are not in the form of a commentary but are a Sanskrit translation of the original. He has also written a few independent stanzas wherein he describes in a nutshell the gist of Amritanubhava— i.e. the self-illumination of the Reality, which is beyond knowledge and ignorance and does not require the proofs of various Pramanas.[12]

(4) *Vireshwar Vallabha:*— Vireshwar was the son of Narasinha Dikshit. He wrote his commentary on Amritanubhava in 1717 Shaka (1795 A.D.) at Channpattan. He was a follower of Shamkar and interpreted Amritanubhava ac-accordingly. The commentary is not yet published.[13]

(5) *Vishwanath Kibe alias Bhayyakaka:*—He has written a prose commentary in Marathi on Amritanubhava in 1882 A.D. The commentary is called "Jyotsna" and is still in manuscript. It is written in Modi script and is in the possession of Mr. M. S. Sanzgiri of Bombay. The author has shown how Jnanadeva differs from thinkers like Shamkar and Vidyāranya in not accepting illusion as the cause of the creation of the universe.

(6) *Harihar:*— The commentary is called Rashtra-Bhashya. It is not in print as yet. The manuscript is in the possession of M. M. Prof. D. V. Potdar. Prof. Potdar believes that the work is written by one named Harihar. The date of composition is uncertain.

The special features of this commentary are:—

1) The commentator has divided the work into four chapters and not into the usual ten. He has made the division in the fashion of the Brahmsutras, and designated the chapters in the same way as Samanvaya, Avirodha, Sadhana, and Phala Adhyayas.

2) He mentions Jnanadeva as Paramahansa Parivrajakacharya!

3) The commentary is written partly in Sanskrit and partly in Marathi.

4) His exposition is from the point of view of Brahma-Vilas.

(7) *Hansarajaswami:*—(1798 to 1855 A.D.)— He was a Rigvedi Brahmin staying at Parabhani on the banks of the Godavari. His commentary is in the form of Sam-ovi i.e. one verse in easy modern Marathi for each verse in the original work. Besides this commentary he has written works like a commentary on Shivagita called Vedeshwari, Kathakalpalata, Agamasar, a commentary upon Shamkar's Sadachar and Laghu-Vakya-Vritti, a commentary on Ishopanishad etc.

(8) *Niranjana Buwa:*— (1782—1855 A.D.)— Niranjana was born at Kalamba in the Hyderabad State in 1782 A.D. His name was "Avadhuta". It was changed into "Niranjana" by his guru Shri Raghunatha Swami. Niranjana was eager to know the meaning of Amritanubhava. At the end of his commentary he tells us how he went to Alandi and weeping like a child prayed to Jnanadeva. He saw Jnanadeva in his dream and was inspired to write his commentary. Besides this he has composed commentaries on Jnaneshwari, Kenopnishad, Mandukyopanishad and Shamkar Bhashya. He has also written biographies of Raghunatha Swami and Keshava Chaitanya, the spiritual teacher of Tukarama. In the introduction of his commentary on Amritanubhava Niranjana calls Brahman with Shakti as Shabal (i.e. inferior) Brahman. He says that the work is written for a Jivan Mukta (a liberated soul). Both the statements

are contrary to the purport of Amritanubhava. Shiva with Shakti is not the inferior form of the Ultimate Reality. Both of them are described by Jnanadeva as Nirupadhik (without limitation). Then again the work is not addressed to a particular class but is written for all people as is stated by Jnanadeva himself in the concluding verses of Amritanubhava.

(9) *Balashastri Huparikar:—* His commentary called Tatparya-Bodhini was published in 1698 A.D. He was a disciple of Balakrishna who was again a disciple of Vishvanatha Kibe, and so his commentary is based upon Kibe's commentary. At the close of his work Balashastri gives his spiritual lineage. Jnanadeva — Satyamalnath — Dinanath Anantraj — Amalnath — Pralhad (Badve) — Bhumanand— Gopal— Vishvanath alias Bhayyakaka — Balkrishna—Balashastri Huparikar. (Tatparya- Bodhini p. 199). In this list we find the names of Pralhad Buva, the author of the Sanskrit translation of Amritanubhava and Vishvanath, the author of "Jyostsna". Balkrishna is also said to have written a commentary on the Changadeva Pasasthi.

(10) *Jivanmukta—Yati:—* Jivanmukta of Uran has written in Shaka 1841, a Sanskrit commentary partly in prose and partly in verse. He says that the aim of Amritanubhava in refuting Mayavada is to establish the Ajatvada.[14]

Besides these there are various expository works on the Amritanubhava by different recent writers like Jog, Sakhare, Kene, Rajarambuwa Brahmachari and Dasganu. Mr. Khasnis has published an English translation under the title of "Elixir of Life". Baba Garde has translated Amritanubhava in Arya metre in modern Marathi.

The philosophy of Jnanadeva deserves a place of honour in the history of Indian Philosophy, but it has not received the attention of prominent writers on the subject like Dr. Dasgupta and Dr. Radhakrishnan. In fact the philosophy of Jnanadeva is not a matter of mere antiquity or a dry skeleton of speculative game. It serves as a foundation for the superstructure of Bhagwatism in Maharashtra, a living creed of more than ten lakhs of people. It is, however, a matter of regret that in the scholarly work of Dr. R. G. Bhandarkar on "Vaishnavism, Shaivism and minor religious systems" the significance of Jnanadeva's work is not taken notice of . We find his name merely mentioned.[15] Dr. Ray Choudhari's "Early History of Vaishnava Sect" ends with Ramanuja. Dr. Kshitimohan Sen's work on "Medieval Mysticism of India" mentions only the name of Jnanadeva[16] and that too is absent in Dr. Dasgupta's "Hindu Mysticism". Dr. Nicol Macnicol has devoted a few pages to Jnanadeva in his "Indian Theism" but it is a very inadequate account.[17]

There are two main reasons for his negligence. Firstly, Jnanadeva has written all his works in Marathi. It was but natural that the historians of Indian philosophy, who have based their works on Sanskrit literature, should have failed to mention his name. Dr. Dasgupta has confessed that he was not able to trace the entire course of the development of Indian Philosophy which includes the views of Vernacular writers.[18] Dr. Radhakrishnan mentions the name of Jnanadeva only as one of the several commentators of the Bhagwadgita and says that "Jnaneshwar makes Patanjali's Yoga the aim of the teaching of the Gita".[19] We find no account of his philosophy except this brief reference in the whole body of the work. The second reason is that Maharashtrian writers have not furnished sufficient material to these writers by translating the complete works of Jnanadeva into English.[20]

Prof. R. D. Ranade's "Mysticism in Maharashtra" is of great importance from this point of view. He has collected several extracts from the writings of Jnanadeva and arranged them so as to bring out metaphysical, ethical and mystical teachings of the great saint. He has devoted a special chapter to Jnanadeva's Amritanubhava where he tells us how the "Sphurtivad" forms Jnanadeva's original contribution to philosophic thought.[21] But the work of prof. Ranade is, as he himself has said, 'historico-analytical' in character and a synthetic work bringing out fully the philosophical significance is yet a desideratum.[22] Dr. D. G. Londhe has written a short but valuable sketch of Jnanadeva's philosophy based upon the Amritanubhava.[23] His conclusion about Jnanadeva's view is that it "can be best described as neither dualism nor monism but a dual monism".[24] Prof. N. R. Phatak, Mr. Chapkhane, and Gulabrao Maharaj have also written on the philosophy of Jnanadeva in their various writings.

Besides various Marathi commentaries already referred to, several Marathi writers have attempted the task of explaining the philosophy of Jnanadeva from their own points of view. Among these there are three important writers — Mr. Pandurang Sharma, Prof. Dandekar and Dr. Pendse. Mr. Pandurang Sharma has written a series of articles in a Marathi monthly on a comparative study of Jnanadeva's philosophy.[25] He compares Jnanadeva with Ramanuja and tries to show the points of similarity in their criticism of Mayavada. His conclusion is that Jnanadeva's philosophy differs from that of Shamkar and is in the line of Ramanuja.

Prof. S. V. Dandekar has written a Marathi work on the life and philosophy of Jnanadeva along with several other articles.[26] He designates the philosophy of Jnanadeva as a perfect monism (Purna-Advait) and tries to show that he is a more thoroughgoing monist than Shamkar. According to him there is only a methodological difference and not a substantial one between Shamkar and Jnanadeva.[27]

Dr. Pendse's work on the philosophy of Jnanadeva is mainly based upon Jnaneshwari though he devotes a separate chapter to Amritanubhava. He tries to prove the identity of the views of Shamkar and Jnanadeva. Criticising his predecessors he concludes that Jnanadeva is no more than Shamkar diluted. Jnanadeva explained the philosophy of Shamkar, according to Dr. Pendse, in easy and poetic vernacular. Prof. R. D. Ranade in his valuable introduction to the work shows his agreement with the author's view.[28]

Mr. Pangarkar has devoted a special chapter to Amritanubhava in his history of Marathi literature where he tells us about the criticism of illusionism by Jnanadeva and his great skill in propounding sphurtivada.[29] Yet in another work he identifies the views of Jnanadeva with those of Shamkar.

The article of Mr. V. M. Potdar appeared in Jnaneshwar Darshan part II on the same topic where the expresses the same opinion and also shows the similarity of Jnanadeva's philosophy with that of Yogavasistha.[30]

It will be seen from the above list of various writers that the majority of them are inclined towards the view that Jnanadeva has merely followed the views of Shamkar and thus have underestimated the distinct individuality of Jnanadeva. So there is a need of re-examining his philosophy independently and to set in clear relief his views on the ultimate problems of life.

1 The manuscript found in possession of Mr. Vipra of Pandharpur has the following opening verse.

निवृत्तिसागरे रम्ये ज्ञानामृतसमुद्भवम् ।
सुरैः सोपान मार्गेण सेवितं मृत्युशांतये ॥

The manuscript is said to have been written by the grandson of a disciple of Sachchidanandbaba, the original writer of Jnaneshwari in Shaka 1275. But it is not clear whether the work is written in Shaka 1275 or 1575. A critical edition of the first chapter is published by Dr. R. G. Harshe in 1947.

2 Jnaneshwari, XV III-1757.

3 "कल्याणप्रद सर्वाप्रती । म्हणूनि म्हणती शांकरी ॥" एकनाथ

The full text of the Ekanatha's commentary is not yet available. But the verses commenting the opening Sanskrit stanzas are quoted in 'Jyotsna' an unpublished commentary on the Amritanubhava by Bhayya Kaka,

4 Ajnanvada is the doctrine of Ajnan or Ignorance. It holds that the appearance of the world is caused by Ajnan or Ignorance. It is supported by Shamkaracharya. Shunyavada is the doctrine of Shunya or Void. It regards the Ultimate Reality to be void. It is upheld by the Madhyamik school of Buddhistic philosophy.

5 Dr. R. D. Ranade:—"Mysticism in Maharashtra" p. 35.

6 Amritanubhava, X - 19, 20, 24; 25, and 31.

ज्ञानदेव म्हणे श्रीमंत । हें अनुभवामृत । ... ॥ १९ ॥
म्हणोनि ज्ञानदेवो म्हणे । अनुभवामृतें येणें ।
सणु भोगिजे सणें । विश्वाचेनि ॥ ३१ ॥

7 Shivakalyan:—Nityanandaikya-Dipika, X-408.

8 Annual Report of Bharat Itihas Samshodhak Mandal 1935. p. 93-97.

9 In the issue of the quarterly of Bharat Itihas Samshodhak Mandal (Volume, XXXIII-No. 1-2) there is an article by Mr. Kanole in which he discusses the point of the arrangement of the Amritanubhava in ten chapters. He tries to establish that it was Shivakalyana who introduced this division.

10 V. L. Bhave:—Maharashtra Saraswat (2nd Ed.) p. 48.

11 Nityanandaikya-Dipika I-158. Cf. Samskshep Sharirak Ch. II-84.

The three view points are described thus—

परिणामबुद्धिमुपमृद्य पुमान् । विनिवर्तयत्यथ विवर्तमतिन् ।
उपमृद्य तामपि पदार्थधिया । परिपूर्णदृष्टिमुपसर्पति सः ॥

[12] Anubhavamrit-Tatparya in Bhakti-Sudha (Published by Badve Samiti Pandharpur-1930).

सदास्वप्रकाशासि कोण प्रकाशी । ... अशी ज्ञान अज्ञान शद्बप्रमाणें ।
स्वतःसिद्ध वस्तुविशी अप्रमाणें । निषेधूनि हीं खंडिलीं ज्ञानराजें ॥

[13] Ramadasi Samsodhan manuscript No. 1041 (Dhulia). One of the manuscript is also in possession of Shri Dhunda Maharaj Deglurkar.

[14] अस्मिन् ग्रंथे श्रीज्ञानराजेन मायावादखण्डनेन अजातसिद्धांत उत्कृष्ट-रीत्या प्रतिपादितोऽस्ति । –उपोद्‌घातः

[15] Dr. R. G. Bhandarkar—Vaishnavism, Saivism and Minor religious Systems, p. 131.

[16] Dr. Kshitimohan Sen—Medieval Mysticism of India, p. 56.

[17] Dr. Nicol Macnicol—Indian Theism (1915) p. 120.

[18] Dr. S. N. Dasgupta—Indian Idealism, p. 198.

[19] Dr. Radhakrishnan:—Indian Philosophy Vol. I, p. 531.

[20] Rev. Edwards has given an English translation of the 18th chapter of Jnaneshwari in his "Jnaneshwar, the Outcast Brahmin". Mr. Manu Subhedar's translation is complete but not adequate. He has mainly relied on Mr. Moghe's versification of Jnaneshwari into current Marathi. Recently Shri. Bhagawat has published his English rendering of the Jnaneshwari which will be more useful to the English readers.

[21] Prof. R. D. Ranade—Mysticism in Maharashtra, p. 158.

[22] Ibid, p. 425.

[23] Proceedings of the 2nd Indian Philosophical Congress p. 297-305.

[24] Ibid, p. 299.

[25] Chitramaya Jagat Magazine from August 1922 to June 1923.

[26] Tatvajnan Mandir Trai-Masik—

श्रीज्ञानदेव. पाश्चात्य तत्ववेत्ते व आत्मानुभवी संत; व १९–१.
श्री ज्ञानेश्वरमहाराजांची जगन्मिथ्यात्वाची कल्पना; व १६, २, ३

[27] Jnaneshwar-Darshan, part II, p. 21-22.

[28] Dr. S. D. Pendse—"Jnaneswaranche Tatvajnan," p. 450.

[29] Mr. L. R. Pangarkar—Marathi Vangmayacha Itihas, Vol. I, p. 732.

[30] Jnaneshwar Darshan Part II—'Shri Jnaneshwar Maharaj Va Anubhavamrit" by Mr. V N. Potdar B. A. LL. B., p. 427.

Chapter IV

METAPHYSICS — THE NATURE OF THE ULTIMATE REALITY.

Limitations of Pramanas

BEFORE considering Jnanadeva's view of Ultimate Reality, it is necessary to take up the problem of Pramanas or the means of ascertaining right knowledge, which occupies an important position in the history of Indian philosophy. Every one of the great Indian philosophers is rightly fond of discussing the different Pramanas first, and then of propounding his views in the light of that discussion. Different schools of Indian Philosophy emphasise or accept different Pramanas or the sources of valid knowledge. Opinions about the nature and the number of these Pramanas differ. Though the maximum number of Pramanas is ten, six of them are common. These are:— (1) Pratyaksha or sense-perception; (2) Anumana or Inference; (3) Shabda or Verbal testimony of sacred texts like the Shrutis; (4) Upaman or analogy; (5) Arthapatti or Presumption and (6) Anupalabdhi or Non-apprehension. The materialists like Charvakas accept perception as the only source of valid knowledge. In addition to perception, Jainas admit inference and testimony, while Naiyayikas add comparison or analogy also to the first three sources. The Mimamsakas of Prabhakar school admit the first five sources while those of Kumaril school admit all the six sources as valid.

Vedant Philosophy includes different schools like monism of Shamkar, qualified monism of Ramanuja, dualism of Madhva and pure monism of Vallabha. All the schools emphasise the third Pramana i.e. the testimony of the

Vedas. Shamkar regards word or testimony as the only Pramana which is philosophically valid, the others having only an empirical value. Only Vedant Texts reveal the true and ultimate nature of the Reality while all the other sources of knowledge are useful in our ordinary life which is based upon super-imposition (Adhyas).[1] Ramanuja, Madhva and Vallabha reject Shamkar's theory of super-imposition and Nescience. Hence the sources of knowledge like perception and inference play more important roles in their systems. These sources, however, have their limited provinces which they cannot transcend. What these Pramanas reveal about cosmos is real but they are powerless in determining the nature of the ultimate Reality or the Supreme Being. The only authority which tells us about the Great Being is the sacred scriptures. The Upanishads, the Bhagawadgita and the Bramhsutras are called Prasthan-trayi and these are regarded as the supreme authority regarding the nature of Brahman or the Ultimate Reality. Besides these Ramanuja regards the Pancharatra Agama and the Prabandhas of the Alvars as authoritative texts.[2] Along with the Vedas, Madhva accepts the authority of some Puranas, Pancharatra Agamas, the Mula Ramayana and the epic Mahabharata.[3] "The Vedas, the words of Lord Shri Krishna, the Sutras composed by Vyas, the Samadhibhasha (the Bhagawat) of Vyas" are the four authorities of Vallabha.[4] Though all the above philosophers i.e. Shamkar, Ramanuja, Madhva and Vallabha consider Prasthan-trayi as the supreme authority, their interpretations differ widely and we see the phenomena of monism, dualism and other schools founded on the same sacred works. Though the foundational texts are the same the view of every Acharya about the ultimate problems is different and their conceptions about God, self and the universe do not agree.

The above mentioned philosophers mainly rely upon the sacred scriptures. But Jnanadeva does not give so much importance to these and relies on his own experience. He says, "And it is not because Shiva or Shri Krishna has spoken this, that we are making our statement. It would have been the same if they had not spoken."[5] Different Pramanas also are of no use in revealing the nature of the ultimate Reality. According to Jnanadeva Reality is self-evident and self-illuminating and hence does not require to be proved by other means. The so called valid sources of knowledge are themselves illuminated by this Reality. We see different objects in the light of the Sun but those objects do not reveal the Sun itself. In the same way the various proofs presuppose the self-luminious Reality and do not prove its existence.[6] The light that enlightens all other things does not require any other thing for its perception.[7] "It is the person who lights the candle and not the candle that creates the person."[8]

Ancient Indian philosophers took up the four Mahavakyas (important sacred texts) like "Thou art that" (Tatvamasi), "I am Brahman" (Aham Brahmasmi), "This self is Brahman" (Ayamatma Brahma), "Knowledge is Brahman" (Prajnanam-Brahma),[9] and tried to interpret them according to their own views. With great skill they all try to show how these sacred texts conform to their own doctrines. Sometimes they have tortured the texts to such a length that they have squeezed a meaning which is quite opposite to the one they indicate. Thus Madhva, while explaining the meaning of "Tatvamasi" says that instead of reading Tatvamasi (That thau art) it should be read as 'Atatvamasi (Thou art not that).[10] Jnanadeva, however, does not build his philosophical structure on the so called revealed words. He strikes at the very root and criticises the efficacy of the "word" itself to reveal the nature of the ultimate Reality. The word is of great use in our daily life. It shows us what we ought to do and what we ought to avoid. It also is useful in reminding the things that are forgotten.[11] But though useful in this way it cannot be brought forth as a proof of the ultimate Reality, which being self-evident and self-existent needs on proof by word. "The Absolute does not prove itself by any means of proof, nor allows itself to be disproved. It is self-evident, beyond proof or disproof. It is, therefore, groundless to believe that the word can gain greatness by enabling the Atman to experience itself." [12]

It is said that the Nescience or Avidya suppresses the nature of Reality and the word has got the power to destroy the darkness of Nescience. But what is the nature of this Nescience itself? The word Avidya itself shows that it is that which does not exist.[13] So to destroy a thing which does not exist is like breaking the horn of a hare or like plucking the sky flower.[14] The word is futile both ways. It can neither destroy ignorance because ignorance does not exist, nor reveal the Reality which requires no aid of any other thing because of its self-luminosity. The word is, therefore, useless like a lamp, lit up in broad daylight, which does not destroy the darkness which is not there, nor light the Sun who is self-effulgent.[15]

In this way the so called gateways of knowledge like perception, inference etc. are not necessary to prove the existence of Reality. Not even sacred words are required for this purpose. These words may point to Reality but cannot be regarded as its proof.

The Conception of Sat, Chit and Ananda

Reality is often designated as Sat Chit and Ananda-Existence, Consciousness and Bliss.[16] Though this is a working conception it is metaphysically inadequate. Jnanadeva has shown this in the fifth chapter of Amritanubhava. Existence, Consciousness and Bliss cannot be real designations of the ultimate Substance. "The poisonousness of a poison is nothing to itself." [17] These are the modes of our apprehension and not the Thing-in-itself. Though there seems to be a triad of Existence, Consciousness and Bliss they denote only one Reality. As lustre, hardness and yellowness together constitute gold, or as viscocity, sweetness and fluidity together constitute nectar, or whiteness, fragrance and softness is only camphor, so the triad of Existence, Consciousness and Bliss is nothing but one Reality.[18]

Moreover these three terms are used by Shruti for telling what the Reality is not and not for indicating what it is. The Reality is called Sat or existence in order to tell that it is not Asat or non-existent. Similarly the words Chit (consciousness) and Ananda (Bliss) are used in order to point out that Reality is not Jada (material) and Dukkha (pain). Hence the word Sachchidananda does not define Reality but is used to differentiate it from the opposites.[19]

In fact, Reality is beyond knowledge and ignorance. Just as the sun is not illuminated by another light or covered by darkness, in the same way, Reality is not brightened by knowledge nor darkened by ignorance. If we say that Reality knows itself that would imply that it was ignorant of itself for some time, because knowledge is always relative to ignorance. Again both existence and non-existence being relative conceptions, they cannot be applied to it.[20]

But to say that Ultimate Reality is beyond existence and non-existence, beyond consciousness and ignorance, beyond bliss and misery, does not mean that it is a void or a Nihil, as the Madhyamik school of Buddhistic Philosophy maintains. Nagarjun was the propounder of Nihilism and his philosophy is neither idealism, nor realism nor absolutism but blank phenomenalism which only accepts the phenomenal world as it is but without any kind of essence, ground or Reality behind it.[21]

Jnanadeva refutes the doctrine of Nihilism and maintains that though Ultimate Reality cannot be called existent or non-existent, it does not mean that there is nothing existing except a void. If it is said that there is nothing but void, there must be some one to say to whom this conviction comes. If the extinguisher of the lamp is extinguished along with the lamp, who will understand that the lamp is extinguished? If, during sleep, the person who sleeps gives up life, then who will, on awaking, remember the happiness of a sound sleep? A jar is visible when intact and equally visible when it is broken. Now when it does not exist it does not mean that the person who sees the non-existence of a jar also does not exist. In the same way that which perceives void does not become void itself. Suppose a man is asleep in a lonely forest where there is no human being. Now he is neither perceived by others nor by himself. But it cannot be maintained on that account that he is not there. Or if a black man stands in pitch darkness he does not see himself and others also cannot see him. But we cannot say that he is not there. Similarly though the words 'being' or 'non-being' do not apply to Ultimate Reality we cannot say that it is nothing or void. The sky is not visible to others and seems to be a vacuum but it stands in its own purity. In a dry lake with a subterranean spring the water is not visible outside but it is still there inside. So Reality though beyond being and non-being is there in its own glory. We say that the ground is with a jar when there is a jar and without a jar when there is no jar. But the presence or the absence of the jar does not affect the existence of the ground itself. So Reality is pure Knowledge which is beyond relative knowledge and ignorance.[22]

To summarise, the terms Sat, Chit and Ananda do not describe the nature of Ultimate Reality. They only show the negation of their opposites and are not positively applicable. In this way Reality is beyond Sat, Chit and Ananda but it does not mean that it is a Nihil.

The Nature of Ultimate Reality

If Ultimate Reality is beyond Sat, Chit and Ananda, what is its nature? Is it knowable or unknowable? Can we tell something positive about it? The answer of Jnanadeva is in the affirmative. The knowledge of Ultimate Reality is possible and it can be described positively. Of course this knowledge is not like the knowledge of some external object but it is like an immediate experience. Ultimate Reality is Pure Consciousness — the substratum of subject-object relation. It is the Experience which manifests itself into the manifold objects in the world. This pure Knowledge or Consciousness is self-evident and self-established. No other proof is required to prove its existence not because it is a blind assumption or a working hypothesis but it is the presupposition of all proofs.

Now this self-illuminating Reality and its self-awareness form as it were a twin which gives birth to the whole universe. These two, though distinguishable, are inseparable. The Ultimate Twin in the form of Knowledge and its self-cognition are called by Jnanadeva, God and Goddess. These two are without limitation (nirupadhik) and parents of the universe. The epithet "without limitation" is most important. Shivakalyan, in his commentary, has brought out the full significance of this word.[23] The God and Goddess. though the words are two, they mean the same Reality and are not two different entities. These are the creators of the universe and they are without limitation. Now here we see a contradiction and two objections can be raised against this statement. First, if the Reality is one why the two names are used? It is superfluous to do so. Secondly, how these two are without limitation? But these objections will be answered if we look into the real nature of the two viz. God and Goddess. The Supreme Reality is Pure Consciousness (Nikhal Drinmatra). Though it cannot be called Sat, Chit and Ananda in a relative sense, we can say so in a transcendent sense. Hence Reality is Pure Existence, Pure Knowledge and Pure Bliss. This is the positive description of Reality. Pure Existence is ever present to Itself and hence It is Pure consciousness. The Existence and Consciousness are inseparable, hence It is Pure Bliss. The knower and the known are not two opposite and separate entities. The one Reality experiences Itself naturally, hence there is the eternal union in the Pure Existence, which is Pure Knowledge and its self-cognition, hence there is the eternal and spontaneous Bliss. As the ocean, assuming the form of garlands of waves, enjoys itself, so Reality naturally manifests itself in the two forms and experiences Its own delight. When one knows oneself it cannot be said that there are two beings, one the knower and the other the known. In the same way, the words God and Goddess do not point to two different realities, but they are the two aspects of the same Experience. Hence we can safely use the two names. Moreover the two i.e. God and Goddess do not delimit or distort each other; hence they are called

Nirupadhik (without limitation). The two are inseparably united, causing not a degradation of the Absolute into the finite existence but the manifestation of the richness of the Absolute in the form of the finite universe.

God and Goddess or Purush and Prakriti

The conception of Purush and Prakriti occupies an important position in the history of Indian Philosophy. Various schools have various conceptions about the two, and these conceptions differentiate them from each other. Jnanadeva's conception of Purush and Prakriti is a peculiar one and has an important bearing upon his whole philosophy.

The author of "Jyotsna" — a commentary upon Amritanubhava — has tried to show similarities of Jnanadeva's view of God and Goddess or Purush and Prakriti with some passages in the Upanishadas. He mentions the Brahadaranyaka, Kena and Svetasvetar Upanishadas. In the Brahadaranyaka Upanishad we get the passage "In the beginning this universe was Self alone in the shape of a person (Purush). Looking round, He saw nothing but His self.... He felt no delight.... He wished for a second. He was as large as man and wife closely embraced. He then made his self fall into two and thence arose husband and wife. Therefore, Yajnyavalkya said, "we two are thus (each of us) like half of a shell". Therefore the space which was there is filled by the wife. He embraced her and human beings were born."[24] In the Kenopanishad a story is told to describe the power of Brahman. Once upon a time there was a fight between Gods and demons and the Gods won the victory. This was due to the power of the Brahman in them, but the Gods thought that they alone won the battle. Hence Brahman, in order to remove their arrogance, presented Himself before them in the form of a Yaksha (spirit). The Gods, being wonderstruck, sent Agni (fire) to Him but Agni could not burn even a small blade of grass before the Brahman. Similarly when Vayu (wind) was sent, he also could not blow away that blade. Lastly when Indra went before the Yaksha, he saw not a Yaksha but a beautiful damsel in his place. She told Indra about the power of Brahman and it was through this power that Gods were able to gain victory.[25] Here the Brahman's assuming the form of a beautiful celestial damsel (Uma Haimavati) appears to be similar to Jnanadeva's conception of God and Goddess. Again, in the Svetasvetara Upanishad, it is said — "Know then Prakriti is Maya and the great Lord the Mayin. The whole world is filled with what are his members."[26] Prakriti is identified with Maya which is also described as the snares of the Godhead inside which all beings are entangled.

Now, if the above passages referred to by the author of "Jyotsna" are closely examined, it will be seen that the passage in the Brahadaranyak has cosmological import and not metaphysical. It tries to explain how the duality of sex is generated from the Atman and does not describe its real nature, and as Prof. Ranade has pointed out, it yet leaves the inorganic generation entirely unexplained.[27] Jnanadeva's God and Goddess are parents of the whole universe containing both organic and inorganic nature. Again, in the same chapter of the Brihadaranyak, it is suggested that the Brahman was alone and hence without delight. So It created the world. It was not strong enough and so It created the four castes. This lack of delight and strength are not found in Jnanadeva's conception of the Ultimate Reality which overflows with delight and manifests itself in the form of the world.

The parable in the Kenopanishad is told to describe the power of the Godhead over the various deities, and the celestial damsel does not represent the eternal aspect of Reality like the Goddess of Jnanadeva. She is only brought forth to proclaim the great power of Brahman and represents the philosophical wisdom which consists in knowing that all physical as well as mental power is to be regarded merely as the manifestation of the power of Brahman.

The description of Prakriti in the Svetasvetar Upanishad is more akin to the Maya of Shamkar than to the Goddess of Jnanadeva. Though Prakriti is described as the creative power of God, that power is identified with Maya — the magic power of God. Who is a great magician that has caught in his meshes (which is no other than Maya) various individuals.[28] In this way the Prakriti or Maya is one who misleads the individual soul, while the Goddess of Jnanadeva is the affectionate mother of the universe.

Jnanadeva's view of God and Goddess, as expressed in his Amritanubhava, is quite distinct from the Samkhya view of Purusha and Prakriti or the Vedantic doctrine of Brahman and Maya. According to Samkhya system, Purusha and Prakriti are two separate entities that are eternal, and cannot be united. One of them i.e. Purusha is a sentient, passive spectator, while the other i.e. Prakriti is material. While Purusha watches her she dances before him and evolves the whole world out of herself. Though Purusha is only a spectator, "he seems to see, to combine, to rejoice, to suffer and to will, does so by misapprehension only, like a spectator who is carried away by his sympathies for Hecuba, but who in the end dries his tears and stops his sighs, leaves the theatre of the world, breathes the fresh air of the night."[29] Vedant (as interpreted by Shamkar) tries to escape this duality; but instead of Prakriti it brings forth Maya or Avidya. This Avidya or Nescience veils and distorts the Brahman and causes the appearance of this world which is no more than an illusion. Avidya itself is of an illusive nature and cannot be called existing or non-existing. Both the views, the views of Samkhya and of Vedant (of Shamkar), are inadequate. Samkhya has the drawback of assuming two eternal principles, and of regarding matter evolving out of itself. There cannot be two Ultimate Realities as they will be limited by each other's existence and hence spoil their absoluteness. Similarly material substance cannot create the world, and if it can, it cannot be called material. The Vedantic view is also marred by the assumption of Avidya, which seems to overpower even Brahman — the Ultimate Reality. Jnanadeva has refuted this doctrine of Avidya in the seventh chapter of Amritanubhava and we shall see his skilful refutation while dealing with his cosmological views.

Discarding both the views Jnanadeva describes the sweet intimacy of the God and Goddess. Jnanadeva himself has not used the words Purusha and Prakriti because of the old associations. He has not used the word Brahman also, to denote Ultimate Reality. His words are "the Self", "The Substance" or 'God'. The word "Brahman" has certain associations and hence he seems to have discarded it. The problem about Ultimate Substance is one of the persistent problems of philosophy, and at the beginning of the Amritanubhava, Jnanadeva deals with it in his own way. While offering his customary salutation to the God and Goddess[30] he says, "I bow down to the two parents of the universe, who are beginningless and without limitation." Apparently it seems that he admits two cosmic substances. But his further description brings out clearly their unique nature. He says that the Lover himself has become the Beloved of his heart and their love is so deep and intense that they swallow each other and again emit. So these two are but the aspects of One and the same Substance. The two complete each other and can not remain without each other. "Oh! how sweet is their union of love! The expanse of the whole universe is insufficient for their play although they reside happily even in a tiny atom. Each is the very life of the other so that nor even a blade of grass is created without their mutual help. Though they appear as two, there is only one Divinity, just as the word is one though the lips are two, or the fragrance is the same though the flowers are two. The sound is one though sticks are two, the light is the same though there are two eyes. So this eternal couple is eternally tasting the sweet nectar in the form of their sweet union. They are inseparable like sugar and sweetness, camphor and fragrance. Shiva is always accompanied by Shakti like wind and motion, gold and lustre, musk and fragrance, fire and warmth."[31] So in the words of Spinoza we can say that the Ultimate fact is "God loves Himself."[32]

So the God and the Goddess are one and the same. Both are identical with the Supreme Being behind the world. For realising Himself the Supreme Being assumes the two forms which, however, are inseparable like light and refulgence, moon and light. Both are responsible for the origination of the world and both of them fill up macrocosm as well as the microcosm. Both of them merge themselves into one form, or if they please they allow the two forms to emerge out of themselves. The unity, intimacy and inseparability of the God and the Goddess will be clearly understood when we bear in mind the identity of God with the pure Consciousness and that of Goddess with its self-cognition. Jnanadeva calls It elsewhere "Svasamvedya" Atmarupa, the self-cognizing Ultimate Reality.[33]

Jnanadeva describes in his Changdeva Pasashthi how the same Reality manifests itself in the triad of knowledge, knower and the known.[34] Though they appear as three, there is only one Reality which Jnanadeva calls "Samvitti" — Pure Knowledge. It is nothing but Reality perceiving Itself. Similar descriptions are also found in the Jnaneshwari.[35]

1 तमेतमविद्याख्यमात्मानात्मनोरितरेतराध्यासं पुरस्कृत्य सर्वे प्रमाणप्रमेयव्यवहाराः लौकिकाः प्रवृत्ताः ।

(It is in the wake of this mutual superimposition of the self and the not-self, which is designated Nescience, that there proceed all empirical usages of the world relating to valid knowledge and the means thereof.)

— Brahmasutra—Bhashyam, Introduction.

2 "As the Pancharatra is the word of God leading to the supreme spiritual goal of godliness, it is as valid as the Veda. The highest proof of the existence of God is the experience of God by godly men. The Alvars like the Vedic Rishis, had a direct experience of God and they invite humanity to share in the joy of their divine life".—Prof. P. N. Shrinivasachari M.A:—The Philosophy of Vishishtadvaita, Introduction, p. XXXI.

3 P. Nagaraj Rao M.A.:—The Schools of Vedant, p. 83.

4 वेदाः श्रीकृष्णवाक्यानि व्याससूत्राणि चैव हि । समाधिभाषा व्यासस्य प्रमाणं तच्चतुष्टयम् ॥ — Tatwadipnibandha Shastra, 7-8.

5 परी शिवें का श्रीवल्लभें । बोलिलें येणेंचि लोभें । मानू तें हे लाभें । न बोलताहि ॥ — Amritanubhava, III, 18.

6 सूर्याचेनि प्रकाशें । जें कांहीं जड भासे । तया तो गिवसे । सूर्य काई ॥ तेवि जेणें तेजें । वाचेसी वाच्य सूजे । तें वाचा प्रकाशिजे । हें कें आहे ॥ Ibid, V, 14-16

7 म्हणोनि स्वयंप्रकाशा यया । आपणपें देखावया । निमित्त हा वान्तोनिया । नाहीच्च मा ॥ Ibid, VII, 234.

[8] दीपु दावितयातें रची । की तेणेंचि सिद्धी दीपाची । तैसी सत्ता निमित्ताची । येणें साच ॥ Ibid, VII, 231.

[9] The four texts are found respectively, in Chandogya Upanishada VI, 7-8; Brihadaranyak Up. I, 4-10; Atharvaveda Part IV and Aitareya Up V-3.

[10] Madhava's commentary on Chchandogyopanishad VI 7-8.

[11] विधिनिषेधाचिया वाटा । दाविता हाचि दिवटा ।...किंबहुना शद्ब । स्मरणदानी प्रसिद्ध । Ibid. VI, 5, 12.

[12] तैसा आत्मा सच्चिदानंदु । आपणया आपण सिध्दु । आतां काय दे शब्दु तयाचें तया ॥ कोणाहि प्रमाणाचेंनि हातें । वस्तु घेना नेघे आपणयातें । जे स्वयें आइते । घेणें ना न घेणें ॥ म्हणोनि आत्मा आत्मलाभे । नांदवूनि शद्ब शोभे । येईल ऐसा न लभे । उमसू घेवो ॥

Ibid, VI, 93-95.

[13] अविद्या येणें नावें । मी विद्यमानचि नव्हें । हें अविद्याचि स्वभावें । सांगतसे ॥ Ibid, VI, 38.

[14] घटाचें नाहीपण फोडू । गगनाचीं फुलें तोडू । सशियाचें मोडू । शिंग सुखें ॥ Ibid, VI, 52.

[15] एवं माध्यान्हीची दिवी । तम धाडी ना दिवो दावी । तैशी उभयता पदवी ॥ शद्बा जाली ॥ आतां अविद्या नाहीपणें । नाही तये नासणें । आत्मा सिध्दुचि मा कोणें । काय साधावें ॥ ऐसां उभयपक्षीं । बोधा न लाहोनि नखी । हारपला प्रळयोदकीं । बोघू जैसा ॥ Ibid, VI 96-98.

[16] सत्यं ज्ञानमनन्तं ब्रम्ह...तैत्तिरीयोप.२... १...१.
यो वै भूमा तत्सुखम्......पंचदशी १... १०.

[17] सत्ता प्रकाश सुख । या तिहीं तीही उणे लेख । जैसे विषपणेचि विख । विखा नाहीं ॥ Amritanubhava, V, 10

[18] कांती काठिण्य कनक । तिन्ही मिळोनि कनक एक । द्राव गोडी पियूख । पियूखचि जेवी ॥ उजाळ दति मार्दव । या तिही तिही उणीव । हें देखिजे सावेव । कापुरीं एके ॥ Amritanubhava, V, 2-7.

[19] तैसे असताचिया व्यावृत्ति। सत् म्हणू आलें श्रुति। जडाचिया समाप्ति। चिद्रुप ऐसें॥ दुखाचेंनि सर्वनाशें। उरलें ते सुख ऐसें। निगदिलें निश्वासें प्रभूचेनि॥ ऐशी सदादि प्रतियोगिये। असदादि तिन्ही बे। लोटितां जाली त्रासे। सत्तादिका॥

Ibid, V, 10-13.

Shamkar, while explaining the already quoted passage of Taittiryopanishad, says that the words Satya, Jnana and Anant are used to differentiate the Brahman from their opposites.

[20] तैसें असणें आणि नसणें। हें नाहीं जया होणें॥

Ibid, IV, 25 also 16, 17,22.23

[21] Dr. S. N. Dasgupta, :—Indian Idealism, p. 79.

[22] तरी कांही नाहीं सर्वथा। ऐसी जरी वेवस्था। तरी नाहीं हें प्रथा। कवणासी पा॥ शून्य सिद्धांत बोधू। कोण्ही सत्ता होय सिध्दू। नसता हा अपवादू। वस्तूशी जो॥ मल्हविता दिवें। मल्हविते जरी मालवे। तरी दीपु नाहीं हें फावें। कोणासी पा॥ सर्वथा नाहीं तें नसें। कोणें म्हणावें॥

Ibid IV, 26-43.

In the Jnaneshwari the self-refusing character of Nihilism is described by comparing it to a naturally broken tusk in one of the hands of God Genesh

एकें हातीं दंतु। जो स्वभावता खंडितु। तो बौद्धमतसंकेतु। वार्तिकांचा।

I. 12.

[23] Amritanubhava I-1, and Shivkalyanas commentary on it.

ऐसी हे निरुपाधिके। जगाची जिये जनके। ते वंदिली मिया मूळिके। देवो देवी॥ (जेथे अर्थु जरी अेकचि जाण। तरी कासया येथें द्विवचन। आणि उपाधिसंबंधा न येवोन। जगत्कारणे कैशी॥ जेवी सागरुचि कल्लोळ झाला। होउनी भोगी कल्लोळ माळा। तेवि आपोआप मांडला। द्विधारुपें॥ .. येथें भेद नाहीं झाला। आपलीया रुपा आपण भाळला। म्हणोनी प्रकृतिपुरुष या बोला। पात्र जालें॥ .. आपआपणिया जाणणें. हें एकचि परी दोन वचनें। अत एव निरुपाधिके कारणें। जगाचि हें॥ –शिवकल्याण)

[24] Brihadaranyakopnishad, I, 4-3.

[25] Kenopanishad. Ch. III.

[26] Svetashvetaropnishad IV - 10.

[27] Prof. R. D. Ranade:—A Constructive Survey of Upanishadic Philosophy. p. 94.

[28] Svetashvetar Upanishad, III-1.

[29] Max Mullar-Six Systems of Indian Philosophy p. 295.

[30] ऐसी हे निरूपाधिके। जगाचि जिथे जनके। ते वंदिली मिया मूळिके। देवोदेवी ॥ Amritanubhava, I-1.

[31] कैसा मेळू आला गोडिये। दोघे न माती जगीं इये। कीं परमाणू-माजीही उवाये। मांडिली आहाती ॥११॥ जीहीं एक एकावीण। न कीजे तृणाचेंहि निर्माण। जिये दोघे जीव प्राण। जिया दोघा ॥१२॥

Amritanubhava, I.

[32] Spinoza:- Ethics; "God loves himself with infinite intellectual love" Part II, Prop. XXXV (Everyman Library edition; p. 219.)

[33] Jnaneshwari, I-1.

[34] तेवि आपणचि आपुला पोटीं। आपणया दृश्य दावीत उठी।
द्रष्टा–दृश्य- दर्शन त्रिपुटी। मांडे ते हे ॥ Changadeva Pasashthi, 18.

आपणिया सन्मुख। आपणचि जो ॥ Ibid, 16.

वस्तुमात्र निहाळे। आपणाशी ॥ Ibid, 28.

[35] ओं नमोजी आद्या। वेदप्रतिपाद्या। जयजय स्वसंवेद्या। आत्मरूपा ॥

Jnaneshwari, I-1.

ज्ञातृज्ञेयाविहीन। नुसधेचि जें ज्ञान। सुखा भरलें गगन। गाळींव जें ॥ जें कार्य ना कारण। जया दुजें ना एकपण। आपणया जें जाण। आपणचि ॥ Ibid, XV, 76-77.

जों आपणपेंचि आपणया। प्रकाशितसे धनंजया। काय बहु बोलो तया। नाहीं दुजें ॥ Ibid, XV, 557.

CHAPTER V

COSMOLOGY — THE NATURE OF THE WORLD

Epistemological Method of Jnanadeva

JNANADEVA is a spiritual monist. He regards Ultimate Reality as One and spiritual. Spirit is pure consciousness — the substratum of the knower and the known. His view so far resembles that of Shamkar, who regards Ultimate Reality as Pure Consciousness without subjective and objective relation (Nirvishaya Jnana). However, the resemblance ends with this common starting point, and their views are widely divergent when they come to deal with the triad of Knowledge, Knower, and the Known or perception, perceiver and the perceived. Jnanadeva has clearly stated his views on this matter in his Changadeva Pasasthi and Amritanubhava. His enquiry begins with the nature and relation of these three things and his method may be adequately called epistemological. He does not emphasise the problem how the world was created or what the stages of its gradual evolution were. According to him the triad of Knowledge, the Known and the Knower is the origin of the universe and so the nature of these three becomes an important topic in his philosophy.

Shamkar maintains that the subjective and objective relation is illusory and is due to Avidya or Nescience.[1] The world also is no more than an appearance though it has a reality for practical purpose (Vyavaharik Satta). His philosophy has rightly been summed up as "Brahman satyam Jaganmithya Jivo Brahmaiva naparah" — (Brahman alone is real, the world is illusory and there is identity between the soul and the Brahman.) Jnanadeva admits the reality of Brahman but rejects the falsity of the world. He clearly states in Changadev Pasasthi "Therefore, I do not understand when it is said that the origin of the perceived and of the one who perceives is Nescience. On the other hand, they are the natural expressions of Reality."[2]

Refutation of Mayavada

In order to defend his position Jnanadeva had to refute the theory of Avidya or Nescience and we find the whole of the seventh chapter of Amritanubhava to have been devoted to this refutation. This chapter is written elaborately and forms more than a third part of the whole work. Out of eight hundred and seven verses of the whole book Jnanadeva devotes two hundred and ninety five verses to this chapter on "Ajnana-Khandan". This "Inquiry into the nature of Ignorance" is the most important part of the philosophy of Jnanadeva. He refutes the Ajnanavada from various points of view, with great logical skill and gives various illustrations to support his refutation.

The concept of Maya is of great importance in the history of Indian Philosophy as it determines the world-view of its propounders or its opponents. Jnanadeva has refuted the doctrine of Ajnan which is identical with Maya of Shamkar. He has clearly declared that the entity which is called Maya by Vedantins is nothing but ignorance.[3]

When a philosopher asserts that Reality is Being which is one without second, he has to explain the appearance of the many or the process of 'becoming' in the universe. Some philosophers deny the one and some the many. Some deny 'being' while others deny 'becoming'. Plato in Greece, his seniors the Upanishadic Sages in India and their followers like Shamkar, denied the reality of all movement.

The Buddhists, on the other hand, as well as the crypto-Buddhists such as the Yogavasisthins pinned their faith on the mere flowing nature of all our experiences and things represented by them. So Shamkar, while propounding the One Absolute, had to account for its appearances. He had to explain the relation of Reality to appearances which he does with the help of his theory of Maya. Though the theory of Maya is found in its fullfledged form in Shamkar we find the germs of Mayavada in Upanishadas. In the Ishopanishad we find the conception of "Real's face being covered over with a golden vessel." In the Brihadaranyakopanishad there is a prayer to God to carry the devotee from Not-being to Being. The passages like "Brahman is one without second" "Here the many do not exist" imply that the Brahman is the only Reality while all the appearances are false. The extreme case of Mayavada is found in Goudpada's doctrine of Ajatvada — the doctrine of Non-creation. While enumerating the different views regarding the world he says, "Some people regard the world as the greatness of God, others as His creation, others as a dream, others as an illusion, others regard it merely as the Will of God, still others the object of His enjoyment, while some people call it the plaything of God, and yet others— regard it as God's nature." Gaudapada's own opinion is that the universe was not created at all.[4] Sometimes he seems to incline towards those who regard the universe as an illusion. Shamkar, however, is definite about his world-view based upon his theory of Maya or Adhyas (super-imposition).

Shamkar distinguishes between Vyavaharika Satta (empirical reality) and Paramarthika Satta (transcendental ideality). The world has only empirical reality. The appearance of the world is caused by Maya or Avidya (cosmic ignorance). Shamkar makes distinction between the two. This cosmic ignorance not only veils Reality, but distorts it and causes the appearance of manifold things in the universe. It is an innate error which is beginningless, positive, and indeterminable, though it can be removed by Jnana (Knowledge). Shamkar does not try to prove the existence of Maya but accepts it as indisputable.[5] It somehow obscures the Pure Consciousness, divides the Absolute and distorts it in the form of the world of difference. The rope appears as a snake, or a conch-shell appears as a piece of silver. So the Pure Brahman appears as the world through illusion. The cause of this illusion cannot be explained, as the concept of causality itself is the effect of the illusion. The Avidya is indefinable. It cannot be called real nor unreal, nor both. It is not real, because it is sublated in the state of liberation. It is not unreal since it is perceived. It can not be both, because to say so would be self-contradictory. According to Shamkar the world is a Parinama (effect) of the Avidya or Maya, while it is a Vivarta (perversion) of Brahman. The world resides in Brahman as the illusion of a snake is said to reside in the rope.

Shamkar's doctrines of Maya, which maintains the phenomenality of God, man and nature and asserts the Reality of Pure Consciousness only, raised a great protest against himself. All the other schools of Vedant viz. Vishishtadwait (qualified monism), Dwait (dualism), Shuddhadwait (pure monism), Dwaitadwait (non-dualism in dualism) have tried to refute it from their own points of view. Jnanadeva's view of Absolute Reality is different from that of Shamkar as well as from the views of the above mentioned schools of Vedant. He has also criticised the doctrine of Maya from his own point of view. In order to appreciate his criticism we shall first have to see, in brief, how other philosophers have refuted it.

Ramanuja

Ramanuja's refutation is known as *Saptavidha Anupapatti* or the sevenfold inadmissibility. The seven charges are as follows:-

1. *Ashraya Anupapatti:-* Avidya has no Ashraya or basis. The seat of Avidya should be either Jiva or Brahman. It cannot be Jiva, because Jiva itself is a fictitious product of Avidya. It cannot be Brahman, for it is self-illumined and can never be enveloped by Avidya.

2. *Tirodhan Anupapatti:-* There cannot be a tirodhan or obscuration of Brahman. If Brahman, which is of the nature of Pure self-illumination, is said to be hidden by Avidya, it means the destruction of the very nature of Brahman.

3. *Swarup Anupapatti:-* It relates to the understanding of Swarup or Nature of Avidya. If the defect of Avidya is real it cannot be destroyed. There will be two Realities and consequently monism will fail. If it is unreal, how is it brought about? If it is brought about by another defect we can ask the same question about that defect, and there will be an endless regression (anvastha). If it is held that the defect is the very essence of intuition of Brahman, the Brahman being eternal, the defect also will be eternal and there will be no emancipation.

4. *Anirvachaniya Anupapatti:-* The nature of Avidya cannot be logically determined. It is neither real nor unreal. To say a thing is indefinable is illogical.

5. *Pramana Anupapatti:-* Avidya is not testified by any means of knowledge (Pramanas) such as perception, inference and revelation.

6. *Nivartak Anupapatti:-* It is the criticism of the theory of the sublation of Avidya. Ajnana cannot be sublated or dispelled by Jnana, as Jnana itself is the product of Ajnana.

7. *Nivritti Anupapatti:-* Avidya is a concrete Reality. The sorrows that are experienced by it are not false. So mere knowledge would not be useful to destroy Avidya, but there is the necessity of God's grace. According to Ramanuja, Jiva is a Prakara (mode) of Brahman. So the knowledge, that Jiva and Brahman are identical, is not a true knowledge but a false cognition which, instead of relieving man from the bondage of Nescience, tightens the knot.

So Ramanuja shows that the concept of Avidya is entirely contradictory to the non-duality of Brahman and his nature as pure consciousness. The concept of Avidya itself is unintelligible and is incapable of being used as a principle of explanation. Avidya is not only logically inexplicable but cannot be proved also as a fact of experience.

Other philosophers like Madhva, Nimbark and Vallabha have also criticised the doctrine of Ajnana in the same way. Though all of them have different views about the nature of the Ultimate Reality, they all agree in rejecting the Advaitin's conception of Avidya.

Madhwa

The Advaitin's conception of Ignorance is refuted by Madhwa on the following grounds:-[7]

(1) Omniscience of the Absolute is incompatible with ignorance. If at any time Omniscience becomes clouded by ignorance, it would cease to be Omniscience.

(2) It is said that though there is identity between the Absolute and the finite, the latter has been alienated from the Absolute by the separating mischief of Upadhi. So, while Brahman is Omniscient, Jiva, under the influence of Upadhi, has ignorance. To this, we may ask, whether the Upadhi is real or imaginary. If it is held to be real, there will be two realities, which is contradictory to the doctrine of monism. If the Upadhi is held to be belonging to the realm of illusion and its origin held to be in ignorance, there would be the fallacy of *regress ad infinitum*. The Upadhi, credited with the power of ignorance, would itself be the effect of ignorance and there would be the fallacy of Ananyashraya i.e. vicious reciprocity of causality.

(3) If it is said that Upadhi creates the difference that produces ignorance, there is the distortion of factual evidence. Really speaking, Upadhi does not create difference *de novo*. It only reveals the difference which is already there. Hence the difference is not illusory, and is, therefore, not the cause of ignorance.

Nimbark

Nimbark is the champion of Bheda-bheda-vada i.e. the theory of the Absolute as Unity-in-difference. He refutes the theory of Avidya in the following way:—[8]

(1) An illusion is possible in a locus only when it has some specific as well as general characters. But, if Brahman is absolutely qualitiless, it is impossible that it should be the locus of any illusion.

(2) It is difficult to explain how Ajnana could have any support or object. Therefore illusion itself becomes inexplicable. Brahman being of the nature of pure knowledge, can hardly be supposed to be the support or the object of Ajnana. Jiva also, being itself the product of Ajnana, cannot be regarded as its support.

(3) Since Brahman is of the nature of pure illumination and Ajnana is darkness, the former cannot legitimately be regarded as the supporter of darkness.

(4) Ajnana is devoid of consciousness. and cannot. therefore, be regarded as the agent of the operation that results in the formation of illusion.

(5) The false appearance of Brahman as a diverse undesirable phenomenon is inexplicable. If Brahman is always conscious and independent, it cannot be admitted to allow itself to suffer through undesirable states.

(6) If Ajnana is regarded as an existent unity, there is the change to dualism, if it is regarded as non-existent, it cannot hide the nature of Brahman.

(7) If Brahman is self-luminous, how can it be hidden and how can there by any illusion about it? If the conch-shell shines forth by its own nature, there cannot be any misconception of its nature as a piece of silver.

(8) If the nature of Brahman is admitted to be hidden by Ajnana, the question arises whether Ajnana hides it as a whole or in part. In the former case the world would be absolutely blind and dark; in the latter. it is not possible because Brahman is a homogenous entity and has no parts.

Vallabha

Vallabha's standpoint is Shuddhadwait-Pure monism. According to him Maya is not Nescience as Shamkar maintains but it is the power of the Lord. The author of Shuddhawaitmartand criticises the conception of nescience as follows:—[9]

(1) Is nescience caused or uncaused? If it is caused. then it must have some originator and that originator must be Brahman, as Shruti has declared. The Brahman of Shamkar is, however, without attributes. and if it is taken to be the originator, it becomes "Savishesh" i.e. with attributes.

(2) Now if the nescience is taken to be uncaused there will be two uncaused substances i.e. Brahman and Maya, and that will destroy the very foundation of Adwaitism.

(3) To hold that Nescience is neither being nor non-being, is inadvisable, for an object must either exist or not exist. It cannot be both at one and the same time.

(4) Nescience is held by advaitins as beginningless but not eternal. But this is mere contradiction. Beginninglessness and endlessness are inseparable concomitants.

(5) It is said that Maya is natural to Brahman. But how is pure knowledge turned into that whose nature is nescience?

(6) That Nescience has a temporary existence, is also inadmissible because one cannot point out when it comes into existence and when it ceases to exist.

Jnanadeva

According to Jnanadeva, knowledge and ignorance are both relative terms. The Ultimate Reality is pure knowledge. Hence the so called knowledge and ignorance are mere words without corresponding existence. They are like gardens in a picture, where we cannot smell the painted flowers or taste the various fruits.[10] Now it is said that though ignorance is not real for all time, it exists for some time at least before its destruction by knowledge, hence its total absence cannot be maintained. Jnanadeva, in his introduction to Chapter VII of Amritanubhava, answers this objection by saying, that if the existence of ignorance is taken for granted before the rise of knowledge, that existence of ignorance does not even become the object of hearing, i.e. nothing can be said about the nature of ignorance because that description itself would not be made without the help of knowledge. The existence of ignorance is illusory like the light of a glow-worm. Though that light appears in the darkness, it does not enlighten and dispel the darkness. Hence, it is not worth the name of a light. In the same way ignorance appears like ignorance but really it is not so because it is not experienced. The thing which cannot be experienced, cannot be called as existing. A dream may be real in the state of dreaming, but its falsity does not diminish on that account. So the imaginary ignorance may have importance in imagination, but not in the real world. The horses in the clouds cannot be used for practical purpose nor can the ornaments produced by an enchanter be really used as one's adornments. So the ignorance does not exist from the beginning and hence, though we think about it, the result will not be anything different. If we assume that ignorance is dispelled as soon as knowledge arises, it means that though ignorance appears to be extinguished, it re-appears in the form of knowledge. Hence that knowledge is nothing but ignorance in another form. Ignorance being false, the knowledge that dispells it, is also false. Hence, both ignorance and knowledge that destroys it, are fictions of the mind.[11]

With this introduction Jnanadeva sets forth in search of ignorance and puts forward following arguments.

(I) Ignorance has no foundation, is unknowable and ineffective.

(a) If Ignorance exists it must exist in some substratum either full of knowledge or full of ignorance. The first alternative is not possible, because it is the nature of ignorance to nullify knowledge and make its substratum ignorant. The second alternative, also, does not hold. If ignorance existed in the beginning no manifestation would have been possible. Manifestation, on the other hand, is quite current with every one. Hence the alternative is invalid.[12]

(b) Ajnana or ignorance is not possible. But, taken for granted its possibility, can it be known? Ignorance cannot know itself since it is non-sentient. If ignorance befools a person how can he know ignorance itself.?[13]

(c) Suppose that ignorance is possible, and also that it can be known. In that case we will have to say that it is non-effective, because it does not nullify knowledge according to its own nature. The clouds do not really eclipse the Sun, who shows them. Sleep does not extinguish the life of the sleeper who experiences its happiness.[14]

(d) If it is assumed that ignorance is effective, it cannot be known i.e. if the ignorance could eclipse the knowledge, there would be all ignorance and none to tell its existence.[15]

(II) Ignorance can neither co-exist with knowledge nor can it exist independently.

(a) The knowledge which distinguishes ignorance cannot be itself ignorance. That which is called ignorance is a kind of knowledge. Hence the word ignorance is meaningless. It cannot be called a cataract that does not impair eye-sight. It cannot be a fire that does not burn. We cannot call it darkness when we see everything before us clearly. Sleep would not be worthy of its designation if it does not do away with our being awake. Night cannot be called night if it does not dispel daylight. Similarly, the ignorance that co-exists with Atman, yet does not conceal its knowledge, cannot be called ignorance.[16]

(b) The same thing is proved by an appeal to the fact that a thing cannot co-exist with another thing which is destroyed by it. Sleep and wakefulness, forgetfulness and memory, cold and heat, death and life cannot co-exist. In the same way ignorance that is densly dark and Atman which is the mine of effulgence cannot exist together.[17]

(c) Ignorance can never co-exist with knowledge. The thing in question co-exists with knowledge. Therefore it can never be ignorance.[18]

(d) Ignorance cannot exist independently, just as a disease cannot exist independent of any patient.[19] Hence, ignorance cannot remain with knowledge, nor without it, just as a fish made of salt, if it becomes alive, can neither live in water nor outside water.[20]

(e) No relation can exist between Atman and Ignorance, as no relation can exist between a rope and the illusory snake. The Rope cannot bind the illusory snake.

(III) Ignorance cannot be proved by any Pramana.

(a) The Pramanas like perception, inference etc., are not Ignorance itself, but they are the results of Ignorance, just like a creeper is the result of a seed, a dream is the result of sleep and the appearance of a double moon is the effect of something being wrong with the eye-sight. So the triad of the Knower, The Known and the Knowledge (Pramata, Prameya and Pramana) is the result of Ignorance. Hence the Pramanas are not entitled to be called Pramanas, because they do not spring from knowledge but from Ignorance.[21]

(b) If the identity of cause and effect is assumed all the things in the world would be non-different from Ignorance, and hence they cannot prove its existence. Both ways we cannot prove Ignorance, and the existence of Ignorance cannot be admitted for want of authoritative evidence. Ignorance neither produces any effect nor is it fit to be the cause of any effect. Hence it is unreal.[22]

(IV) Ignorance cannot dwell in Atman in its Pure state.

(a) It can be maintained that Ignorance dwells in Atman in its pure state, as fire dwells in the wood before churning. But this is not possible since even the word Atman has no room in that pure state, much less would there be room for Ignorance. It would be as futile as removing the burnt part of the wick before the lamp is lighted, or cleanse a mirror which has not yet been made.[23]

(b) To say that Ignorance existed in Atman when It was neither a being nor non-being, would be tantamount to saying that the non-entity of a jar was broken into thousand pieces.[24]

(c) One, who seeks to prove Ignorance in pure intelligence, seeks to defeat his own purpose just like a person who seeks to prove the existence of darkness in broad daylight. He is self-stultified.[25]

(d) And if it is not sought to be proved, its existence stands self-condemned.[26]

(V) Ignorance cannot be proved with reference to the manifestation of the Objective World.

(a) Objection:- Though it is difficult to call Atman by name, there is spread out before us this wide world, and not only it is spread out but is directly seen in front of us. It is true that Ignorance is not visible, but we cannot doubt its existence, for we can easily apprehend it by inference from the vast expanse of the visible world. If there is one moon in the sky and it appears as two, we infer that there is a disease of the eye-sight. Trees are fresh and green and though we do not see the source of water, still we infer that their roots are taking water which exists deep under the soil. So the existence of Ignorance is known from the visible world as the cause from the effect. Then again, though a man who is asleep is not conscious of the sleep which goes away at the time of awakening, still, his sleep can be inferred from the dreams. In the same way, Atman is pure, yet there is the appearance of the world. So we can infer that Ignorance exists.[27] Ignorance corresponds with sleep, and dream with the worldly appearance.

(b) Answer:- The argument, that the existence of Ignorance must be known by the process of mediate inference by reference to the vast expanse of the objective world, can be opposed with a counter-argument, — that the very existence of the objective world, far from being the outcome of Ignorance, speaks volumes for the existence of a counter-entity, which is diametrically opposite in character to the Ignorance in question. And one is not required to seek far to prove the existence of Knowledge, as its existence has got self-credentials. To call knowledge ignorance is a absurd as to call a thing dark collyrium when it makes all other things brighter and whiter than the moon. It is like saying that water performs the function of fire and that ambrosia produces poison. When we see in front of us Knowledge pervading all wordly activity, how can the flood of Ignorance ever come there? [28]

(VI) If Ignorance has the Power of Presentation, It Cannot be Called Ignorance.

When it is maintained that Ignorance presents the multiple existence to the perverted human eye, the Ajnanvadi still unconsciously and inspite of himself has as good as admitted that Ignorance has the power of presentation. Solid human experience shows that Ignorance cannot have the power of presentation. On the other hand, it is Knowledge which has been universally characterised with that power. Since that characteristic is admitted in a particular thing, it is immaterial to us if you call that particular thing by a different name. The so called Anjana (collyrium), which shows the treasure-trove, does not cease to have its peculiar power simply because it is called Anjana. The name Anjan, i.e. a black pigment, does not prevent us from seeing the treasure. In the same way the gold figure of Goddess Ambika, though it is resplendent with lustre, is ungrudgingly called Kalika which signifies Parvati associated with a dark colour.

As a matter of fact it is the light of the Absolute Sun that enlightens everything from Shiva to the clod of the earth, that causes the existence of wordly knowledge and gives birth to all insight. Who would try to point it out as Ignorance except a wretched person trying to shroud the Sun in a cloth of darkness?[29]

(VII) Ajnanvadin's Mal-apropism

Ajnanavadi describes Jnana, not with the word Jnana but with the word Ajnan i.e. "A" simply prefixed to the proper word Jnana without any particular meaning of its own. This verges on mal-appropism. Delimiting Atman by calling Ignorance is as fruitless as confining the fire in a lac-box. Just as fire reduces to ashes the lac-box and blazes aflame as usual, in the same way, the Atman breaks through the incrustation of the words of the Ajnanavadin and flourishes as self-luminous as ever.

The Ajnanavadi gains nothing by his wrong way of argumentation, but commits two sins—one, of misnaming a thing and the other, of utter falsehood by ascribing to the purest thing the most despicable name which signifies a filthy attribute. If pearls can be prepared out of water or a lamp lit with the help of burnt cow-dung, then alone can one attribute Ignorance to Pure intelligence.[30]

(VIII) Though Ignorance is supposed to be born out of Knowledge, it vanishes at its very birth.

Even granting that there was Ignorance in the beginning, Knowledge must have put an end to it. Hence there can be no talk of Ignorance. Knowledge cannot give birth to Ignorance, but suppose that it did so, still, at its very birth, Ignorance would die away in the presence of knowledge and there would remain Knowledge only. So it is useless to discuss about ignorance also from this point of view.[31]

(IX) The Support of the Shruti.

We have already seen that Jnanadeva does not rely upon the Sacred Scriptures for his thesis. However, in one verse, he says that the Vedas also say, "This world is illuminated by His light."[32] After putting forth all the arguments, this quotation comes at the end of the chapter. It shows that his reliance upon it is only secondary. The verse which is quoted occurs thrice in different Upanishadas.[33] It tells us that Brahman is "the light of lights".

> There no sun shines, no moon, nor glimmering star,
> Nor yonder lightening, the fire of each is quenched;
> From him, who alone shines, all else borrows its brightness,
>
> The whole world bursts into splendour at his shining.[34]

It is to be noted that Shamkar interpretes the above passage to denote the Reality of Brahman and falsity of the world.[35]

But Jnanadeva quotes the verse to support his theory of the world as the delightful expression of the Reality and not its illusory appearance.

(X) Atman would never meet Ignorance though he purposely tries to do so.

The non-existent Ignorance cannot be in any casual relation with the expanse of things, just as darkness can have no connection whatsoever with the Sun, Even though the Sun retires to its abode. The Sun will not come into contact with darkness though it retires to its abode, in the same way Atman can never come in contact with Ignorance though he might offer to take the help of Ignorance in fashioning the world.[36]

It will be seen, from the various criticisms of Ajnanvad given above that Madhva, Nimbark and Vallabha are following almost the same line of criticism as adopted by Ramanuja. Shri Pandurang Sharma in his articles on Jnaneshwar and other philosophers, has tried to show similarities between Ramanuja's various Anupapattis and the points of criticism adopted by Jnanadeva. Dr. Pendse has critically examined the views of Pandurang Sharma and his conclusions are as follows:—[37]

(1) The verses VII-10, 11 cited by Pandurang Sharma, as similar to Ramanuja's Ashrayanupatti, have only a partial similarity. Jnanadeva omits the part of 'Jiva's impossibility of being the locus of Avidya" which Ramanuja maintains.

(2) In the case of Tirodhananupapatti, Jnanadeva does not mention the name Tirodhan, but the criticism of Ramanuja is included in Jnanadeva's criticism of the locus of Avidya. Though there is no similarity in expression, the purport is similar. So there is a partial similarity also in this case.

(3) Swarupanupapatti—Here Pandurang Sharma cites the verses VII-5, 23, 35. Now these verses are instances of first two Anupapattis. Only the last line of the 35th verse which means "Ajnan cannot be proved independently," bears some resemblance, but the lines of argument followed by Ramanuja and Jnanadeva are different. Hence here also there is a partial likeness.

(4) Anirvachaniyatvanupapatti-VII-36, 39, 40 are quoted as its instances but these can be included under Ashra-

yanupapatti and Anupapatti of perception. Jnanadeva acknowledges that Nescience is Anirvachaniya; Ramanuja does not agree with him on this point. Hence there is no similarity between the two thinkers.

(5) Pramananupapatti:— Ramanuja criticises the view of the Advaitin who says that Ajnana being positive, is the object of Anupalabdhi Pramana, and shows that we cannot experience the positivity of Ajnana, while Jnanadeva shows all the Pramanas as invalid because they spring from nescience (as his opponent says).

(6) Anumananupapatti:— Same is the case as above. Dr. Pendse shows a point of similarity which is not noted by Pandurang Sharma. That is the argument from the appearance of the world. Ramanuja has not refuted the point while Jnanadeva has done so. Hence the similarity is not complete.

Dr. Pendse also shows how the other refutations are also dissimilar. But while doing so he tries to show similarities between the views of Jnanadeva and Shamkar which are not well-founded. He says that both Shamkar and Jnanadeva regard nescience as non-existent, hence Jnanadeva's Amritanubhava is nothing but an elaborate exposition of the Adhyasa-bhashya of Shamkar.[38] He quotes as his support two verses-VII-38 and VI-39. The first verse has the illustration of the rope and the serpent. But this illustration is given only to show that no relation can exist between Atman and Ignorance and not as Shankarites usually give it to show the illusory nature of the world. In the second verse Jnanadeva says that to call nescience as Anirvachaniya is as good as saying that it does not exist and by that very name it proves its non-existence. Shamkar also says, in his Adhyasbhashya, that Adhyasa which is called Avidya is false. But

Avidya is false from the point of view of those that have attained liberation, and not from the point of view of worldly people who are Ignorant; and all the categories of knowledge, knower and the known which pervade worldly appearance are the outcome of nescience.[39]

Now we have seen how Jnanadeva has criticised the view that Ajnana exists before the rise of knowledge, is his introduction to the Ajnana Khandan.[40] Then again, he has clearly stated that the manifestation of the world is not due to nescience but is the very expression of pure intelligence, and as such the triad of Knower, Knowledge and the Known does not spring from Ignorance, but is enlightened by the Atman. To Shamkar, the world is the outcome of Avidya, while to Jnanadeva, it is "Chidvilas." — The Play of the Absolute. Shamkar posits Ajnana between Atman and the world, while Jnanadeva, in his refutation, shows the utter futility of the idea and considers it to be not only unnecessary but even perverse, because Atman itself vibrates in the form of the Universe.[41]

So it must be said that Dr. Pendse has not interpreted the facts fairly when he has tried to identify the views of Jnanadeva and Shamkar. We can agree with him in so far as he says that Jnanadeva has not followed Ramanuja. In fact, though Ramanuja was a predecessor of Jnanadeva, the criticism about the locus of Avidya is such as can be independently suggested by the works of the Advaitins themselves, amongst whom there is a difference of opinion on this point. The followers of the old school like Sarvajnatmamuni, Prakashatman and Anandabodh maintain that Avidya is located in the Absolute Consciousness, while Vachaspati and his school hold that it is located in the Jiva-Consciousness. Jnanadeva has refuted the very existence of Avidya in his elaborate, subtle and skilful argument against the theory of Ajnana. He has taken great pains to show that the conception of Ignorance, as existing and causing the manifestation of the world, is logically absurd as well as distorting the facts of experience. Here we get the negative aspect of Jnanadeva's cosmological view. It tells us what the world is not, and warns us not to underestimate its content. It strikes at the root of Mayavada or Avidyavada of Shamkar which regards the world as caused by Nescience and, therefore, illusory.

The World-as the Expression of Divine Love and Joy

a) Atman is beyond description

While stating that the cause of the manifestation of the universe cannot be Ignorance, Jnanadeva describes the nature of Atman. Atman is not proved by any other means but His existence is self-established. He is beyond existence and non-existence. But He is not a void on that account. He sees without seeing anything. Though some try to establish His non-existence, He bears it calmly. In any state, even in deep sleep, His omniscience is not affected. The Veda cannot apprehend Him, the Sun cannot show Him, and the Sky cannot pervade Him. Ego-consciousness cannot catch Him. Intellect knows everything except Him. The Mind cannot imagine His being and various sense organs cannot taste how sweet He is. But His perfection is such that it swallows this incomprehensibility as well as its one-ness.[42]

b) The World as the sport of Atman.

Setting aside all these difficulties of indescribability, the doors of illumination are opened for the glorious display of Atman who becomes the Knower and the Known without being transformed. Visions upon Visions are displayed, but all of them rest upon one Pure Intelligence. The Atman is so intoxicated by the glorious spectacle of His creation that He does not wish to see the same scene over again in the mirror of the objective universe. Every moment He wears, as if, new and beautiful apparels. He expands Himself and shines forth as the world. The Observer, in the guise of the objects, comes to visit Himself. The thread of the unity is not the least disturbed. As water sports with itself under the guise of waves, the Atman plays with Himself by becoming the process of the universe and feels happy. No difference is created in the fire when it wears a garland of flames. The Sun cannot be held to be separated from its rays when it is thickly surrounded by them. The unity of the Moon is not disturbed even when enveloped by its light. The lotus is still a lotus even though it blossoms into a thousand petals. The king Sahasrarjuna has thousand hands but he does not become one thousand and one persons. Even when there are spread on a loom a number of threads, there is found in them nothing but thread. Though in the residence of speech there is a meeting of crore of words, still it is all speech. Similarly there is no difference in the Atman when He presents Himself either as the seer of the world, or as the world that He sees, for it is all Atman Himself. If a lump of sugar is broken to pieces it is nothing but sugar.[43]

c) No parallel can be found to this sport.

If the seed of a Banyan tree had been able to produce the full-grown tree without breaking itself, then it would have been possible to illustrate how the Atman expands Itself into the manifold world without disturbing Its unity.[44] The Atman is incomparable in Its richness or glory. It could have been compared with the sun if its rays had not gone out of it. Cotton cannot come out and produce cloth without the bursting of the cotton-boll. A gold bar cannot be turned into ornaments without changing itself. Water cannot pass from one place to another without surpassing the obstacles. So Atman cannot be compared with these. There is, therefore, no parallel to the sport of Atman and all that we can say about It is, It is like Itself.[45]

So in the evolution and involution of the world the self-illumination of the Atman is not changed and there is no other cause present except Him. The process of the universe is nothing but Atman's love for Himself and we have already seen how Jnanadeva has described the sweet union of God and Goddess which gives birth to the offspring in the form of the Universe. God and Goddess are one and it is as much as to say that God loves Himself. The whole Universe is not an enchanting deception of Avidya, but the expression of that Supreme Love.

[1] Shamkar; Brahmasutra Bhashya — Introduction.

[2] म्हणोनि अविद्यानिमित्तें । दृश्य दृष्टत्वें वर्तें । तें मी नेणें, --आइतें । ऐसेंचि असें । Changadeva Pasasthi.

[3] वेदांती इयेतें माया । असें म्हणिजें प्राज्ञराया । असो किती बोलो वागा । अज्ञान हें ॥ Jnaneshwari XIV. 71.

[4] Gaudapad — Mandukyakarika II-32.

[5] Dr. S. N. Dasgupta — History of Indian Phiiosophy Vol. I. p. 435.

[6] Ramanuja:—Shri Bhashya, p. 178.

[7] Madhwacharya:—Upadhi Khandan with Jaytirtha's Commentary; St. 1-3.

[8] Shrinivasa:—commentary on Nimbarka's Vedant-Parijat-Saurabh: I-1.

[9] Giridhar:—Shuddhadvait-Martand; p. 23, 25.

[10] एवं शब्दैकजीवनें । आपुडीं ज्ञानें अज्ञानें । साचपणें वनें । चित्रींचीं जैशीं ॥ Amritanubhava; VI-102.

[11] एऱ्हवी तरी अज्ञाना । जै ज्ञानाची नसे क्षोभना । तै तरी काना । खालीच दडे ॥ Ibid; VII-1, also 2-7

[12] Ibid; VII, 8-11.

[13] Ibid; VII, 12-14.

[14] Ibid; VII, 15-16.

[15] तैसें अज्ञान असें जेथें । तेंच जरी अज्ञान आते । तरी अज्ञान अज्ञानातें । नेणतां गेलें ॥ Ibid; VII-17.

[16] Ibid; VII, 18-24.

[17] Ibid; VII, 25-30.

[18] आत्मेनशी विरोधी । म्हणोनि नुरेचि इये संबंधीं ॥ Ibid; VII-34.

[19] वेगळें तरी सिद्धी । जायेच्चिना ॥ Ibid; VII, 35-36.

[20] लवणाची मासोळीं । जऱ्ही होय जिव्हाळी । तरी जळी ना वेगळी । न जिये जेवी ॥ Ibid; VII, 38-39.

[21] Ibid; VII, 42-47.

[22] Ibid; VII, 48-56.

[23] Ibid; VII, 58-64.

[24] Ibid; VII, 66-67.

[25] कां सूर्य कोणा लाहे । अंधाराते ॥ ७२. तैसा चिन्मात्रीं चोखडा । भलतैसा अज्ञानाचा झाडा । घेतला तरी पवाडा । येअील काअी॥७३.
Ibid; VII, 72-73.

[26] Ibid; VII, 76.

[27] Ibid; VII, 88-94.

[28] अगा ऐसिया ज्ञानातें । अज्ञान म्हणणें केउतें । काय दिवो करी तयातें । अंधारू म्हणिपे ॥ ९५. तैसा जाणणेयाचा वेव्हारू । जेथें भासला समोरू । तेथ आणिजे पूरू । अज्ञानाचा ॥ १००
Ibid; VII, 95-100.

[29] ऐसा निरूपमावरी । आपुलिये विलासवरी । आत्मा राणीव करी । आपुलें ठायीं ॥ २६८. येऱ्हवी शिवोनि पृथ्वीवरी । तत्वाच्या वानेपरी । जयाच्या रश्मिकरी । उजाळा येती ॥ २७२. Ibid; VII, 267-72.

[30] तें कोणें निकृष्टें । दाविलें अज्ञानाचेनि ब्रोटे । ना तमें सूर्या मोटें । बांधिना निके ॥ २७४. Ibid; VII, 274-86.

[31] ना ज्ञानीं अज्ञान जालें । ते होतांचि अज्ञान गेलें । पुढति ज्ञान एकलें । अज्ञान नाहीं ॥ Ibid; VII, 287

[32] विभाति यस्य भासा। सर्वमिदं हा ऐसा । श्रुति काय वायसा। ढेकर देती॥ Ibid; VII, 290.

[33] Kathopanishad, V-15; Svetasvetarop, VI-14; Mundakop, II-2-10.

[34] Duessen:—Philosophy of the Upanishadas; p. 137.

[35] Shamkar Bhashya on Mundakop. II-2, 10-11.

[36] अज्ञान कीर वावो । पाहो ठेलियाही ॥ परी तमाचा विसुरा । न जोडेचि दिनकरा । रात्रीचिया घरा । गेलियाही ॥

Amritanubhava; VII, 293-94.

[37] Dr. Pendse—Shri Jnaneshwaranche Tatvajnana; Ch. VII. p. 300-310.

[38] Ibid, p. 312.

[39] तमेतमविद्याख्यमात्मानात्मनोरितरेतराध्यासं पुरस्कृत्य सर्वे प्रमाणप्रमेय-व्यवहारा लौकिका वैदिकाश्च प्रवृत्ता...ब्रम्हसूत्र शांकर भाष्य, उपोद्घात,

[40] Amritanubhava; VII, 1-8

[41] तैसा जाणणेयाचा वेव्हारू । जेथें माखला समोरू । तेथ आणिजे प्रूरू । अज्ञानाचा ॥ १००.
यालागी वस्तुप्रभा । वस्तूचि पावे शोभा । जात असे लाभा । वस्तूचिया ॥ २९१. Ibid; VII, 100-291.

[42] कोण कोणा भेटे । दिठी कैची फुटे । ऐक्यासगट पोटें । आटोनि गेली ॥ १२२. Ibid; VII, 103-33.

[43] एवढें हि सांकडे । जेणें सारुनि एकिकडे । उघडली कवाडें । प्रकाशाची ॥ १२३. पाणी कल्लोळाचेनि मिसें । आपणपे वेल्हावे जैसें । वस्तु वस्तूत्वे खेळो ये तैसें । सुखे लाहे ॥ १३५. Ibid; VII, 123-143

[44] न फुटता बीज कणिका । माजी विस्तारे वटु असिका । तरी अद्वैत फाका । उपमा आथि ॥ Ibid; VII, 149.

[45] म्हणोनि इये आत्मलीळे । नाहीं आन कांटाळे । आता येयाचिये तुळे । हाचि यया ॥ २६६. Ibid; VII, 262-266.

Chapter VI

THE NATURE OF THE JIVA

Importance of the Problem

THE nature of the Jiva or the individual self is one of the main problems of Philosophy. The nature of God, man and the world are three outstanding problems and the value of any philosophy depends upon their satisfactory solution. The goal of any philosophical thinking is not merely an intellectual solution of a question but to guide man through weal and woe by showing him the beacon-light of his true nature, and by pointing out to him his real dignity and status in the whole universe and his relation with the Supreme Being. "Man, Know thy self" was the watchword of the teaching of Socrates. Only Knowledge of the Self was worth the name of Knowledge with the Upanishadic thinkers. Every other kind of Knowledge was a sign of poverty of the soul which did not know itself. A man may be versed in all sciences, may know the constituents of the atoms and the stars, may know all the fine arts, yet if he does not know himself it becomes all a vain parody of knowledge. Hence the test of all supreme philosophy is that it should be able to give man the knowledge of his own self.

The Various Conceptions of the Jiva

Various systems have, however, various conceptions of the Jiva or the individual soul. Though the nature of the self forms one of the persistent problems of philosophy it is also one of the most difficult problems and hence when we turn to the various answers to this question by different systems of philosophy, we find their bewildering variety. Charvakas consider consciousness as a function of the physical body, hence they identify the soul with it. The Yogachara school of Buddhists acknowledge the aggregate of ideas but deny their unifying principle in the form of the soul. The pluralistic realists like Naiyayikas regard the soul as a substance of which knowledge is an attribute and not the essence. The Samkhya philosophy regards the self as a pure, continuous, immutable consciousness and tries to explain the experience of activity and alterations of personality by stating that these are due to the false identification of the self with the Prakriti.

Different exponents of the Vedant philosophy have also different conceptions.

Shamkar:- He analyses the nature of the self and separates its noumenal and phenomenal aspects. The noumenal aspect is its consciousness without which there would be no sense of "I" or egoism. Ultimately the self is identical with Brahman, and at the dawn of true knowledge its selfhood vanishes. The empirical portion of the self is contributed by Maya. Hence the self has the spiritual element as well as physical and psychical adjuncts. These are all illusory and only the spirit is real.[1]

Ramanuja:- He regards the soul as the self-conscious atom different from its physical, psychical and vital functionings. The Relation between Brahman and Jiva is not that of the reality and its appearance but that of the soul and its body. As the soul controls, supports, and utilises its body for its own ends, in the same way Ishwar controls supports and utilises the selves for His purpose. The soul has very intimate and organic relation with Ishwar and is inseparable from Him.

Madhwa:— He sets forth a scheme of fivefold difference of which the first and foremost is the difference between Jiva and Ishwar. There are vital differences between the two. God is ever free from samsara, all-knowing and all-powerful creater of the universe, while the Jiva is comparatively ignorant, dependent and bound to the samsara. These limitations really pertain to the soul and are not merely due to our misapprehension. Some of these, like comparative ignorance and dependence, persist even in liberation.[2]

Nimbark:—He maintains that individual souls are infinite in number and atomic in size. All-pervading knowledge being their attribute, they can cognize various sensations in different parts of their bodies. The individual souls are, in one sense, different from God and in another sense, constituent parts of Him. Though atomic and partless in their nature they are completely pervaded by God through His all-pervading nature. They are bound with the beginningless girdle of Karma but are emancipated through the grace of God. In emancipation they feel themselves like one with Him and abide in Him as a part of His energy.[3]

Vallabha:—He regards Jiva as an emanation of Brahman and as atomic. It has no separate existence. The finite centres of consciousness and inert existence emanate from Brahman out of His innate desire of self-expression. Consciousness and bliss are absent in the inert while in a Jiva bliss only is absent.[4]

Jnanadeva's Conception of the Jiva or Finite self

Jnanadeva's conception of the finite self is different and at the same time more clear and dignified than those of the other Indian philosophers. Finite self, though each has its different content, is an experiencing subject and partakes the nature of the Infinite or the Ultimate Reality. It is not a mere appearance, as Advaitins like Śhamkar maintain, that ultimately dissolves in the Absolute. The relation of the Absolute and the finite self is also peculiar. Ramanuja says that this relation is that of "Aprathak-siddhi" and not that of "Samavaya." It is the internal relation and not external. He uses the analogy of the soul and its body to denote this intimate relation. So the Soul of souls controls and sustains them and in this way there exists a vital relation between the two. Still we feel a gap in this view and according to Jnanadeva the relation between them is more intimate and inseparable than Ramanuja would imagine.

We have already seen how Jnanadeva describes the Absolute as splitting itself into subject and object and experiencing Itself. Now the subjective aspect differentiates between so many finite selves through which the Reality enjoys Its own wealth. So the real nature of an individual is the experiencing of the Being. While describing the real status of the individual, Jnanadeva makes the point clear by using various beautiful similies. He says, "There is as it were fragrance became a nose and smelt itself, or sound became an ear and heard itself, or the mirror became an eye to see itself. Air by its own motion became a fan, or the head became the Champaka flower to decorate itself. The tongue became the taste, the lotus became the Sun, the Chakora bird became the Moon, flowers became the bees, the damsel became the youth or the sleeper became the bed. The sprout of the mango tree became the Cuckoo, or the limbs became the Malaya breeze".[5] In this way Jnanadeva describes how the enjoyer and the enjoyed, the seer and the seen are merged in one Absolute. But this merging does not mean extinction. It implies that amid this diversity the Unity of Experience is not broken like "the Shevanti flower that remains one though it blossoms into a thousand petals."[6]

So the finite self expresses the innate nature of the Ultimate Reality to manifest Itself through duality. "Unity comes of its own accord in the court-yard of duality and as diversity increases the unity is deepened".[7] The relation between the individual self and the Absolute is not imaginary as Shamkar believes, nor physical as Ramanuja would have it. It is also not of a mere dependence as Madhwa puts forth. There is no negative relation due to the absence of bliss in the self as Vallabha thinks. It is not fragmentary as Nimbark imagines. According to Jnanadeva, the relation is more intimate and natural. The finiteness of the individual does not mean that it is a degradation of Reality but it implies that the Reality determines Itself in order to realize itself in various forms. So the end of life is not emancipation (Mukti) but to realize this real dignity and act up to its real worth. God-realization means understanding how God realizes Himself through one's being and this is the secret of natural devotion, before which Yoga and Knowledge grow pale like the Moon in broad day-light.[8]

[1] Dr. P. T. Raju—Thought and Reality, p. 60.

[2] B. N. Krishnamurti M. A. — Madhwa's Theistic Realism, p. 6-7.

[3] Dr. S. N. Dasagupta:—History of Indian Philosophy Vol. II p. 413-414.

[4] Dr. M. N. Sarkar,:—Vedantism, p. 44.

[5] Amritanubhava, IX, 1-5.

[6] Ibid; IX, 7-8.

[7] द्वैत दशेचें आंगण । अद्वैत वोळगे आपण। भेदु तंव तंव दूण । अभेदासी॥ Ibid; IX, 29.

[8] कोणी एक अकृत्रिम । भक्तीचें हें वर्म । योगज्ञानादि-विश्राम । -भूमिका हें ॥ Ibid; IX, 61
प्रत्याहारादि अंगीं । अंग टेकिले योगी। ते जाले येया मार्गीं । दिहाचा चांदू ॥ Ibid; IX, 27.

CHAPTER VII

BHAKTI OR GOD-REALIZATION

THE conception of Bhakti has played an important role in the religious history of India. It has also dominated the various schools of philosophy. So before we propound Jnanadeva's view, it will be useful to trace its history from the earlier Vedic period down to the age of Jnanadeva.

Vedic Age

In the Hymns of the Rigveda, natural powers are regarded as so many deities. Sayaṅa has classified them in three divisions. (1) Celestial deities e.g. Varun, Sun, Ushas etc. (2) Intermundane-deities e.g. Indra and Maruts, (3) Terrestrial deities e.g. Agni and Soma. There is a polytheistic as well as a Henotheistic tendency, and these Gods are worshipped for the sake of worldly benefits such as wealth, offspring, cattle, victory in their struggles, as well as for heavenly happiness. Of all these Gods Varuna and Indra are more prominent. Varuna is the upholder of moral and physical order. The rivers keep their bounds, the ocean does not oversweep, the Sun and the Moon follow their courses at his behest. He commands the regularity of the noumena. He is omniscient, knows the hearts of men, and people cannot escape him. He punishes sinners but forgives those that repent. So Dr. Radhakrishnan aptly remarks that the theism of the Vaishnavas and the Bhagawatas with its emphasis on Bhakti is to be traced to the Vedic worship of Varun with its consciousness of sin and trust in divine forgiveness.[1] Indra is regarded as the national and war-god. The position of Agni is different. He is a great friend of men and mediates between God and man. Vedic sages talk to him as to a dear companion and ask him the blessings which a kind father bestows upon his dear children. So in these Vedic hymns we breathe an atmosphere of hearts full of devotion though it has not found the right direction and its adequate philosophical background.[2] Gradually, however, there is a change in this atmosphere and those simple hymns are used for the purpose of various sacrifices. The word acquires more significance than the underlying emotion. Even the Gods pale into insignificance before the power of sacrifice. It is not the grace of God that is powerful but the various sacrificial rites and the hymns recited as prescribed in the Brahmanas or ritualistic manuals.

Side by side there is also a tendency of scepticism about the existence of so many Gods. The existence of even Indra is doubted.[3] Thoughts were expressed about one Substance underlying various divinities.[4] At the end of the Rigveda we find something like an agnostic atmosphere in the famous Nasadiya Sukta.[5]

The Upanishadas

In the Vedic age itself polytheism was giving way to monotheism. The same tendency is carried out in the Upanishadas. The supreme Godhead, however, is not some cosmic outward force but forms the very basis of human life. He is the inward Atman who manifests Itself in the form of subjective and objective worlds. Atman is identical with Brahman to whom all the Gods were subordinated. Agni has no power to burn a blade of grass nor Vayu has any strength to blow it without the help of Brahman.[6]

The age of the Upanishadas was the age of speculation, hence there are no prayers for material prosperity but meditations on the One Spirit,[7] Who is worshipped for leading one from unreal to the real, from darkness to light, from death to immortality.[8] Nachiket, to whom Yama offers a boon of wealth, offspring, celestial damsels with chariots and musical instruments, does not accept these transitory blessings but insists on knowing the real nature of the Atman. He is convinced that man is not really satisfied unless he is in possession of this highest knowledge.[9] This Self-knowledge is not obtained by any other means but by the grace of Atman Itself. "The Self cannot be realized by the study of the Vedas, nor by intelligence, nor by deep learning. It can be realized by him only whom It chooses or favours. To him the Self reveals its own nature."[10] The doctrine of grace finds its clearest expression in this verse. There is an atmosphere of personal warmth and affection when the great philosopher Yajnyavalkya propounds the doctrine of Atman and says that the husband, wife, sons and other objects of love are not dear for their own sake, but they are dear for the love of Atman.[11] So Atman is the true object of love. Every lover of any worldly object is unconsciously a lover of Atman. Hence by self-analysis he should find the true nature of this love and the Atman. The word Bhakti occurs for the first time in the Upanishadas.[12] The doctrine of grace and self-surrender is emphasised in the Svetashvetaropanishad, and Brahman is described as of the nature of bliss and the source of all human joys, in the Taittiriya and Brihadaranyak Upanishadas.

The Upanishadas do not teach a set theory of philosophy. These are various suggestions at truth and "the bubbling up of the thoughts of numerous sages of antiquity, each of whom tried to express as naively, as simply and as directly as possible, the thoughts which were uppermost in his mind."[13] For this reason, we find in them the roots of the later day systems of philosophy. In this way we also find in the Upanishadic doctrine of divine immanence and of Atman's nature of bliss, the germs of the later day philosophy of Bhakti-yoga.

Muktikopanishada gives a list of 108 Upanishadas of which only thirteen are major and others are minor works that were composed to support Yoga, Shaivism, Vaishnavism, Shaktism and Vedantism. In the Kalisantaranopanishad the Lord's name is extolled as capable of removing all sins.[14]

The Bhagavadgita

The Doctrine of Bhakti is found explicitly stated in the Bhagavadgita. In the Upanishadas different Upasanas or meditations upon objects like the mind, the person in the sun or moon, food, vital breath-supposing them to be Brahman-are prescribed.[15] In Chapter X of the Bhagavadgita various Vibhutis or excellent forms of God are described. God is the Self dwelling in all beings that are born. He is Vishnu among Adityas, the radiant Sun among various forms of light, the Moon among the nightly luminaries.[16] Everything that is potent, prosperous or forceful springs from a portion of His splendour.[17] In the next chapter Arjuna is described to have seen the vision of His splendour in its fullness. He sees the Virat form of God—the form in which Arjuna himself is swallowed up. In the beginning of the chapter XII we see him asking who were superior —the worshippers of the Personal or of the Impersonal.[18] Krishna tells him that both of them reach the same goal but the path of those that follow the impersonal aspect of God is strewn with great difficulties.[19] Thus the Gita recommends the Path of Bhakti, or approach to the Reality through love and devotion, as superior, and at the same time without any risk, for God Himself is ready to help His devotee at every step. At the end of the Gita, Arjuna is advised to set aside all the other means of salvation and surrender himself with all his heart to God, Who abides in the hearts of all things and moves them, so that he may be liberated from all the sins by His Grace. This is the secret that the Lord wishes to disclose to his dear disciple.[20]

With all the catholicity of the Gita we find there also the advice not to disclose its teachings to an unbeliever.[21] Then again, though God is described as Purushottam who only is fit to be worshipped, those that worship lower deities also reach the same goal.[22] In this way the Gita has indirectly, encouraged these lower forms of worship.

The philosophical background of the Gita seems to be indefinite and this indefiniteness is the source of various interpretations of it by different commentators like Shamkar, Ramanuja and others. God is the ultimate Reality according to the Gita, but when we come to the descriptions about His nature we find that He is described both ways. He is described as personal as well as impersonal, the actor as well as the spectator, transcendent as well as immanent.

In the chapter XIII we find the conception of the impersonal. God is omnipresent. He is Nirguna. He moves and moves not, is near and far off. We have passages where the Personal God is described as under Vedantic and Samkhya influence. Under Vedantic influence we find three kinds of Purushas-Kshara, Akshara and Uttama Purusha i.e. the mutable beings of the world, the immutable self inside us and the supernal God.[23] Here God as well as nature personified. Under Samkhya influence there is the description of two Prakritis i.e. Apara or nature and Para or Selves, and of one Purusha who is God.[24] We also find a third kind of description in the Ch. XII of a Purush, a Prikriti and a Para Purush or Paramatma who is above them.

God is described both as an actor and as a spectator. In the Ch. XVIII it is said that he who sees God as the doer, does not see the Reality.[25] Also in Ch. V "God only looks on and leaves all things to nature."[26] On the other hand in the Ch. XVIII God is described as the supreme, doer, the great potter of the universe parallel to Plato's God as "demi-urge" at work on his "spindle".[27]

Then again God is described as transcendent and immanent. In the Ch. XIII it is said that just as the sky is untainted by any other thing, similarly God is not contaminated. On the other hand we get in Ch. VII, "All these things are woven on me as pearls on a thread......I am the seed of all beings."[28] Because of these two kinds of descriptions we find that the same Gita is interpreted by Holtsman as pantheistic and by Garde as theistic out and out.

As regards Bhakti, though the Gita praises it so much, it is not regarded as the Alpha and Omega of spiritual life but as a means to liberation or Moksha. The same state is described as Nistraigunya or beyond three gunas. Naishkarmya or purposeless action and Sthitaprajna or equanimous intellect. The sum and substance of Gita, then, is that intense devotion brings God's grace and by God's grace an individual gets liberation.[29]

The Bhagawata

"The Gita is universally accepted as the true guide; the Shrimat Bhagwata is accepted only by Bhaktas. The latter (Bhaktas)......consider the Gita as only the seed from which the other book the Shrimat Bhagawata, has sprung. Indeed, where the Gita ends, the Bhagawata begins."[30] So says a biographer of the famous Vaishnava Saint Chaitanya. Not only does Bhagawata begin where the Gita ends but it gives more prominence to Bhakti than the Gita does. Disinterested action and knowledge without the presence of devotion to the Lord are worthless.[31] Bhakti is the supreme goal of life.[32] A true Bhakta does not desire heavenly pleasures, kingdom on earth, different Yogic powers or even Moksha. All these pale into insignificance before the bliss he enjoys. So Bhakti is superior even to Moksha or liberation.[33] Sinners like Ajamil and even dumb animals like the elephant Gajendra are entitled to the path of Bhakti, and we find in the Bhagawat their life stories along with those of great devotees like Pralhad, Dhruva, Uddhava and the Cowherds and Maidens of Brindavan.

Along with this tendency in the Bhagawata to give supremacy to Bhakti we find that it inclines sometimes to extreme asceticism represented by men like Jad-Bharat and Kadaryu. These people, with their utter disregard of their bodies, are more like extreme Jain ascetics than true devotees. Then again the author of the Bhagawata seems doubtful about the supreme significance of Bhakti when he says that the path of action is suitable for the worldly minded, the path of knowledge is for those who have aversion to the pleasures of the world, while the path of devotion is for those that are not inclined to both the extremes.[34]

It is to be noted that the Chatusloki Bhagawata is regarded as the quintessence of the Bhagawata. God has told Brahma the great secret in four stanzas.[35] This secret ought to contain the secret of devotion but we find there the teaching of 'Anvyaya-Vyatirek-Jnana,' though, the commentator Shridhar interprets the meaning of "Secret" as "Devotion" and Vishwanath Chakravarti, another great commentator who was a follower of the Chaitanya sect, interprets it as "Loving devotion" (Prem-Bhakti).

The Shandilya Sutras

Though nothing is definitely known about the priority among the two sets of sutras-the sutras of Shandilya and those of Narada, we can infer from some internal evidence the priority of the Shandilya Sutras. Narada Sutras mention Shandilya Sutras but not *vice versa*.[36] Unlike Narada, Shandilya discusses the philosophic background of Bhakti. Carpenter rightly says, "The Sutras of Shandilya interpreted by Svapneshwar occupy a middle position between the philosophies of Shamkar and Ramanuja. With the former, Svapneshwar declares at the outset the ultimate identity of the soul and Brahman. With the latter, he vindicates the Reality of the world."[37] According to Shandilya, Brahman is Pure consciousness and Maya is the power of Brahman and not a mere illusion.[38] Both are real and eternal and both are the necessary and inter-dependent causes of the world.[39] As regards the conception of Jiva and its relation with Brahman, Shandilya mentions the views of other two thinkers viz. Kashyapa and Badarayan. The former maintains the absolute difference between Jiva and Brahman, while the latter considers both as identical. Shandilya himself rejects both the views and tries to reconcile them by holding that the Jiva and Brahman are distinct from each other, yet one in essence. The finite soul is potentially infinite while Brahman is actually infinite. The finite soul is capable of attaining the state of Brahman. Therefore they are identical in essence, though they are actually different from each other.[40]

Unlike Shamkar Shandilya holds that the empirical life of the Jiva (Samsara) is not due to ignorance (Ajnana) but to the absence of devotion (Abhakti), and so Bhakti and not Jnana is the means of liberation.[41]

The Narada Bhakti-Sutras

The author of these sutras is God-intoxicated. Instead of raising and discussing the questions about the nature of Brahman, Jiva and Jagat he goes straight into the heart of Bhakti and describes its nature, means and effects. He also explains the criterion of Bhakti and its relation with Yoga, Jnana and Karma.

While defining Bhakti, Narada mentions the definitions given by other authors. According to Vyas, Bhakti is the worship of God, according to Garga it is narrating God's exploits, while Shandilya defines it as meditation on the self. Narada himself defines it as the highest Love for God, a surrender of all actions to Him and agony in His forgetfulness.[42] Narada regards Bhakti as superior to action, knowledge and meditation. Devotion is not a means of knowledge. Knowledge does not lead to devotion. They are not interdependent on each other. Devotion is the fruit of itself. So the most important point which Narada emphasizes is that Devotion is not a means to something else e.g. liberation but it is an end in itself.[43] However, he does not try to base his doctrine on a philosophical foundation.

Renunciation of worldly objects and of their contact, incessant prayer, hearing and singing of the Lord's qualities, the grace of saints and of God are the means of devotion.[44] Narada describes the devotees who are wholly attached to God in these words, "With their throats choked and tears running down their cheeks they talk lovingly with each other. They sanctify not only their family but the whole world. Sacred waters are holy because of their contact. Among the devotees of God there is no distinction of birth, learning, appearance, family, wealth, religious observances and the like, since they all belong to Him."[45]

Narada's conception of Bhakti is more elevated than that of Shandilya. But Narada has propounded renunciation as a means of devotion, and he also advises Karma-Sanyas-giving up of actions, which is against the tenets of the Bhakti school of Maharashtra.

The Bhakti-Mimamsa-Sutras

The author of these Sutras published by M. M. Gopinatha Kaviraj[46] is unknown. The date of their composition is also uncertain and hence it cannot be ascertained whether the work is really one of those associated with the name of the acharyas whose references are often met with in Sanskrit literature. But it belongs to a school of thought distinct from that of Shandilya or of Narada.

In these Sutras Bhakti is regarded as a kind of Ulhas of the mind.[47] It is of the nature of Rasa, is eternal, hence an end in itself. Here we find a conception of Bhakti different from that found in some of the old Alankar treatises like those of Mammat and others who regard Bhakti as a Bhava and not a Rasa. The result of Bhakti is the attraction of God (Ishwaravashikara) and not the cessation of evil (Anaratha-nivritti), not even Jivanmukti.[48] The highest object of human striving should not be Moksha or liberation, but Bhakti itself.[49] The effort towards the absence of misery or freedom from pain is regarded as only an enlightened form of selfishness. So the view of the author of Bhakti Mimansa Sutras is more allied to that of Narada than to that of Shandilya M. M. Gopinath Kaviraj rightly observes, "The rejection of Moksha as the supreme end of human aspirations, follows as a necessary corollary from the conception of Bhakti as in itself the highest form of Bliss, higher indeed—so it is boldly declared-than Brahmananda which is revealed in Moksha."[50]

Jnanadeva's Conception of Bhakti

The commonsense view of Bhakti is that it is a whole-hearted devotion to God. Though God is the object of such a devotion, the feeling of devotion itself is not objective but subjective. So Bhakti amounts ultimately to a kind of subjective feeling. We have already seen how the conception of Bhakti has evolved from Vedic times to the sutras of Narada and Bhakti-Mimansa, and how it is regarded as an end in itself and not as a means to something else by these later authors. Narada regards Bhakti as the highest love for God and the author of the Bhakti-Mimansa-Sutras regards it as of the nature of Rasa or the Highest form of Bliss. But after all, if it is a subjective sentiment its objective value is doubtful.

Jnanadeva's conception of Bhakti as propounded in his Amritanubhava is more fundamental and has an intrinsic or absolute value. To him Bhakti is not some external mode of approach to Reality or God, but it forms the very essence[51] of Reality which is self-experiencing (Swasamvedya) and self-illuminating (Swaprakash). Now this self-experiencing is nothing but Bhakti or Love of God towards Himself. The Goddess described in the chapter I of Amritanubhava is nothing but this Bhakti which is not only inseparable form of God but forms the very core of Divinity. The whole world, animate as well as inanimate, is Its manifestation. "What is termed Swasamvitti (self-illumination) by philosophers and Shakti (Dynamic power) by Shaivas is nothing but Bhakti from our point of view." Bhakti is not an act of devotion but the very nature of God.

According to Jnanadeva, the Absolute of philosophy and the God of religion are identical. The Ultimate Reality is Pure consciousness, Love and Creative Energy. It is the nature of Love to express itself and creation is nothing but this expression. This Love is not something material. It is a living spirit, hence self conscious and self-realizing. So in the words of Prof. Bergson, "Divine Love is not a thing of God; it is God Himself."[52] In this way God can be said to be a person. Bergson makes this point clear in these illuminating words — "It is upon this point (i.e. Love is God Himself and not a thing of Him) that the philosopher must fasten who holds God to be a person and yet wishes to avoid anything like a gross assimilation with man."[53] "To call God a person is not a sign of anthropomorphism, because He is not an image of the human being who is himself God's image." Webb tells us that the personality attributed to God is different from man's personality, for the relation of man to man in social experience is one of mutual exclusion whereas the relation of man and God in religious experience is one of mutual inclusion.[54] But Jnanadeva's view of the relation of the Absolute person and finite soul is more deep, and the relation is not merely that of mutual inclusion i.e. the finite self dwelling in God as a separate self, but the existence of that self means the very manifestation of God whose essence is Love.

To experience this Love is the goal and the final fulfilment of life. Before this ideal even the ideal of Jivan-Mukti pales into insignificance. Bhakti (realization of divine Love) and not Mukti (liberation from wordly bondage) is the culmination of spiritual experience. Plurality in the world is not merely an illusory appearance to be discarded, but is the manifestation or expression of the Absolute playfulness. Hence a liberated soul is devoid of that bliss which a devotee living in the world enjoys.[55] Every object in the world is significant to a devotee. It is not a mere object of sensual enjoyment as a materialist thinks, but is the expression of divine Love which is also the very source of his life. If Moksha or Liberation is the fourth Purushartha (value of life), Bhakti is the fifth i.e. the highest.[56]

So Jnanadeva has fully brought out the objective significance of Bhakti. It is the highest value not only from our human standpoint, but also from the point of the Absolute Experience. Hence here the highest value and reality coincide. According to Jnanadeva, the sense of numena is not the core of religious experience as Dr. Otto maintains in his "The Idea of the Holy,"[57] but it is the sense and appreciation of Divine Love that forms the very stuff of religion. "The Holy" of Dr. Otto, by its supernatural power evokes a feeling of awe, wonder and humility but "The God" of Jnanadeva evokes a feeling of intimacy and Love. Then again Otto's Holy is the object of religious experience in the sense of something other than the individual who experiences it while the God of Jnanadeva is the object of religious consciousness not like something other, but He is the true self of him who feels his loving presence.

Difference between Jnanadeva and other Acharyas

Bhakti, according to Shamkar, is meditation upon one's supreme Self.[58] Ramanuja takes it to be a continuous meditation accompanied by the practice of eight Yoga-processes.[59] Bhakti leads to Mukti, the alternative path to it being Prapatti or self surrendering.[60] According to Madhwa, Bhakti is a method of service and is the perception of Hari.

Vallabha thinks Pushtibhakti as supreme. The frame of mind generated by such a kind of devotion is the desire of the attainment of God to the exclusion of everything else. The fruit of this devotion is an admission to Goloka where one can participate in the eternal sport of Krishna.[61] The first three Acharyas regard Bhakti as a means to Mukti, though their conceptions of Mukti differ from one another. Vallabha rejects the four kinds of Mukti and considers Bhakti as superior to all. But this Pushti Bhakti has its fruit in the ideal world where God's Divine sport goes on eternally.

Jnanadeva's conception of Bhakti differs from that of all these Acharyas. He does not think of Bhakti as a means to Mukti. He rejects the ideal of Mukti. The realization of Bhakti does not require the renouncing of this world. It can be realized in this very life. God's eternal play is not going in some ideal plane, as a Vallabha believes, but is going on in this very world. The world is nothing but the manifestation of God's Eternal Sport.

[1] Dr. Radhakrishnan:—History of Indian Philosophy Vol. I p. 78.

[2] Ranade & Belwalkar — History of Indian Philosophy:— Creative Period, p. 409,

[3] Rigveda VIII-89.

[4] Ibid; I, 164-46.

[5] Ibid; X, 129,

[6] Kenopanishad, ch. III.

[7] Chhandogya Upanishada III-14.

[8] Brihadaranyak Upanishada I-3-27.

[9] Kath Upanishada ch. I.

[10] Kath Upanishada ch. II-23 Mundak. Up. III, 2-3.

[11] Brihadaranyak Up. II, 4, 1-5.

[12] Swetashwetar Upanishada; VI, 23.

[13] Prof. R. D. Ranade:—A Constructive Survey of Upanishadic Philosophy; p. 178.

[14] Dr. T. M. Mahadevan M. A. Ph. D.—Upanishadas (selections) p. 351.

[15] Taittiriya Up. III, 2-6, Chchandogya Up. VII.

[16] Bhagavadgita X, 20-21.

[17] Ibid; X, 41.

[18] Ibid; XII, 1.

[19] Ibid; XII, 2-5, 7.

[20] Ibid; XVIII, 64-66.

[21] *Ibid;* XVIII, 67.

[22] Ibid; IX, 23.

[23] Ibid; XV, 16-17.

[24] Ibid; VII, 4-5.

[25] Ibid; XVIII, 16.

[26] Ibid; V, 14.

[27] Ibid; XVIII, 61.

[28] Ibid; VII, 7.

[29] Ibid; XVIII, 54-56, 66.

[30] S. K. Ghosh:—Lord Gourang, Vol. II; p. 327.

[31] नैष्कर्म्यमप्यच्युतभाववर्जितम् । न शोभते ज्ञानमलं निरंजनम् ॥

Bhagawat; I, 5-12.

[32] स वै पुंसां परो धर्मःयतो भक्तिरधोक्षजे ॥ Ibid; I, 2-5.

[33] Ibid; II, 14-14.

[34] Ibid; XI, 20-7-8.

[35] Ibid; II, 9, 32-35.

[36] Narada Sutras:—18,

[37] Carpenter:—Theism in Mediaeval India p. 419.

[38] Shandilya Sutras:—85-86.

[39] Ibid; 39 and Commentary.

[40] Ibid; 29-31.

[41] Ibid; 98.

[42] Narada Bhakti Sutras, 16-19.

[43] Ibid; 25-30.

[44] Narada Bhakti Sutra, 34-40.

[45] Ibid, 67-73.

[46] Saraswati Bhawan Studies Vol. II Edited by Dr. Ganganath Zha and M. M. Gopinath Kaviraj.

[47] Bhakti Mimansa Sutra 1-1-2. भक्तिर्मनस उल्लास विशेषः ।

[48] Ibid; 4-1-16.

[49] भक्तिरेव परमपुरुषार्थः मोक्षस्याऽपुरुषार्थत्वादिति तु भागवताः ।

Ibid; 4-1-7

[50] Saraswati Bhavan Studies Vol. II:—"A New Bhakti Sutra;" p. 69.

[51] कोण्ही अेक अकृत्रिम । भक्तीचें हें वर्म । योगज्ञानादि–विश्राम ।
–भूमिका हे ॥ अमृ. ९–५९.
(येथील स्वसंवेद्यखूण । ते लोपली नाही जाण । तेंचि अकृत्रिम भजन ।
वर्म एथिंचें ॥ शिवकल्याण.)
आता भक्ति अभक्ति । जाले ताट अेके पाती । कर्माकर्माचिया वाती ।
मालवूनिया ॥ अमृ. ९–४८.
(स्वरूपाची स्वरूपासी प्रीति । ते स्वरूपींच असे निजभक्ति । ते भक्तीनें
भजन स्थिती । वेल्हावत असे ॥ किंवा न भजोनि असता निवांत ।
तो मूळ भक्तीसी होवुनि रत । एवं न भजता न ढळत । मुळींची
भक्ति ॥ --शिवकल्याण.)
क्रिया कीर न साहे । परी अद्वैती भक्ति आहे ॥

Jnaneshwari; XVIII. 1151.

ज्ञानी इयेतें स्वसंविति । शैव म्हणती शक्ति । आम्ही परमभक्ति ।
आपुली म्हणो ॥ Ibid; XVIII, 1133.
ऐसा हा सहज माझा । प्रकाशु जो कपिध्वजा । तो भक्ति या वोजा ।
बोलिजे गा ॥ Ibid; XVIII, 1117.
...माझिये सहज स्थिती । भक्ति नाम ॥ Ibid; XVIII. 1113.

[52] Bergson—Two sources of Morality and Religion. p. 216.

[53] Ibid; p. 216.

Prof. Bergson's position in this work is made clear by Dr, Radhakrishnan. He says, "In his latest work on the Two Sources of Morality and Religion, Bergson argues that the principle of life in general which inward intuition reveals, is to be defined as Love and is God Himself."
(Contemporary Indian Philosophy p. 280.)

[51] Dr. Rudolf Metz-A Hundred Years of British Philosophy p. 410.

[55] कैवल्याही चढावा । करीत विषयसेवा । जाहला भृत्य भज्यु कालोवा । भक्तिच्या घरीं ॥ Amritanubhava; IX, 29.

[56] चहू पुरुषार्थां शिरीं । भक्ति जैसी ॥ Jnaneshwari; XVIII, 867.
जया भक्तीची येतुली प्राप्ती । जे कैवल्यातें परौतें सर म्हणती ॥
Ibid; IX, 192.

[57] Dr. Otto-The Idea of the Holy, p. 12.

[58] स्वस्वरुपानुसंघानं भक्तिरित्यभिधीयते । मोक्षकारणसामग्रयां भक्तिरेव गरीयसी ॥ विवेकचूडामणी.

[59] भक्तियोगो नाम यमनियमासनप्राणायामप्रत्याहारधारणाध्यानसमाधिरूपाष्टांगवांस्तैलधारावदविच्छिन्नस्मृतिसंतानरूपः ॥ यतींद्रमतदीपिका प्र. ७ पा. ६२

[60] Prof. P. Shrinivasachari—The Philosophy of Vishishtadwait, p. 382.

[61] Dr. R. G. Bhandarkar — Vaishnavism, Shaivism and Minor Religious Systems, p. 112-113.

Chapter VIII

INFLUENCES OF THE PHILOSOPHY OF JNANADEVA

The Upanishadas

JNANADEVA does not base his Amritanubhava upon the sacred scriptures but upon his own experience along with its logical defence. There is only one quotation from Shruti[1] and that too comes after he has logically refuted Ajnanvadin, to state that the Shruti or the sacred scriptures also say the same thing. The verse quoted is, as we have already seen, "Vibhati Yasya Bhasa Sarva Midam etc." We have also seen how Jnanadeva differs from Shamkar in interpreting it. Shamkar, as usual, interprets it on the basis of his theory of illusion, while Jnanadeva quotes it in support of his view that the world is the manifestation of the Ultimate Reality and not the outcome of Maya or Ajnana.[2] In the last chapter of Amritanubhava there is a reference to the ten Upanishadas, but it is only to state that all of them do not say anything more than what is contained in his own composition.[3] "So my expression" says Jnanadeva "is the deepest silence like the picture of a crocodile drawn on the surface of water."[4] The same is the case with the Upanishadas.

The Upanishadas declare that Atman is beyond the reach of thought and speech. "That from which our speech turns back along with mind, being unable to comprehend its fulness, is the Ultimate Reality."[5] Of that to which the eye is unable to go, which neither speech nor mind is able to reach — what conception can we have, except that it is beyond all that is known and beyond all that is unknown?"[6] In the same strain Jnanadeva says that Atman is not illuminated by the Sun who illumines all the other things, is not enveloped by the sky which envelops everything, and is not embraced by egoism. The understanding, the mind or the senses fail to grasp the Atman who baffles all description by means of words.[7] As soon as thought reaches the Atman it disappears like a great warrior who wins success for his master by sacrificing his life.[8]

We find another side to the same subject in the Upanishadas. Atman is unknowable because He is the eternal subject who knows. "How could the Eternal knower be an object of knowledge? " asks the great philosopher Yajnyavalkya.[9] "Who can know him, who Himself knows? " says Svetasvatara Upanishad.[10] Jnanadeva also describes Atman as the eternal subject who knows Himself though He is not an object of others' knowledge.[11] With Yajnyavalkya he agrees that self-consciousness is the Ultimate fact of experience. The Ultimate Reality or Atman is self-conscious (Swasamvedya)[12] and His unity is not lost even if He comes to pervade the whole universe. There is no second line drawn thereby.[13]

The Yogavasishtha

According to Dr. Pendse there are striking similarities between the Yogavasishtha and Amritanubhava.[14] Hence he opines that Jnanadeva must have based his work on Yoga Vasishtha. Probably he might have written a work on Yoga Vasishtha of which the Amritanubhava forms a chapter. His reasons for the adoption of this view are as follow:—

a) The name of Jnanadeva's work i.e. Anubhavamrit seems to be suggested by stanzas in the Yogavasistha (St. 6-10-70 and 71).

b) Similarity of the description of Shunya or void in both the works.

c) Similarity of the view about the illusory nature of the world.

d) Similar descriptions of Shiva and Shakti.

e) The Sphurtivada of Jnanadeva is not his original contribution as Prof. Ranade believes. It is found in the Yogavasishtha from which Jnanadeva must have borrowed.

Dr. Pendse also thinks that he gets support in drawing the conclusion about the identity of Shamkar's Philosophy with that of Jnanadeva from the fact that both of them base their philosophical doctrines on the Yogavasistha.

Dr. Pendse's view cannot be accepted for the following reasons:-

a) Jnanadeva himself has said that he does not base his work on some authority like that of Shiva or Shrikrishna. He is expouding his own experience, hence adopts the title Anubhavamrit significantly. So the mere similarity of words like Anubhava and Amrit in certain verses of Yogavasishtha do not prove that Jnanadeva has borrowed his title.

b) Both Jnanadeva and the author of the Yogavasishtha have designated the Ultimate Reality as "Shunya" to denote its absolute nature. But the Absolute of Yogavasishtha is the ground of world appearance, which is essenceless like a mirage, while Jnanadeva's Absolute manifests itself in the form of the world in which It is immanent.

c) With regard to the world-appearance, the standpoint of the Yogavasishtha is that of "Ajatavada." The world is not only illusory but has not even come into being also. It is utterly non-existent.[15] Jnanadeva, on the other hand, considers the world as Chidvilas, and not as something which has no existence but appears to exist through our ignorance.

d) The Prakriti in the Yogavasishtha is the creative impulse out of which waves of wordly appearance arise. This creative power is called by various names, Spanda-Shakti, Samkalpa-Shakti, Jaganmaya and Prakriti. Now this Shakti is nearer to Shamkar's Maya than to Jnanadeva's Goddess who is nothing but God's Love towards Himself.[16]

e) There is a difference between the conception of the Shakti in the Yogavasishtha and of the Goddess in the Amritanubhava. In the same way the word Sphurti also has not the same meaning in both the works. Both Shakti and Goddess are Sphurtis of One Reality but in a different sense, as stated above. Prof. Ranade is right in his statement about Jnanadeva's original contribution of Sphurtivada.

It is clear from the above criticism that Jnanadeva has written his work independently and does not base it, like Shamkar, upon Yogavasishtha. Hence we cannot draw any conclusion from this about the identity of the views of Jnanadeva and Shamkar as Dr. Pendse tries to do. There is a work on the Yogavasishtha in Marathi Ovi metre published by Mr. Chandorkar and its authorship is attributed to Jnanadeva but the very language of it is so rough, so modern and so prosaic that even Dr. Pendse denies its authenticity.

Besides these there are some other points also to be noted in connection with the different standpoints of the two works. The author of the Yogavasishtha has written his work for a certain class of readers. He tells us that the proper person to study this work is he who has become aware of his bondage and longs to be free, who is no longer in utter ignorance, but has not yet attained wisdom (Y. V. 1-2-1).[17] Jnanadeva, on the other hand, proclaims that he has received the spiritual dish from his spiritual teacher so that all might taste and enjoy its sweetness. (Amt. X-1-6). The cause of all suffering, according to the Yogavasishtha, is "trishna" or desire for worldly objects. Jnanadeva does not despise worldly objects. He tells us that a true devotee is aware of their real nature, i.e. they are the expressions of Divine Love, and enjoys them in a spirit of worship.[18] Liberation is the goal of Yogavasishtha which advises tranquility, contentment, company of the wise and reflection as the four gate keepers of liberation (Moksha-Dwarpalak).[19] Jnanadeva criticise the conception of liberation and bondage and sets forth the ideal of Bhakti.

According to the author of the Yogavasishtha, the world as such never existed in the past, nor exists now, nor will exist hereafter. Yet there is the appearance of a wonderful creation and it has to be explained somehow. The answer given by the Yogavasishtha is that the course of appearing events takes place merely by accident (Kakataliyayoga).[20] Jnanadeva, on the other hand, does not regard the world as appearing accidently but regards it as the expression of the very nature of God or Ultimate Reality.

The Shivasutras

The Shivasutras are the fountain-head of Kashmir Shaivism. They are said to be revealed to Vasugupta by God Shiva Himself. The time of Vasugupta is ascertained as the end of the 8th century or the beginning of the 9th. Jnanadeva was acquainted with these Sutras and he refers to one of them in his Amritanubhava (III-16). The Sutra "Jnanam Bandhah" which literally means "Knowledge is a bondage" occurs twice in the Shivasutras (1-2 and 3-2), and the commentator Kshemendra interprets "Jnanam" as the perverted knowledge which imposes not-self upon self and *vice versa*.[21] Jnanadeva has interpreted "Jnana" in a different sense. In the third chapter of Amritanubhava he is criticising the conception of Moksha. The conception of bondage itself is wrong. Hence if bondage is unreal, freedom is also unreal. Hence, the knowledge (Jnana) which regards this unreal freedom as real is bondage and here he passingly refers to the above Sutra.

आणि ज्ञान बंधु ऐसें। शिवसूत्राचेनि मिसें। म्हणितलें असें। सदाशिवें ॥ ३–१६.

(In the course of revealing the Shiva Sutras, Sadashiva has said that knowledge is a bondage.)[22]

Looking to the philosophy of Kashmir Shaivism as revealed in the Shivasutras with its commentary, and other later works, we find that Jnanadeva's views in the Amritanubhava about the ultimate questions are similar to those in Kashmir Shaivism. In the Shiva Sutras the Ultimate Reality is the Chaitanya or Shiva.[23] It is self-illuminating and requires no other proof.[24] Shakti is its inseparable aspect and the universe is nothing but the manifestation of this Shakti. It has no other basis or ingredient like Maya or Ajnan in it.[25] Jnanadeva's description of Shiva and Shakti is similar. Both are Ultimate principles, of the same nature, inseparable and both give birth to the universe.[26]

Kashmir Shaivism assumes 36 principles or Tatvas. Jnanadeva does not give the figure or a detailed list of these, but mentions them as "From Shiva to the Earth", and says that they are illuminated by the Ultimate Reality.[27] Jnanadeva uses the simile of moon and its light to show the relation of Shiva and the universe. The same simile is used by the author of Shivasutra-vimarshini.[28]

Kashmir Shaivism differs from the Adwaitins who support the theory of Vivartavada which regards appearances of names and forms as real under no circumstances, because these are not existent in the supreme Reality. The theory of Kashmir Shaivism is called "Abhasavada" or "Swatantryavada" and regards appearances as real in the sense that they are aspects of the ultimate Reality "The appearances, therefore, are not the forms of some indescribable (Sadasadbhyam Anirvachaniya) Maya, but real (Sat) in essence.[29] Jnanadeva agrees to the latter view and rejects the former.

Shakti (power) is Para Samvit (the supreme knowledge) as well. Jnanadeva recognises this and says that a Jnani calls it Svasamvitti and a Shaiva calls it Shakti, but it is also Bhakti (Love). So what Shaivas call the energy of Shiva is also His Love towards Himself. It is "Praneshwari" (Beloved), hence the Universe is not only the manifestation of the power of the Supreme Being, but is also the expression of The Supreme Love.[30] So, though Jnanadeva has endorsed the Shaiva view of Shiva and Shakti, he fully brings out the nature of Shakti and shows that this Shakti is not only the creative Power but also the creative Love which is the impetus to the world's manifestation.

Gorakhanath

The relation of Jnanadeva with the Nath-cult is well-known. At the end of Jnaneshwari, he gives his spiritual lineage beginning from God Shamkar. The historical figures, however, are from Matsyendranath. Gorakhanath was his disciple. In the Amritanubhava no names of these Nath-Yogis are mentioned. But it is interesting to notice the similarities between the philosophical background of the Nath-cult as found in the works of Matsyendranath and Gorakhanath, and that of Jnanadeva's Amritanubhava.

Mr. Bhingarkar, in his biography of Jnanadeva, quotes some verses from Matsyendrasamhita where it is told that the universe arises out of the power (Chit-shakti) of Brahman.[31] This shows his divergence from the Mayavada of Shamkar. Again there is a Sanskrit work called Siddha-Siddhant-Paddhati published by Shri Purnath of Haridwar with learned commentaries in Sanskrit and Hindi. The author of this work was Gorakhanath as we see from the first verse.[32] In this work we get not only the account of the religious discipline of the Nath-cult but also its philosophical foundation.

According to Gorakhanath, the Ultimate Reality is "Shakti Yukta Shiva"—Shiva accompanied by Shakti. Shakti, however, is not some outword force but is the power inherent in the Supreme Spirit. Hence both Shiva and Shakti are inseparable and eternally united. "At the heart of Shiva there is Shakti and at the heart of Shakti there is Shiva. See no difference between them as between the moon and it light"[33]. There are similar descriptions in Jnanadeva's Amritanubhava. Instead of the Moon and Its light we get there the instance of Sun and its light.[34] Again there is the similar description of the inseperability of the two.[35]

Gorakhanath does not regard the Supreme power that gives birth to the world as Maya or Ingorance. Vedantic

Maya is neither real nor unreal. It is an incomprehensible entity, while the Supreme energy of the Absolute is the dynamic aspect of His noumenal consciousness. The power has the tendency of self-expansion as well as self-contraction and these constitute the cosmic order.[36] Hence the cosmos is not illusory but the real expression of the Absolute Energy.

The Absolute spirit, according to Gorakhanath, conceived as being, is Shiva and conceived as becoming is Shakti. The conception of Shiva divorced from Shakti is incomplete and the conception of Shakti divorced from Shiva is meaningless. Shiva with his own Shakti, which is non-different from Himself, is the sole ground and the true self of all the phenomenal existence.[37]

In this way the philosophical background of Gorakhanath as propounded in his Siddha-Siddhant-Paddhati is similar to that of Amritanubhava. Gorakhanath lays stress on the Power-aspect and hence his philosophy culminates in the path of Yoga, while in the Amritanubhava the Power or Shakti is also the Love of the Supreme towards Himself. Jnanadeva has stressed this aspect of Reality which he considers to be Its essence. So His philosophy culminates in the path of Bhakti before which the eight-fold Yoga pales into insignificance like the Moon in broad daylight.[38]

Shamkar

Jnanadeva had great reverence for Shamkar. In his Jnaneshwari he says that he is merely following the footsteps of the great Bhashyakar (i.e. commentator). It does not mean that he slavishly imitated Shamkar. The statement is expressive of his humility, and though sometimes he follows Shamkar, he has his own way of expounding the

Gita. In the Amritanubhava there is no mention of Shamkar, and he has his own line of philosophic thinking. We are reminded of Aristotle's remark about Plato that though Plato was dear to him, truth was dearer to him than Plato. In the same way though Jnanadeva paid great homage to Shamkar, he had to criticise his theory of Mayavad which he found to be logically untenable as well as contradicting experience. Though Amritanubhava does not mention the name of Shamkar, we find in it some traces of Shamkar's influence as well as an elaborate criticism of his point of view.

This influence is seen when we notice how Jnanadeva describes the Ultimate Reality as self-established, beyond all the proofs because It is their own presupposition and beyond all conceptual constructions.[39] Shamkar has expressed the same idea in his commentary on the Vedant Sutras.[40] Jnanadeva has criticised the doctrine of nihilism in the same way as Shamkar.[41]

In spite of these similarities there are fundamental differences between the two philosophers. Both are Absolutists but their conceptions about the nature of the Absolute differ. Shamkar's Absolute is undifferentiated consciousness (Nirvishesh Chinmatra), while Jnanadeva's Absolute is the perfect consciousness (Bhariva Jnanamatra). Shamkar's Absolute is static and unchanging, and the multiplicity of the world is in truth nothing but an illusory appearance on that substratum, while Jnanadeva's Absolute is dynamic and expresses Itself in the form of becoming or the process of the Universe. According to Shamkar the triad of Knower, Knowledge and the Known is merely an illusion while Jnanadeva thinks it to be the very nature of Reality or Experience.

The God of Shamkar is a limitation of Brahman, hence Ultimately unreal, while Jnanadeva's God is without limitation and is the real expression of the Absolute. The Maya of Shankar is nothing but limitation itself, but the Goddess of Jnanadeva is without limitation and is not a limiting power but the essential aspect of the Absolute. According to Shamkar the Jiva or the empirical ego is an appearance to be finally dissolved in the Absolute, while to Jnanadeva it forms as it were a focus through which the Absolute enjoys itself.[42]

[1] In the Jnaneshwari Jnanadeva describes the ten upanishadas as the flowers, with the noble fragrance of wisdom, decorating the crown of the deity. उपरी दशोपनिषदें । जियें उदार ज्ञानमकरंदे । तियें कुसुमें मुकुटी सुगंधें । शोभती भली ॥ I; 18 While Commenting on the 45th verse in the second chapter of the Gita, he says that the Vedas are covered by three gunas. The upanishadas, therefore, are Satvik or full of wisdom and the portion of the Veda, dealing with rituals, is full of egoistic tendencies. तिहीं गुणीं आवृत । हे वेद जाण निभ्रांत । म्हणोनि उपनिषदादि समस्त । सात्विक ते ॥ येर रजतमात्मक । जेथ निरूपिजे कर्मादिक । II; 256-57. In the 18th chapter of Jnaneshwari, while describing how the temple of the Gita was erected, Jnanadeva compares the upanishadas to a plateau on the jewel-mountain of the Vedas which was quarried by the clever artist Vyas. व्यास सहजे सूत्री चळी । तेणें निगमरत्नाचळी । उपनिषदार्थाची माळी । माजी खांडिली ॥ XVIII-35.

In the Abhangas, Jnanadeva says that God is the inner core of the upanishadas उपनिषदाचा गाभा । Abg. 52. In the Haripatha he says, "My Lord is all-powerful and the Upanishadas cannot comprehend Him" ज्ञानदेव म्हणे हरि माझा समर्थ । न करवेचि अर्थ उपनिषदा ॥

विभाति यस्य भासा । सर्वमिदं हा ऐसा । श्रुति काय वायसा ढेकर देती ॥ Amritanubhava, VII-290.

According to Shamkar the gist of the verse in the Upanishadas is (Shamkar's Commentary on Mundak, 2-2-10.)

यत्तज्ज्योतिषां ज्योतिर्ब्रम्ह तदेव सत्यं सर्वं तद्विकारं वाचारंभणं विकारो नामधेयमात्रमनृतमितरत्...।

Jnanadeva's own view is—

प्रकाश तो प्रकाश की । यासी न चुके घेई चुकी । म्हणोनि जग असकी । वस्तुप्रभा ॥ Amritanubhava VII, 279.

—This is immediately supported by the above verse which again is followed by—

यालागी वस्तुप्रभा । वस्तूचि पावे शोभा । जात असे लाभा । वस्तूचिया ॥

वाचून वस्तु यया । आपणपे प्रकाशावया । अज्ञान हेतु वाया । अवघेंचि ॥ Ibid; VII, 291, 292.

3 Ibid; X, 18.

4 Ibid; X, 17.

5 Taittiriya Upanishada II, 4.

6 Kenopanishad I, 3.

7 Amritanubhava; VII, 107-122

8 Ibid; V. 57. विज्ञातारमरे केन विजानीयात् । स वेत्ति वेद्यं नच तस्यास्ति ।

9 Brihadaranyak Up. II, 4-14.

10 Svetasvetar Up. III, 19.

11 Amritanubhava; VI, 87. 89 with Shivkalyana's Commentary.

12 Ibid; VI, 13-93.

13 Ibid; V, 146.

14 Dr. Pendse—Shri Jnaneshwaranche Tatvajnana Ch. VIII.

15 Yogavasishtha:—3-7-20.

अत्यंताभाव एवास्ति संसारस्य यथास्थिते ।
यस्मिन्बोधमहांभोधौ तद्रूपं परमात्मनः ॥

16 Yogavasishtha $\frac{6}{2}$ —85—14.

सा राम प्रकृतिः प्रोक्ता शिवेच्छा पारमेश्वरी ।
जगन्मायेति विख्याता स्पन्दशक्तिरकृत्रिमा ॥

— Yogavasishtha VI-2-85-14.

17 Dr. B. L. Atreya M. A. D. Litt—The Yogavasishtha and its Philosophy, p. 39.

18 कैवल्याही चढावा । करीत विषयसेवा । झाला भृत्य-भज्यु-कालोवा। भक्तीच्या घरीं ॥ अमृ. ७. ३०.

19 Dr. Atreya—The Yogavasishtha and its Philosophy p. 48.

20 Dr. S. N. Dasgupta—A History of Indian Philosophy Vol. II. p. 239.

21 Shiva Sutra Vimarshini—p. 13.

एवमात्मनि अनात्मताभिमानरूपाख्यातिलक्षणाज्ञानात्मकं ज्ञानं न केवलं बंध : यावद् अनात्मनि शरीरादौ आत्मताभिमानात्मकम् अज्ञानमूलं ज्ञानमपि बंधः एव ।

22 Amritanubhava III, 16.

23 Shiva Sutra I, 1. चैतन्यमात्मा.

24 Shiva Sutra—Vimarshini, p. 9.

25 Pratyabhijna—Hridaya, p. 2-8.

26 Amritanubhava I, 1.

27 Ibid; VII,—272; Cf. Shivasutra Vimarshini p. 99.

28 Ibid; VII,—138; Cf. Shivasutra Vimarshini p. 88.

29 J. C. Chatterji M. A.—Kashmir Shaivism p. 55.

Dr. K. C. Pandey calls this theory of Abhasavada the realistic idealism and explains it thus—"The world of experience is real because it is a manifestation of the All-inclusive Universal Consciousness or Self; it is ideal, because it is nothing but an experience of the self and has its being in the Self exactly as our own ideas have within us"—Abhinavagupta—An Historical & Philosophical study. p. 196.

30 Jnaneshwari XVIII—1113. 89. Amt. I-2, 12.

31 Quoted by Dr. Pendse in his Shri Jnaneshwaranche Tatvajnan p. 408.

[32] Prof. A. K. Banerji M. A.—"The Shiva-Shakti cult of Yogiguru Gorakhanath" in Prabuddha Bharat (Oct. and Nov. 1943).

आदिनाथं नमस्कृत्य शक्तियुक्तं जगद्गुरुम् ।
वक्ष्ये गोरक्षनाथोऽहं सिद्धसिद्धांतपद्धतिम् ॥

[33] शिवस्याभ्यंतरे शक्तिः शक्तेरभ्यंतरे शिवः । अंतरं नैव जानीयात् चंद्रचंद्रिकयोरिव ॥

[34] Amritanubhava I, 25.

[35] Ibid; I, 41.

[36] Cf. Amritanubhava, VII-257.

[37] Siddha Siddhant Paddhati IV-13 Cf. Amritanubhava I, 17.

[38] Amritanubhava IX.-26, 59-60.

[39] Amritanubhava V, 16-17; VI, 94; VII, 119.

[40] Brahm-Sutra, Shamkar Bhashya on II-3-7.

न हि आत्मागंतुकः कस्यचित्, स्वयंसिद्धत्वात्...आत्मा तु प्रमाणादि... व्यवहाराश्रयत्वात् प्रागेव प्रमाणादिव्यवहारात् सिद्ध्यति.

[41] Amritanubhava IV, 26-31. Cf. Brahma Sutra Shamkar Bhashya II, 3-7.

य एव हि निराकर्ता तदेव तस्य स्वरुपम् ।

[42] Pringle Pattison:—Idea of God—"The intelligent being is rather to be regarded as the organ through which the Universe beholds and enjoys itself" p. 211. Instead of "Universe" we may substitute "God" in the case of Jnanadeva.

CHAPTER IX

AMRITANUBHAVA AND OTHER WORKS OF JNANADEVA

Changadeva-Pasasthi and Amritanubhava

CHANGADEVA-Pasasthi is a small work of Jnanadeva containing 65 verses addressed to Changadeva who was famous for his Yogic powers. Though small in size, the work is most important as it contains a clear cut view of Jnanadeva's attitude to the ultimate problems of philosophy. And it is truly said that what Jnanadeva has told in nine thousand verses of Jnaneshwari and in eight hundred verses of Amritanubhava, is contained in the sixty five verses of Changadeva-Pasasthi. In this way Pasasthi can be called a quintessence of the philosophy of Jnanadeva.

There are, however, two main points absent in the Pasasthi which we find in his other works. First, there is the absence of a logical argumentation or the refutation of opposite views. In the Amritanubhava the greater part of the work is devoted to the refutation of Ajnana, while in the Pasasthi there is only a summary statement about the absurdity of those who regard "Avidya" as the cause of the world.[1] The second is the absence of any statement about the nature of Bhakti which we find both in the Jnaneshwari and Amritanubhava. Hence the Pasasthi in itself is not sufficient to convey the view point of Jnanadeva completely.

The Ultimate Reality is described in the Pasasthi in the same way as in the Amritanubhava. "Nothing can be said about it. It cannot be known in any way (that does not mean, however, that it does not exist). It is the pure existence or Being. The eye is unable to see itself though it has the power of seeing other objects. In the same way it is powerless in the matter of self-knowledge. It is knowledge itself where there is no room for ignorance. But being knowledge itself It cannot be said to be an object to itself. Therefore if anything has to be spoken about it, it should be done in the form of silence."[2] His existence, appearance and enjoyment do not depend on anything else.[3]

The main object of Pasasthi is to state that the triad of knower, knowledge and the known is the manifestation of one Samvitti (consciousness). Hence the world is not caused by Avidya, but it is the natural manifestation of Reality. God is not hidden by His manifestation. His splendour is not diminished on that account. Gold itself becomes an ornament without diminishing its quality. In the same way He Himself has become the world without losing anything. Though there are aggregates of tiny particles of clay, their material nature is not annihilated. In the same way He is not concealed by His own vibrations in the form of the universe. The Moon is not covered by its rays; fire does not become something else though it appears in the form of flames. I do not, therefore, understand the meaning of the saying that the manifestation of the subject and the object is caused by Avidya. On the contrary they are the natural expressions of the One Reality."[4]

So the relation between Reality and the cosmos is not like that between a rope and a serpent. Reality is not the ground of an illusion in the form of the world but it is the very stuff of the Universe. "Though we call cloth by its name it is nothing but thread. The earthen pot is nothing but earth. So the Pure-Consciousness (Samvitti) which is above the subjective and objective conditions, manifests itself in the form of subject and object. The pure Gold exists in the form of an ornament, or a person appears in the form of an aggregate of several organs. In the same way all the objects from Shiva to the earth are simultaneous illuminations of one Samvitti. Though sugar appears in the form of several lumps its sweetness is not divided; in the same manner, the one Samvitti is not divided though there are so many objects in the universe. The same Samvitti manifests Itself in the form of the knower, knowledge and the known.[5] "

The Unity of Samvitti is not broken. "In a bundle of thread there is nothing but thread inside and outside. So in the threefold manifestation there are no three separate entities. Nothing but one's own complexion is seen in a mirror. Hence the seeing seems to be without any purpose. So the one Samvitti appears threefold without losing its Uniqueness." [6]

Jnaneshwari and Amritanubhava

Though Jnaneshwari is a commentary on the Gita and Amritanubhava is an independent work, both of them reveal the same metaphysical standpoint. Jnanadeva describes the Ultimate Reality or the Absolute Existence in Jnaneshwari in the following manner — "The Absolute Being is sound without being heard, fragrance without being scented, joy without being experienced. What is behind it is before it; what is before it is behind it; which itself unseen, sees without there being any object to be seen; which is knowledge without being either the knower or the known; which is neither effect nor cause, which is neither the second nor the first; which is alone to itself." [7] So the

Ultimate Reality is Pure Knowledge or Spirit. It is the presupposition of all proofs, and experiences Itself.[8]

Amritanubhava describes the cosmos as a sport of the Absolute. It is not something that hides Reality but manifests It. In the same way Jnanadeva says in his Jnaneshwari that the world is related to God as waves are related to the sea, limbs to the body, branches to a tree, or flames to a fire. The lustre of a jewel does not hide it. In the same manner this world does not hide God. Gold does not lose itself though several ornaments are made. Lotus when bloomed is the same lotus. As it is not necessary to destroy the petals in order to see the lotus, it is also not necessary to set aside the world in order to have a vision of God, because everything is His manifestation.[9]

Sometimes, while describing the relation of the world to God or the Ultimate Reality, Jnanadeva uses the similies of Vivartvada e.g. of rope and snake, in Jnaneshwari. That does not mean, however, that he follows Maya-Vada. He also uses the similies of Parinamvada e.g. milk and curds, or a seed and a tree. That also does not mean that he follows the Samkhya system. He has used both kinds of similies, but he has also shown that these are insufficient to point out the relation between God and the Universe by using the similies like the Sun and its rays, which illustrate his own view of "Chidvilas" (Play of the pure consciousness).[10]

There is a description of Ajnan or Nescience in some passages of Jnaneshwari, hence there is a difference of opinion as regards Jnanadeva's philosophical point of view as expressed in it. Out of humility Jnanadeva says at the end of the work that he has followed the foot steps of his predecessors like Vyas and Shamkar in writing his commentary. Hence some critics urge that Jnanadeva's metaphysical conceptions are identical with those of the great Vedantist Shamkar. Jnanadeva had a great reverence for Shamkar no doubt, but that does not mean that he did nothing but blindly followed him. Though Jnanadeva expresses his humility, he is also conscious of his own intellectual powers and of the grace of his own spiritual teacher, for he says in the same passage that by the grace of Shri Guru every breath of his will become a new treatise.[11]

The passages where we find the description of Ajnan or Maya, are those in which Jnanadeva is explaining the Vedantic standpoint, just as he has explained the Samkhya view of Prakriti in the 13th chapter of Jnaneshwari.[12] He says that what the Samkhyas call Prakriti is called Maya by Vedantins.[13] Jnanadeva's Goddess is different from both the Maya of Vedantin and the Prakriti of Samkhyas. The contradiction of Jnaneshwari to Amritanubhava, on account of the description of Ajnan in the former is only apparent and not real. The description of Ajnan is only an exposition of Vedantic standpoint and does not show that Jnanadeva himself was an Ajnanvadin. How can he be an Ajnanvadin like Shamkar, whose view he has refuted in his Amritanubhava and when there are passages in the Jnaneshwari itself, describing the universe as the manifestation of the Supreme Being?

Again, it might be said that these two works, written one after another, show the evolution of the author's thought. While writing Jnaneshwari Jnanadeva was an Ajnanvadin; afterwards his thought gained maturity, and he gave up his old conception, nay, not only that, but he refuted it in his Amritanubhava. But this view is also not tenable. In the first place, Jnanadeva's span of life was brief i.e. of barely twenty two years. Jnaneshwari was written when he was only sixteen years old. Then there remain only six years during which Amritanubhava, Pasasthi, Haripath and other devotional lyrics were composed. So the interval between the composition of Jnaneshwari and Amritanubhava could not have been a long one. Jnaneshwari is also a work of maturity as Jnanadeva himself says that the work reveals the majesty of the grace of his Guru.[14] So both of them are works of maturity and the idea of an evolution in his thought is inconceivable.

The same conception of Bhakti, which is found in the Amritanubhava, is expressed in the Jnaneshwari also. Bhakti is not merely a pathway to God, an external means of attaining God-Realization, but is the very nature of God or Ultimate Reality. Bhakti is Divine Life.[15] To regard appearances in this world as separate existences is a sign of ignorance. As a matter of fact God is experiencing Himself through Bhakti i.e. the Knower and the Known (Appearances) are the two aspects of the same Divine Experience.[16] To apprehend this Divine Love is the highest achievement of Human Life, and he who has achieved this is a true Bhakta. Jnanadeva has depicted beautifully the life of such a devotee, who, becoming one with the Lord, enjoys Him. The sweet unitive experience of the devotee can be compared to the waters of the Ganges that mingle with the ocean and yet play upon its bosom. When a mirror is placed before another mirror the beauty of the perception is enhanced. Similarly there is the enhancement of Divine Love in the heart of the devotee. Again his experience can be compared to that of a person looking at his fair complexion in a mirror. The person's eyesight discards the glass of the mirror and perceives the reflection. No sooner is the reflection perceived than the man gives it up and enjoys the pure delight of his own simple existence. So the devotee enjoys Divine Joy without duality. He enjoys it as a damsel enjoys her youth. The ripples of water on every side kiss the water. Light everywhere delights in the Sun and space pervades the sky. Without actions he worships God as ornaments worship gold, as fragrance worship sandal wood, or as the moon light worships the moon. Though there is no action there is Bhakti in non-duality.[17]

Some one might object the possibility of enjoyment in such way and say that it is impossible to enjoy a thing by becoming one with it and hence Bhakti in non-duality is also impossible. Jnanadeva definitely answers the objection by stating that it is possible to enjoy God only by uniting with Him. If one does not become united with Him one cannot enjoy Him. Just as royal dignity cannot be enjoyed without possessing a royal personality, so Divine sweetness cannot be enjoyed without union with God.[18]

Amritanubhava and Abhangas

The Abhangas of Jnanadeva express the same metaphysical standpoint as that of Amritanubhava. The Ultimate Reality is described as Pure consciousness that manifests Itself as a subject as well as an object.[19] It is self-established and requires no other proof.[20] God is the Ultimate Being. There is no other besides Him. Every becoming is his manifestation.[21] He is cosmic as well as acosmic.[22] He is beyond our conception and is enjoying Himself.[23]

The Universe is nothing but His manifestation. It is as if His ornaments.[24] It is His play.[25] In one of His Abhangas Jnanadeva regards the whole Universe as a Lingam and gives a sublime description of it. He says that the basin of the Lingam is the heaven and its water line the ocean. It is as fixed as Shesha and is the support of the three worlds. There Clouds pour water on it and it is worshipped by flowers in the form of stars. The Moon is the fruit offered to it, the Sun is the light waved before it and the individual self the oblation offered to it.[26] So God pervades the whole Universe as well as transcends it.[27]

Amritanubhava and Virahinis

Virahinis are, as we have already seen (P. 22), the religious lyrics in which Jnanadeva has expressed the pangs of his love-lorn heart. In the Amritanubhava he puts forth the theory of Chidvilas upon which he bases his conception of natural devotion (Akritrim Bhakti). Virahini is the mature fruit of this devotion. Writers like Dr. Ranade believe that this विरहावस्था (love-lornness) is a degenerated form of the attitude of submission.[28] But this interpretation is misleading. Jnanadeva himself warns us not to look upon this experience as insignificant. In one of his Virahinis he says; "I am waiting alone and my heart is burning with love. This condition should not be considered as a trifling matter."[29] In the same Virahini he compares this state with the soil which is dried up and is thirsty for sweet showers.[30] So this experience of the Virahini is the sweetest of religious experiences where the deep calls unto deep and the devotee is drinking the droughts of Love Divine in the form of his yearnings.[31] The Viraha is at the same time the sweet embrace of the beloved Lord. This is called by Jnanadeva the Sweetness of Divine Experience (अनुभव सौरसु).[32] It is union in separation. (वियोगी संयोग).[33]

[1] Changadeva Pasashthi, 8.

[2] Ibid; 30-33, Cf. Amritanubhava VII, 103; IV, 37, 18, 22; VI, 87-88.

[3] Ibid; 36, Cf. Amritanubhava VII, 104.

[4] Ibid; 4-8, Cf. Amritanubhava VII, 234-292-289.
[5] Ibid; p. 9-12; 14, 18.
[6] Ibid; p. 19-21, Cf. Amritanubhava VII, 205.
[7] Jnaneshwari XV, 72-79.
[8] Ibid; I, 1. Cf. Amritanubhava V, 40, 41, 52.
[9] Ibid; XIV, 118-128. Cf. Amritanubhava VII, 289.
[10] Ibid; IX, 64-88.
[11] Ibid; XVIII, 1735.
[12] Ibid; XIII, 960-1025.
[13] Ibid; XIV, 70.
[14] Ibid; XVIII, 1751.
[15] Ibid; XVIII, 1117.
[16] Ibid; XVIII, 1128.
[17] Ibid; XVIII, 1137-1151, Cf. Amritanubhava IX, 38-41; 57-59.
[18] Ibid; XVIII, 1142-46.
[19] पाहातें पाहाण्यामाजि स्वयेंचि विस्तारलासि । की देखणेंचि होवुनि अंगे । सहजसिद्ध तें तू आपणपे पाही । Gatha of Jnanadeva, Abg; 351.
[20] Gatha of Jnanadeva, Abg. 332.
[21] Ibid; सर्व होणें तुज अेकाचें । दुजेपण तेथे आणावे कैचे ॥
[22] Ibid; सगुण निर्गुण अेक गोविंदु रे । 40
[23] Gatha of Jnanadeva Abg. 7. आपेआप सोहळा भोगीतसे.
[24] Ibid; 348. विश्वी अळंकारला देव.
[25] Ibid; 334. आदि पुरुषा...नानापरी तुझा खेळू.
[26] Ibid; 44
[27] Ibid; 26. निवृत्ति म्हणे लीळा । विश्वव्यापक निराळा ॥
[28] Dr. R. D. Ranade:—Pathway to God in Hindi Literature, (p. 179).
[29] वाट पाहे मी एकली मज मदन जाकळी । अवस्था धाकुली म्हणो नये ॥ (ओळीचे अभंग क्र. ३८७७).
[30] वाफा शिंपिलीया वाळुनिया जाये । Ibid.
[31] ज्ञानदेव निळी हृदयीं सावळी । प्रेमरसें कल्लोळीं बुडी देत ।
Ibid; Abg. 3835.
[32] बापरखुमादेवीवरू हृदयीचा जाणुनी । अनुभव सौरसु केला ॥
Ibid; Abg. 63.
[33] बापरखुमादेवीवरा विठ्ठला संयोगी। तोचि तो त्यागुन भोगी गे माये ॥
Ibid; Abg. 3858.

CHAPTER X

DIFFERENT INTERPRETATIONS OF JNANADEVA'S PHILOSOPHY—A CRITICAL SURVEY

Jnanadeva's philosophy is differently interpreted by various scholars among whom the important names are those of Dr. Pendse, Prof. Ranade, Prof. Dandekar and Shri Pandurang Sharma. All of them have deeply studied the works of Jnanadeva. Each of them, however, has his bias which colours his interpretation and leads him to adopt his own peculiar point of view. Hence it is important to know their interpretations and to see whether they rightly bring out the spirit of the philosophy of Jnanadeva.

Dr. Pendse in his "Shri Jnaneshwaramche Tatvajnana" (Philosophy of Shri Jnaneshwar) has devoted a special chapter to the Amritanubhava.[1] He tries to identify the metaphysical standpoint of Jnanadeva with that of Shamkar. According to his estimate Amritanubhava is like a detailed exposition of Shamkar's Adhyas-Bhashya (Introductory portion of Shamkar's commentary on the Braham-Sutra).[2] The positions of Shamkar and Jnanadeva, however, are different in dealing with the triad of Knower, Knowledge, and the Known. Shamkar regards this triad as due to Superimposition or Avidya. Jnanadeva, on the other hand, disproves the existence of Avidya and the cause of the trio is not an imaginary ignorance but the Pure consciousness itself.[3]

According to Dr. Pendse, Jnanadeva and Shamkar both regard Ultimate Reality as one Pure Consciousness and both of them admit the Unreality of the world. Sometimes

Jnanadeva speaks as if the world is the real expression of the Absolute.

How are these contradictory views to be reconciled? Dr. Pendse tries to solve this riddle by the method of Anvaya-Vyatirek (affirmation and negation). These are the two ways of propounding the same thing i.e. the Reality of Brahman and the Unreality of the world. To say that everything is Brahman is equal to saying that Brahman transcends everything. "Sarvam Khalvidam Brahm" and "Neti Neti" mean the same thing. Jnanadeva in his Amritanubhava mainly employs the Anvaya (affirmative) method while Shamkar uses Vyatirek (negative) method prominently. Sometimes Shamkar also uses the affirmative method.[4] The purpose of both these methods, according to Dr. Pendse, is that the negative method takes for granted ignorant people's conception about the world and refutes it, while the affirmative method uses the standpoint of one who has attained Knowledge.[5] Thus Amritanubhava is rightly called "Siddhanuvad" — utterances of one who has attained the highest stage of life.[6]

Dr. Pendse's solution seems to have been suggested by Shamkar's own solution of the difficulty found in the interpretation of the different Upanishadic texts. Some passages in the Upanishadas describe Brahman as acosmic, while others as cosmic. Both these descriptions, according to Shamkar, mean the same thing. Brahman, from the empirical standpoint is cosmic, while from the transcendent standpoint is acosmic.[7] In this way Shamkar tries to synthesise the Upanishadic teachings. The same kind of synthesis, in the case of Jnanadeva, is fallacious. It is true that both Jnanadeva and Shamkar say that the world is unreal. But their meaning of the word "unreal" is not the same. Hence "Atman or Spirit" which is regarded by both as ultimately real does not convey the same thing.

Dr. Dasgupta has discussed the question of the cardinal principle of Idealism in his "Indian Idealism."[8] The cardinal principle of Idealism is the spirituality of the real. There are different varieties of Idealism according to the meaning attached to the word "Spirituality". The proposition "Reality is Spiritual" has for its corollary the proposition that the external world of our perceptions is in some sense illusory.[9] This discussion helps us to make clear the positions of Shamkar and Jnanadeva. Both are Idealists. Both regard the Ultimate Reality as spiritual. Both regard the world as in some sense unreal. The question arises about the meaning of the Spirit and Unreality, as understood by these two thinkers. According to Shamkar, the spirit or Atman is pure consciousness which is static and unchanging. It is pure being and has no room for becoming. The unchanging has no room for change. Hence it is but natural that he regards the world which is ever changing and ever active as the product of ignorance or Avidya. This is the meaning of his conception of the unreality. Therefore he employs mainly Vyatirek or negative method and though at times he seems to adopt Anvaya or the affirmative one, he always means by affirmation nothing more than negation e.g. to say that "all is Brahman" (Sarvam Khalvidam Brahm) means nothing more than that "All is not. Only Brahman is." The Spirit or Atman of Jnanadeva is dynamic. It expresses Itself in the form of the world. 'The world is ever changing' means that the Absolute is ever manifesting itself spontaneously in novel forms. Hence the world is called "Chidvilas" (the playfulness of the Absolute). The unreality of the world in the case of Jnanadeva bears a different meaning. The world is unreal means that it has no meaning apart from the Atman or the Absolute in whom it finds its full significance and ground. It has no separate existence. In another sense the world is real. It is real in the sense of being a real manifestation of the Absolute.[10] Hence Jnanadeva seems to adopt the affirmative method. Though he sometimes uses the negative method, his negation means an affirmation. Though he sometimes uses the conception of Maya, he only conveys the sense of Chidvilas.

This doctrine of the play of the Absolute can be easily misconstrued. Dr. P. T. Raju in his "Thought and Reality" has identified "Lila" of the Upanishadas with "Maya" of Shamkar. "Lila" according to him is something inexplicable. So the world is "Lila" (play) of the Absolute means that it is inexplicable i.e. Anirvachaniya. Maya is Anirvachaniya (inexplicable). So "Lila" is Maya.[11] But to explain the play of the Absolute in this fashion is nothing but playing upon words without taking into consideration the underlying significance. In the same way Dr. Pendse also misses the significance of Jnanadeva's positive statements and construes them as negative ones in the light of Shamkar's method of explanation.

To sum up, the unreality of the world in the case of Shamkar means that the world is the effect of ignorance or Avidya, while in the case of Jnanadeva it means that the world is not some independent entity apart from the Atman. It is the experience of the Atman beholding Itself.[12]

Dr. Pendse himself is conscious of the differences between Shamkar and Jnanadeva. He admits that the main points where they differ are that Jnanadeva identifies God with the Absolute, and Jnana (knowledge) with Bhakti (Devotion), while Shamkar regards these as different. Absolutism and Monotheism are regarded by Jnanadeva as one and the same, while Shamkar denies it. Jnanadeva sets forth Bhakti as the Direct pathway to Moksha, while to Shamkar it is only indirectly that Bhakti is useful and the final emancipation is attained only through the pathway of Jnana or knowledge.[13] Inspite of his admitting these differences, Dr. Pendse wrongly insists upon the identity of the views of both the thinkers. He also admits that Shamker lays stress on Sannyas (renunciation) while Jnanadeva on Bhakti or Loving devotion.[14] Dr. Pendse does not go deeper into the matter to inquire into the root cause of this emphasis.

The reason for these differences, which Dr. Pendse admits, is no other than the difference in the conceptions of Atman or the Ultimate Reality held by these philosophers. The conception of one naturally leads to the ideal of renunciation while that of other ends in the ideal of Loving Devotion. Their conceptions of Moksha also differ. Dr. Pendse fails to notice this. Jnanadeva's Moksha or final emancipation finds room for action and devotion while that of Shamkar debars them.

Prof. S. V. Dandekar has written a learned article on "Jnanadeva's Philosophy."[15] He terms Jnanadeva's Advaita as Purna (complete) Advaita or Monism pure and simple. He rightly contrasts his teachings with those of other Acharyas like Ramanuja and Vallabha. Both these Acharyas, though agreeing with each other in not accepting Shamkar's conception of Avidya, have different philosophical backgrounds. Ramanuja calls himself a qualified monist, but as a matter of fact, he is a dualist because of his tripartite division of the one Reality into God, man and the world. Vallabhacharya's philosophy is called pure monism, but his point of view also is not similar to that of Jnanadeva. He regards Vasudeva's son Krishna as the Highest

God and advocates what is called Pushti-marga, the goal of which is to offer to your Guru your body, mind and wealth. Jnanadeva, on the other hand, is a devotee of the same-Krishna, but his Bhakti is related to that Supreme Spirit which transcends Guru, place and time, as shown by him in his Amritanubhava.[16]

For these reasons Shamkar is nearer to Jnanadeva than Ramanuja or Vallabha. The circumstances in which Shamkar lived were different from those of Jnanadeva. He had to refute Buddhists, Mimansakas and Samkhyas. His work, therefore, is mainly polemic in character. He had to use the conception of Ajnan. Shamkar and Jnanadeva, both of them, are non-dualists though they use different methods of proving their theory. One proves Advaita by accepting Ajnan while the other proves it by rejecting it; so it can be said, according to Prof. Dandekar, that Jnanadeva revived the philosophy of Shamkar in an independent way.

But by maintaining that there is only a methodological difference between the two, Prof. Dandekar does not do full justice to the concrete character of Jnanadeva's monism. Shamkar's monism is abstract. So the difference between the theories of these two philosophers is not one of method only. It is more fundamental. Prof. Dandekar also compares Jnanadeva with Goudapada and tries to show that because of his criticism of Ajnana Jnanadeva reverts to the Ajatavada of Goudapada, who maintains that the world is never produced at all. Its appearance is due to our imagination. But the Ajatavada of Goudapada and the Chidvilas of Jnanadeva are not the same. According to Goudapada there is no world at all, while Jnanadeva says that there is the world, though it is not independent. It is the real manifestation of the Absolute as the rays of the sun are its manifestations.

A special chapter is devoted to the Amritanubhava "one of the greatest philosophical works in Marathi literature," in Prof. R. D. Ranade's "Mysticism in Maharastra."[17] The Sphurtivada is rightly regarded by him as Jnanadeva's original contribution to philosophic thought.[18] Later on, however, he says that the Sphurtivada, which regards the world as coming from God as light from a jewel and it is real to the same extent as a light is, is advanced by Jnanadeva metaphysically, and we should not suppose that he (Jnanadeva) did not believe Mayavada in its ethical and mystical aspects.[19] Prof. Ranade acknowledges that Jnanadeva has shaken the metaphysical foundation of Mayavada by his arguments against Ajnanvada in the VIIth chapter of Amritanubhava. Once this is admitted it cannot be said that Jnanadeva believed Mayavada in its ethical and mystical aspects. If he had done so, he would have preached the path of renunciation and not of Bhakti, which does not require the giving up of the worldly life. In the first chapter of Amritanubhava Jnanadeva describes Goddess instead of Maya. When Jnanadeva sometimes speaks about the unreality of the world it is to be understood that he wants to bring to our notice that the world has a deeper significance than we know. It is the expression of the Spirit and is to be experienced as such. So what is Maya to a believer in abstract monism is the expression of Divine Love to a Bhakta. Hence Jnanadeva says in the Jnaneshwari that to a devotee the water of Maya disappears on its very bank.[20]

Though Shri Huparikar Shastri has contrasted the philosophy of Jnanadeva with that of Shamkar and Vidyaranya in his writings, it was Pandurang Sharma who drew the attention to this point by his forcible argument and deep erudition. He wrote many articles in the Chitramaya Jagat — a Marathi monthly — on the philosophy of

Jnanadeva as expounded in his Amritanubhava. He rightly showed that though each thinker uses the same words, they have different meanings according to their points of view. Hence we should not confound their perspectives and identify the views of philosophers like Shamkar and Jnanadeva by their verbal semblance. Jnanadeva has his own view and his statements should be interpreted accordingly. Otherwise contradition would result.

Shri Pandurang Sharma has made a noteworthy contribution to the study of Amritanubhava but he does not make clear the meaning in which Jnanadeva regards the world as real. Instead of fully bringing out the significance of Jnanadeva's positive contribution and making explicit the implications of the conception of chidvilas, he tries to enter into the question of the influences of other schools of thought like those of Kashmir Shaivism, Pancharatra and Ramanuja, on Jnanadeva.

It cannot be said, on account of some similarities, that Jnanadeva borrowed his refutation, as Shri Pandurang Sharma maintains, from Shri Bhashya of Ramanuja. His philosophical background is different and it is possible that he should have criticized independently. The conceptions of Radha and Krishna are not found in the Amritanubhava, hence it is futile to look, as Shri Pandurang Sharma does, to the Pancharatra as the source of God and Goddess of Jnanadeva. As for Kashmir-Shaivism, some influence of these works is likely because Jnanadeva mentions Shiva-sutras. However Jnanadeva goes deeper into the nature of Shakti mentioned in Shaivism where it is treated as the energy of the Supreme Shiva. To Jnanadeva she is not mere energy. She is also the Love Divine which manifests the multiple universe.

In this way it will be seen that Dr. Pendse has misinterpreted Jnanadeva's standpoint. Prof. Dandekar and Prof. Ranade give only a half hearted consent to its originality. Pandurang Sharma, though he tries to show its originality, does not look deeper into its valuable implications that laid the foundation of the Bhakti cult in Maharashtra.

[1] Dr. Pendse — Jnaneshwaranche Tatvajnana Ch. VI.

[2] Ibid; p. 312.

[3] Amritanubhava, VII, 131-133, 146, 162 etc.

[4] Dr. Pendse:—Shri Jnaneshwaranche Tatvajnana p. 441.

[5] Ibid; p. 199.

[6] Amritanubhava, X, 12

[7] Prof. Hiriyanna — Outlines of Indian Philosophy; p. 61-62.

[8] Dr. Dasgupta — Indian Idealism — "Upanishadic Idealism" Ch. II.

[9] Ibid; p. 27.

[10] Amritanubhava, VII, 289. जग असकी वस्तुप्रभा ।

[11] Dr. P. T. Raju — Thought & Reality, p. 274.

[12] Amritanubhava, VII, 280.
असो हे आत्मराजे । आपणापे जेणें तेजें । आपणचि देखिजे ।

[13] Dr. Pendse; Shri Jnaneshwaranche Tatvajnan p. 448.

[14] Ibid p. 450.

[15] Shri Jnaneshwar Darshan vol, II, p. 8-26.

[16] Amt. IX, 37.

[17] Prof. R. D. Ranade—Mysticism in Maharashtra p. 140.

[18] Prof. R. D. Ranade—Mysticism in Maharashtra p. 158.

[19] Ibid. p. 179.

[20] Jnaneshwari VII. 79.
तया ऐलीच थडी सरले । मायाजळ ॥

CHAPTER XI

JNANADEVA AND SOME WESTERN PHILOSOPHERS

The philosophy of Jnanadeva may now be compared with that of some western philosophers. A philosopher, he may be born in the West or in the East, has before him some persistent problems to be solved, problems that affect the whole of mankind. A comparative study of different thinkers is useful in clarifying and appreciating the solutions of various problems by them. Hence we would do well to compare the views of Jnanadeva with those of some prominent thinkers of the west.

Plotinus and Jnanadeva

Plotinus (204-269 A.D.) was the leader of Neo-Platonism that arose during the last period of Greek philosophy and had great influence upon the growth of the later Christian theology. The philosophy of Plotinus is the culmination of Greek philosophy. The founder of Neo-Platonism was Ammonius Saccas. But no works were written by him. Plotinus was his disciple He passed his eleven years in the company of his teacher and studied his doctrines. In 243 A.D. he went to Rome where he founded a school and presided over it until his death. The composition of his work began in his fiftieth year, and they were not published during his life time. Porphyry, his famous disciple, wrote his master's Biography, arranged and published the writings of Plotinus. These are called Enneades. There are six Enneades, each being a group of nine treatises. Plotinus was a mystic as well as a Philosopher. Porphyry tells us that his master had experienced mystic trances four times during his lifetime. He was greatly influenced by Yogic and Buddhistic systems of Indian philosophy. According to Dean Inge Plotinus holds a more undisputed place than Plato in the history of Mysticism.[1]

Generally there is a tendency among mystics to enjoy their contact with the Divine and not to discuss philosophical problems. It does not, however, mean that "there is a radical difference between the metaphysician and saint"[2] as Baron Von Hugel says. Both Jnanadeva and Plotinus were great mystics and both of them have written philosophical works.

The philosophical thinking of Plotinus is spun round the triad of the One, the Nous and the world-soul. Plotinus begins from the One. The One is God. He is good. He is infinite. He is the Ultimate source of all being and knowledge but He himself is outside all being and knowledge. God is the Absolute to whom thought or will cannot be predicated. Even self-consciousness cannot be attributed to him. He is the source of the world. Plotinus does not accept the idea of creation or evolution. He uses the word "Emanation." "Being perfect by reason of neither seeking, nor possessing nor needing anything, the One overflows as it were and what overflows forms another hypostatis."[3] The idea of emanation is akin to Jnanadeva's conception of sphurtivada. There is again a striking similarity between Jnanadeva and Plotinus in the use of the similes for describing the relation between the world and the One. "We are to think of it as a radiance proceeding from the One abiding in its changelessness, just as the light about and surrounding the sun is eternally generated without any change or motion in the solar substance".[4] Jnanadeva uses the same simile of the sun and its beams in the Jnaneshwari and again tells us how this simile is also inadequate to describe the relation between the world and the Reality, in his Amritanubhava.[5] The rays of the sun go out of it but the world does not go out somewhere from their ground.

Both Jnanadeva and Plotinus are monists. Both regard God-realization as the supreme end of human life. The description of the One as beyond thought and existence is akin to that of Jnanadeva who says that the Ultimate Reality is beyond Sat, Chit and Ananda.[6] Again Plotinus describes the One as happiness and he explains "The One seeks nothing in order that it may exist or be happy nor yet anything to support it. Since it is the cause of all else, owes its own existence to nothing else. For the same reason why should its happiness be an object external to itself? It follows that happiness is not an attribute of the One. The One is happiness,"[7] In the same way Jnanadeva tells us that if the Ultimate Reality is called Being (Satta), Knowledge (Prakash) and Happiness (Sukha), it does not mean that these are three different parts. Though the words are different they denote the same Reality. "Beauty, hardness and yellowness — these combined express one thing — gold.[8] Liquidity, sweetness, indicate one nectar."

To sum up, the two philosophers agree in holding (a) The Ultimate Reality is one, (b) The world is "emanation" or "Sphurti" of the One and (c) The mystic experience is the highest end of life. There are however, certain differences between the two. These are as follows:—

1) The theory of emanation, put forth by Plotinus, lays stress upon the simile of rays. As the rays go farther from the sun of Reality they become dimmer and dimmer until at last there is nothing but darkness. This darkness is what

we call matter. Jnanadeva does not hold such a negative conception of matter. Matter or everything knowable is nothing but "Sphurti".[9] Every particle of matter is surcharged with it. Hence he describes that "God and Goddess live happily even in a tiny atom."[10]

2) The highest mystic experience, according to Plotinus is "a flight of the alone to the Alone." [11] He means by flight different stages of contemplation culminating in the experience of ecstasy. This ecstasy is akin to the path of Dhyan or meditation. In the case of Jnanadeva, he himself was a great Yogi as well as a great Bhakta. He had experienced both the states and by comparing the two he found that Yogic Samadhi pales into insignificance before loving devotion. In the presence of spontaneous Divine Love, Yoga is like the Moon in a broad daylight.[12] So though both Jnanadeva and Plotinus are mystics, the types of their mysticism are different. One is devotional while the other is contemplative.

3) The ideal of Plotinus being ecstasy, he inclines towards giving up the wordly life. It is said that he limited his sleep and food to the minimum and fasted every second day to realize the Cynical ideal of freedom from needs.[13] He recognises that sensual beauty can lead us to supersensual. "But the whole of his ethics is dominated by the idea that the basis of all evil for the soul is its combination with the body and that every activity has more value the less it brings us into contact with the world of the sensual." [14] Plotinus regards this world as a shadowy copy of the supersensual world which is true and real. His ethical teaching is consistent with his own conception. Jnanadeva, on the other hand, regards this world as the expression of Divine Love. So he does not repudiate worldly

life. Instead of escaping from the world he teaches us to experience God's presence in every object. Bhakti is superior to Mukti and so he says:— "His (Bhakta's) enjoyment of objects surpasses even salvation and in the abode of Bhakti the devotee and the object of devotion are intermingled." [15]

Spinoza and Jnanadeva

It was Novalis, "One of the lights of early Romantic School" who first designated Spinoza a God-intoxicated man. The views of Spinoza were against orthodox religion — the Judaism in which he was born — and he was excommunicated. He was considered as a dangerous atheist and his great book "Ethic" was not published during his lifetime. These incidents in the life of Spinoza remind us of similar events in the life of Jnanadeva. Orthodoxy excommunicated Jnanadeva because his father sinned against their superstitions by accepting a householder's life after Sannyas. His monumental work like Jnaneshwari was practically unknown until Ekanath investigated the manuscript and proclaimed its greatness after three centuries.

To Spinoza philosophy was not merely a way of thinking but a way of life. Descartes, the father of Western modern philosophy, was inspired by intellectual curiosity. Spinoza was in search of a permanent object of love which would give him everlasting happiness.[16] He resorted to the rational thinking not as a speculative game but as a means to a perfect life. The name 'Ethic' is significant from this point of view. Jnanadeva has also the same goal. The name "Amritanubhava" itself suggests that it shows the pathway to the experience of unending bliss.[17]

Spinoza and Jnanadeva both are monists. Spinoza calls Ultimate Reality "the substance"[18] while Jnanadeva calls it "Vastu".[19] Spinoza identifies "substance" with God. The Vastu of Jnanadeva and God are the same. The culmination of Spinoza's philosophy is in "the intellectual love of God"[20] while Jnanadeva's philosophy ends in "Natural Devotion"[21] (Akritrim Bhakti). Both regard, 'God loving Himself', as the Ultimate fact.

In spite of these similarities there are some notable differences. Spinoza uses the geometrical method in the exposition of his theory. The substance or God is the ground of the world. The world necessarily follows from the substance as the conclusion of a Syllogism follows from the premises. The conception of Jnanadeva is more flexible than that of Spinoza. The world is not such a rigid necessity but is the playful expression of the abundance in the Absolute.[22] Then again if we examine Spinoza's conception of the intellectual Love of God and God's Love towards Himself, we find that it differs from the conception of Jnanadeva, which is more positive. To Spinoza the intellectual Love is more like a joy of resignation. "The philosopher cannot help loving God; at least, he cannot but feel perfectly contented, peaceful and resigned in contemplating Him." This complete acquiescence of the thinker in the supreme law, this reconciliation of the soul with the necessities of life, this entire devotion to the nature of things — is what Spinoza, by accommodation, without doubt, calls the intellectual Love of God, the source of eternal happiness.[23] To Jnanadeva, God is the ocean of Love as we find in the description of the first chapter in the Amritanubhava, and human life is meant for tasting this ambrosia of Experience.[24]

Bradley and Jnanadeva

The Philosophy of Jnanadeva can be compared to that of Bradley — the modern Absolute Idealist. Both of them regard Experience as the Ultimate Reality and try to determine its nature by analysing it. In his "Appearance and Reality' Bradley starts with a critical examination of the various ways of accepting Reality. Primary qualities, secondary qualities, time, space, — all are examined and found to be self-contradictory. Although this critique of Bradley discredits most of the categories of commonsense and philosophy, and compels us to relegate them to "appearance" as distinguished from Reality. the result is not wholly negative. Bradley positively discovered that "Ultimate Reality is such that it does not contradict itself."[25] It is self-consistent. Secondly it must contain appearances. Thirdly, Reality must be one, and fourthly it is sentient Experience. "There is no being or fact outside of that which is commonly called psychical existence."[26] There is but One Reality and Its being consists in Experience."[27]

So behind the destructive criticism of Bradley there is a vision of Reality as a harmonious undivided whole of experience. The experience is a whole which is not merely reason or thought, but also feeling and willing, all of which remain merged in one undifferented Absolute. Both Bradley and Jnanadeva maintain that thought cannot grasp the nature of the Absolute.[28] Jnanadeva tells us that Reality is non-dual whose nature is to manifest itself in duality.[29] To Bradley this duality or appearances are fragmentary and full of contradictions. Jnanadeva looks at these appearances from a different angle of vision. Unity enjoys its own reflection in duality. So according to him, the status of duality or diverse phenomena is more significant than Bradley believes. Shamkar regards diversity as illusory, Bradley gives it more prominence and says that Reality appears through appearances. Jnanadeva goes a step further and brings out fully their real significance. Every appearance, according to him, is surcharged with divine immanance.

Bradley recognises the feeling aspect of the Absolute but he does not say anything more than that the Absolute must also be emotionally satisfying, that there must be the absence of pain and a balance of pleasure. Jnanadeva, on the other hand, brings out fully the implication of this side of the Absolute and shows how Love is its very essence.

Again the philosophy of Jnanadeva is the outcome of a profound religious experience. Bradley had no close or vital relation with religious matter and what he says about it is the product of an "arm-chair thinking.[30]

[1] Dean Inge-Christian Mystician p. 91.

[2] Baron von Hugel-Eternal Life p. 85.

[3] Bakewell-source Book in Ancient Philosophy p. 401.

[4] Ibid p. 402.

[5] Jnaneshwari XIV, 384.

तेजाच्या तेजौनि निघाला । तेजीच्च असे लागला ।
तया रश्मी ऐसा भला । बोध होआवा ॥

Amritanubhava VII 262. रश्मी सूर्याची आथी । परी दिवा बाहेर जाती ।
म्हणोनि बोधसंपत्ति । उपमा नोहे ।

[6] Amt. V, 13.

एवंसच्चिदानंदु । आत्माहा ऐसा शब्दु । अन्यथाव्यात्रृत्ती सिध्दु । वाचकुनव्हे ।

[7] Bakewell-Source Book in Ancient Philosophy p. 399.

[8] Amt. 1-2

सत्ताप्रकाशसुख । या तिहीं उणे लेख ।
जसें विखपणेंचि विख । विखा नाहीं ॥
कांति काठिण्यकनक । तिन्हि मिळोनि कनक एक ।
द्राव गोडी पियूख । पियूखचि जेवी ॥

[9] Amt. VII, 245 इये स्फूर्तीकडुनी नाही । स्फूर्तीमात्रवाचुनी

[10] Amt. I, 11 की परमाणुमाजी उवाये । मांडिली आहाती ॥

[11] Benjamin Rand — The classical Moralists (Selection) "This therefore, is the life of the Gods, and of divine and happy men, a liberation from all terrene concerns a life unaccompanied with human pleasures, and a flight of the alone to the alone p. 175.

[12] Amt. IX, 26, 50,

प्रत्याहारादि आंगी । टेकिले योगी । तो जाला इये मार्गी । दिहाचा चांदु ॥ कोण्ही एक अकृत्रीम । भक्तिचे हे वर्म । योगज्ञानादि विश्राम । भूमिका हे ।

[13] Zeller — Outlines of The History of Greek Philosophy p. 292.

[14] Ibid p. 296.

[15] Amt. IX, 30.

[16] Spinoza (Selections) "On the Improvement of Understanding p. 1.

[17] Amt. X, 19.

[18] Ethic — Part I, prop. XI.

[19] Amt. VI, 94. VII, 110, 135, 163, Cf. p. 28.

[20] Ethic Part V prop. XXXIII.

[21] Amt. IX, 60

[22] Amt. VII, 136.

पाणी कल्लोळाचेनि मिषे । आपणापें वेल्हावे जैसे । वस्तु वस्तुत्वें खेळो ये तैसे । सुखे लाहे ॥

[23] Weber — History of Philosophy, p. 273.

[24] Gatha of Jnanadeva Abg.

बापरखमादेवीवरु हृदयीचा जाणुनि । अनुभव सौरसु केला ।

[25] Bradley — Appearance and Reality p. 120.

[26] Ibid p. 127

[27] Ibid p. 403.

बुद्धि बोध्या सोके । ते येवढी वस्तु चुकेळ

[28] Amt. VII, — 110.

[29] Amt. IX. 28

द्वैत दशेचें आंगण । अद्वैत वोळगे आपण । भेदु तंव तंव दूण ।
अभेदासी ।

[30] Motz — A Hundred years of British Philosophy p. 343.

CHAPTER XII

JNANADEVA'S PLACE IN THE HISTORY OF INDIAN PHILOSOPHY

Negligence of Jnanadeva's philosophy

The various historians of Indian Philosophy like Dr. Radhakrishnan and Dr. Dasgupta do not mention Jnanadeva because they have relied upon Sanskrit works only. Jnanadeva has written all his works in Marathi, hence his name is neglected by these writers. The significance of any philosophical system does not depend upon the language in which it is couched but upon the vitality of its meaning. Jnanadeva has purposely written in Marathi. In a democratic spirit he wished that his message should be understood by a Pandit as well as a layman. He was proud of his mother tongue and said that his Marathi words are more sweet than Sanskrit words.[1] It is not the expression of a vain glory but of a real feeling. Both Jnaneshwari and Amritanubhava are written in Ovi meter. Jnanadeva's Ovi is incomparable. Prof. Patwardhan is thrilled by its beauty and cadence. He says: "With Jnanadeva the Ovi trips, it dances, it whirls, ... it takes long jumps, it halts and sweeps along, evolves a hundred and one graces of movement at the master's command. In the music of sound too it reveals a mysterious capacity of manifold evolution."[2] The Amritanubhava is a purely philosophical work, hence these literary excellences are found there in a lesser degree than in Jnaneshwari. Still we find there beautiful similes and literary graces by which the author has tried his best to make the subject as interesting and as lively as possible.

The culmination of Indian idealism

The dominant note of Indian philosophy is idealistic. This idealism has its source in the Upanishads. Aruni and his disciple Yajnavalkya were the prominent teachers of Idealistic monism. The cardinal principle of the idealism is the spirituality of the Real. Yajnavalkya interpreted Spirit or Atman as the Pure Intelligence — the ontological substratum of all existence as well as the epistemological nucleus of all knowledge.[3] Later on Shamkar accepted the same interpretation but regarded the manifestations of the Pure Intelligence as illusions. His Idealism was Absolute but one sided. Kashmir Shaivism tried to correct this defect and regarded Maya as the power or the dynamic aspect of the Ultimate Reality. Jnanadeva has endorsed both the aspects of the Absolute i.e. Knowledge and Power but he introduces a new element in his theory. He draws attention to another more vital aspect of the Absolute. That aspect is the emotional one. The Absolute is not mere knowledge and will, but also affection or love. The Absolute is a person in a higher sense. He is the Shiva, the blessed Divine, who loves to manifest Himself as the knower and the known. In this way the Whole is the Experience saturated with Love Divine. Thus Idealism of Jnanadeva is the mature fruit of Upanishadic Idealism and deserves an important place in the history of Indian Idealism.

Ethical teaching

The ethical teachings of Jnanadeva are in consonance with his metaphysics. The world, being a divine manifestation, is not to be despised. Hence Jnanadeva does not teach the gospel of renunciation.[5] One should not give up one's duties but should do them in a spirit of worship.[6] Every act should be performed in an attitude of prayer. The world is neither something heinous nor it is the object of mere sensual enjoyment. Every object is surcharged with divine significance. The ideal man of Jnanadeva is One whose heart overflows with divine Love at the sight of any object in the world.[7]

Religion of love

The religious implications of Jnanadeva's philosophy are also of great importance. With him the God of religion and the Absolute of Philosophy are identical.[8] The ideal of life is not Moksha or liberation but Bhakti or the realization of Love Divine in this very life. Rituals or Yogic practices are of no use.[9] Our life is not something sinful or a degradation of the Absolute but the medium through which Divine Love experiences Itself. To know this, to remember this with longing is the way of intermingling our little self with the Divine.[10] This is the highest summum bonum of life which is within the reach of every human being. No barriers of caste or creed, time and space hinder his path. In this way the Philosophy of Jnanadeva is the bed rock on which the lofty and noble temple of the Bhakti cult in Maharashtra is erected.

Influence on later writers.

The influence of Jnanadeva upon the writers of the later periods was profound. Namadeva was his contemporary who was greatly influenced by Jnanadeva's philosophy, as was the the latter by his devotion. The Abhangas of Namadeva bear testimony to his assimilation of the philosophy of Chidvilas. In one of the religious lyrics Namadeva says: "He (God) gave birth to Himself out of his own sweetwill."[11] Ekanatha was a great devotee of Jnanadeva who carried out the same line of teaching. His famous commentary upon the eleventh chapter of Shri Bhagawat Puran bears the stamp of Jnaneshwari and his "Hastamalak" and "Swatmsukha" show the influence of the Amritanubhava.[12] Tukaram who is rightly regarded as the pinnacle of the temple of Bhagwata Dharma, has absorbed Jnanadeva's teachings and explained them in his own way, e.g. he seems to have summarised the whole chapter of the Amritanubhava on the refutation of Ajnana in one famous line of one of his Abhangas where he says, "People look out for darkness taking a lighted torch in their hand. How strange is their notion that they will meet darkness in this way! "[13]

No influence of Jnanadeva is found upon Ramadasa who was more orthodox and accepted Shamkar's Maya-vada. The name of Jnanadeva is not even mentioned in his works. An indirect reference is found in his Dasbodha,[14] where he describes the miracle of the movement of an inanimate object. This, certainly, refers to Jnanadeva who is said to have performed the miracle of moving a wall, by his Yogic powers, when Changadeva had come to see him. Here Ramadasa is not showing his respect to Jnanadeva but is rather inclined to belittle him.

The universal significance of Jnanadeva's philosophy

We have so far dealt at some length with the salient features of Jnanadeva's philosophy. We have seen how the Chidvilas theory propounded by him is his notable contribution to Indian Philosophy by a scheme of Idealism which must always remain one of the greatest achievements of the human mind. The blend of Bhakti, Jnana and Karma was adumbrated by Jnanadeva into a consistent and an all embracing philosophy. It stressed the feeling aspect in philosophy without the loss of intellectual heights attained by philosophers who laid stress purely on the aspect of Jnana. It is interesting to note that this blend had its natural effects in liberating the conative forces which were so far inhibited by the over emphasis on purely Jnana aspect of Reality. This new outlook was also responsible for an entire change in the attitude towards the worldly things. The World, the existence of which no person could deny or refuse to take into account, whose living and active presence was equally felt and experienced by both the learned and unlearned and which had the capacity to stir the highest emotions and stimulate the passions of the deepest die, was required to be regarded as a mere appearance. This the common man could not do. Naturally philosophic thought became alien and strange to him and philosophy became the pursuit of a few. This in turn made philosophy more and more unrealistic. The philosophic thought was in the main moving in the grooves of Shamkar's Philosophy. Jnanadeva tried to change this course of thought.

The dynamic aspect of Jnanadeva's philosophy consists in his recognition of the feeling aspect in philosophy pari passu with the aspect of Jnana and Shakti. This dynamic nature is further accentuated by his adoption of a healthy, positive and realistic outlook of looking towards the objects in the world. For him the world is not a mirage or a cobweb of human imagination. According to his teachings God takes delight in manifesting in and realizing Himself through the infinite variety of forms of existence. Every form of existence, therefore, becomes at once endowed with the wealth and beauty of the Infinite. Again, the relation of the ultimate Reality or God with our finite-selves is one of deep sympathy and love. God is regarded as the embodiment of love. Hence to know him is to love Him, and this love is the inspiration of noble deeds and the highest social service. So the philosophy of Jnanadeva has not only a considerable historical importance but there are also elements in it that have a lasting universal significance.

[1] Jn. VI, 14.
माझा मऱ्हाठाचि बोलु कौतुकें। अमृतातेंही पैजा जिंके। ऐसीं अक्षरें रसिकें। मेळविन ॥

[2] Prof. W. B. Patwardhan — "Wilson Philological Lectures" — quoted in Prof. R. D. Ranade's "Mysticism in Maharashtra" p. 36.

[3] Brihadaranyak Upanishada II, 41-1.

[4] Dr. M. N. Sarkar — Hindu Mysticism — (Studies in Vaishnavism and Tantricism) "Hegel speaks of Absolute Life as the eternal play of Love with itself" p. 159.

[5] आतां गृहादिक आघवें। कांहीं न लगे त्यजावे Jnaneshwari V, 22
कां सांडिसी गृहाश्रम । कां सांडिसी क्रीयाकर्म ।
आहे तें वर्म वेगळेंची ॥ Gatha of Jnanadeva abg. 466
घरदार वोखटें त्यजू म्हणसी तरी शरीरा एवढे जाड ।
मायबाप वोखटें त्यजू म्हणसी तरी अहंकार अविद्येचें कोड ।
बंधू सखे त्यजू म्हणसी तरी कामक्रोधमद मत्सर अवघड ।
बहिणी पाठीच्या त्यजू म्हणसी तरी आशा तृष्णा माया अवघडरया ॥
त्यजिलें तें काय कासया म्हणिजे । सांग पा मजपाशी ऐसे ॥
जया भेणें जासी तू वनांतरा । तें तव तुजचि सरिसें रया ॥ Ibid 462
असोनि संसारीं जिव्हे वेगु करी। Haripatha. I

[6] हें विहितकर्म पांडवा। आपुला अनन्य वोलावा ।
आणि हेचि परमसेवा। सर्वात्मकाची ॥ Jnaneshwari XVIII, 906
अगा जया जे विहित । तें ईश्वराचें मनोगत ।
म्हणौनि केलिया निभ्रांत । सांपडेचि तो ॥ Ibid, 911

तया सर्वात्मका ईश्वरा। स्वकर्मकुसुमांची वीरा।
पूजा केली होय अपारा। तोषालागी ॥ Ibid, 917

[7] Amt. IX, 30. कैवल्याही चढावा। करित विषय सेवा। झाला भृत्यभज्यू कालोवा। भक्तीच्या घरीं ॥

[8] अगा ब्रह्म या नावा। अभिप्राय मी पांडवा ॥
पै मंडळ आणि चंद्रमा। दोनी नव्हती सुवर्मा।
तैसा मज आणि ब्रह्मा। भेद नाहीं ॥ Ibid XIV, 405, 6.

[9] योग याग विधि येणे नोहे सिद्धी।
वायाचि उपाधि दंभ धर्म ॥ Haripatha 5
अष्टांगयोगें न सिणिजे। यम नेम निरोध न कीजे रया ॥
वाचा गीत गाइजे। गातां वातां श्रवणीं ऐकिजें रया ॥
गीताछंदे अंग डोलिजे। लीला विनोदें संसार तारिजे रया ॥
Gatha of Jnanadeva, Abg 417.

[10] घडोनि सिंधूचिया अंगा। सिंधूवरी तळपे गंगा।
तैसा पाड तया भोगा। अवधारी जो। Jnaneshwari XVIII, 1138, Amt. IX, 29.

[11] आपलीच आवडी धरुनि खेळिया आपआपणाते व्याले रे। —नामदेव
आवडी धरोनी आलेली आकार। केला हा पसारा याजसाठीं॥ —तुकाराम

[12] Ekanath-Bhagwat II, 370.

[13] दीप घेउनिया धुंडिती अंधार। भेटे हा विचार अघटित॥ —तुकाराम

[14] Ramdas—Dasabodha; I, 10-9

APPENDIX A

THE AMRITANUBHAVA

(An English Rendering)

The Invocatory Sanskrit Verses

1 I take shelter in the deity, who is well-known as the glorious Nivrittinatha, who is indestructible, indescribable, the bliss itself, unborn and imperishable.

2 I pay my homage to the very Divine Wisdom who showers blessings, who is known in the world as Guru (the spiritual teacher), whose command is ever victorious and who overflows with compassion.

3 Shiva and Shakti are identical but frequently appear as two. So it is not possible to know whose half part is united with the half part of the other.

4 I bow to the parents of the worlds, who reveal their essential unity to each other, so that I may understand the same.

5 I respectfully salute the Perfect Shambhu who is the cause of the beginning, the preservation and the end of the world, who is the manifestation of the beginning, the middle and the end, and who is also the dissolution of the three.

CHAPTER I

The Union of Shiva and Shakti

1 Thus have I paid my homage to the God and Goddess who are the limitless primal parents of the universe.

2 On the charming spot, the Lover Himself, out of overflowing love, becomes the Beloved, who is made up of the same flesh, and who eats the same food.

3 Out of deep longing they swallow each other, and again emit each other because they like to be two.
4 They are neither completely identical nor completely different. We do not know their real nature.

5 How strong is their desire to enjoy themselves ! They become one through it and never allow their unity to be disturbed even in jest.

6 They are so afraid of their separation that although they have given birth to the child in the form of the universe their duality is not disturbed.

7 Even though they perceive the animate and the inanimate nature emanating from them, they do not allow any third object to touch them.

8 They are seated on the same ground (existence) and they wear the same ornament of light (knowledge). From time immemorial they dwell happily in union.

9 The difference itself, that tried to discover duality for enjoying it, was abashed to see their intimacy merged itself in their sweet union.

10 It is through God that the other is Goddess and without her the Lord is nowhere. As a matter of fact their existence is due to each other.

11 Oh ! How sweet is their union ! The great world is too small for them to live in, while they live happily even in the smallest particle.

12 They treat each other as their very life and they do not create even a blade of grass without mutual help.

13 These are the only two inmates in the home of the universe. When the Lord goes to sleep, the mistress remains awake and plays herself the part of both.

14 If either of them happens to wake up, the whole house is swallowed up and nothing is left behind.

15 Each became a half part of the whole for the process of diversity. Both are trying to melt their forms into one.

16 Both of them are objects to each other. Both are subjects to each other. Both are happy in each other's company.

17 Shiva alone lives happily in the nominally different forms of the male and female. The whole universe is due to the coupling of the half part of each.

18 Two lutes produce one musical note. The flowers are two but the fragrance is one. Though the lamps are two the light is one.

19 Two lips utter but one word and two eyes give but one vision. In the same way the two (Shiva and Shakti) create one world.

20 So the eternal couple manifesting duality is enjoying the dish of the same flavour.

21 The chaste and well devoted Shakti cannot live without her Lord. Without her the all-doer has no existence.

22 The two cannot be distinguished because the appearance of her Lord is due to her while her existence is due to him.

23 We cannot distinguish sugar and sweetness, camphor and fragrance.

24 While trying to gather the rays we get hold of the flame itself. We get Shiva while trying to catch hold of her essence.

25 The sun shines on account of his lustre, but the essence of lustre is nothing but the sun. So the One Supreme Beauty shines swallowing all the difference.

26 An object is the cause of its reflection. The reflection is the cause of the inference of the object. (The one object appears as an object and its reflection). In the same way the one Reality shines as two.

27 The essence of all void became Purusha through her, while the Shakti got her peculiar existence through the Lord.

28 Shiva Himself formed His beloved without whom Shiva loses his own personality.

29 Her form is the cause of God and His glory manifested in the process of the world. But Her form itself is created by Him out of Himself.

30 Blushing at her formless husband and her own graceful form, she adorned him with the ornament of names and forms as great as the universe.

31 There was scarcity even of unity. But she, the fortunate one, playfully presented the rich manifold of the world.

32 She manifested the glory of her Lord by melting her own body, while by belittling himself he made her wellknown.

33 He assumes the form of a seer through his love to see her. If he fails to see her he throws himself away.

34 He assumes the form of the universe through her importunities and he is left naked without her.

35 He is so subtle that he is not visible though manifest. He assumed the form of the universe through her grace.

36 The Shiva awakened by her, is satisfied when he eats the dishes in the form of the objects that are perceived as well as one who serves him.

37 When her husband is asleep she gives birth to all the things living and non-living. When she takes rest the husband himself vanishes.

38 When the husband hides himself, he is not discovered without her. Both of them are like mirrors to each other.

39 Shiva enjoys his own bliss by embracing her. Though he is all enjoyer he enjoys nothing without her.

40 She is his form while her beauty is due to him who is her lover. They are enjoying the feast by intermingling with each other.

41 Shiva and Shakti make up one whole just like air and its motion, gold and its lustre.

42 Shakti is inseparable from Shiva just like the musk and its fragrance, fire and its heat.

43 If night and day would go to the abode of the sun, both of them would vanish. In the same way their duality would vanish in their real essence.

44 As a matter of fact, Shiva and Shakti (because of their duality) are antagonistic to the state from which the sprout of Pranawa (the letter Om) springs.

45 Jnanadeva says, "I show my respect to the couple of Shiva and Shakti who by swallowing the sweet dish of name and form, enlighten the underlying essence."

46 By embracing each other both of them merge into one unity, just as the darkness of night is transformed into light at the break of day.

47 Para with Vaikhari remains silent in the process of discovering their real nature, just as the ocean merges along with the Ganges into the waters of Pralaya.

48 The air with its motion merged in the sky. The sun with its lustre is merged in the light of Pralaya times.

49 In the same way while trying to see them, the seer and his sight vanish. I pay homage to the inmates of the universe again and again.

50 Both of them are like a stream where not only the knower cannot drink its water in the form of the known but also throws himself away.

51 Under these circumstances if I remain separate to pay my homage, it would be a meaningless verbal separation.

52 But my salutation is like that of an ornament which is not different from gold and yet worships it.

53 When the word 'tongue' is uttered by the tongue, is there any difference between the word and the object meant by it ?

54 The Ocean and the Ganges intermingle and though their names are different, would there be any difference in their waters ?

55 The Sun shows in himself the object as well as the subject of illumination, yet he does not lose his singleness.

56 If moonlight brightens the surface of the moon, or if a lamp is enmeshed in its rays, is there any degradation ?

57 When the lustre of a pearl plays upon it, its beauty and purity is enhanced.

58 Is Pranava (the letter Om) divided into different parts because it contains three components ? Or is the letter 'N' divided into three parts because it is formed of three lines.

59 If the capital of unity is not lessened and the advantage of gracefulness is obtained, why should not water smell the buds of flower in the form of its own ripples ?

60 Therefore, without differentiating Shiva and Shakti, I proceed to bow to them in this manner.

61 By giving up the mirror, the image merges in its object. A ripple vanishes when the air is still.

62 A man comes to his own as soon he wakes from his sleep. In the same way I have bowed to the God and Goddess by giving up my ego.

63 The salt giving up itself becomes the ocean, so giving up my ego I am united with Shiva and Shakti.

64 I have paid my homage to Shiva and Shakti by uniting with them just as the inner empty space of the plantain tree is united with the outward one.

CHAPTER II

Paying Homage to Shri Nivrittinatha

1 Now (I bow to Him) who is the spring to the garden of spiritual endeavours, an auspicious thread of Divine Command and though formless the very incarnation of compassion.

2 (I bow to Him), who mercifully runs to help the Pure Consciousness who is experiencing the self-hood by wandering in the wilderness of Avidya.

3 I bow to the spiritual teacher Nivritti, who by killing the elephant in the form of Maya, offers him the dish of the pearls taken from its temple.

4 By whose glance the bondage is turned into liberation and the Knower realizes himself.

5 He makes no difference between great and small in distributing the gold of liberation. He is the cause of the knower's vision..

6 As for his powers, he surpasses even the greatness of Shiva. He is like a mirror in which Atman sees his own bliss.

7 It is through his grace that the scattered digits of the Moon of spiritual knowledge are brought together to form the play of full moon night.

8 All the efforts of the spiritual aspirant cease as soon as he meets him (the spiritual teacher.) He is like the sea where the Ganges in the form of activity ceases to flow.

9 In his absence the seer wears the lovely ornament of appearance. All the diversity disappears as soon as he appears.

10 The darkness of Avidya is transformed into the blessed daylight of self-knowledge at the touch of the Sun of his grace.

11 By the water of his grace the individual self becomes so pure that he regards even the state of Shiva as impure and does not allow himself to be touched by it.

12 He gave up his greatness to save his disciple yet his real greatness does not forsake him.

13 There was no happiness in being alone. So the Pure consciousness sees Itself assuming the forms of a teacher and a disciple.

14 By the sprinkling of whose grace the poison of Avidya is turned into the nectar of infinite knowledge.

15 His insight swallows the knower himself as soon as it embraces the knowable. Still it does not become impure.

16 With his help the individual self attains the status of Brahman, while if he is indifferent the Brahman becomes more insignificant than a blade of grass.

17 Those who faithfully endeavour and regard his will as all in all, gain the ripe fruit of their efforts.

18 Unless the spring of his graceful glance touches the garden of the Vedas, the aspirant does not get his own fruit in his hand.

19 By casting his glance he causes the appearance to recede and vanish. Though his conquest is great he does not call it his own.

20 He has attained the greatness of a spiritual teacher through the unworthiness (of his disciple). He is so fortunate as to destroy that which does not exist !

21 He is like a solid substance which saves anyone from drowning in the water that does not exist, and the individual thus saved remains nowhere.

22 The ordinary sky (ether) with its component parts cannot equal Him who is like a spiritual sky that is ever full.

23 The moon with her cool rays is formed out of his light. The brilliance of the sun is due to a ray of his light.

24 He is like an astrologer to whom even Shiva, who is tired of assuming the form of an individual self, asks for the auspicious moment to regain his own status.

25 He is like the moon whose manifest form is not diminished by wearing the apparel of her own light that enhances her lustre.

26 Though manifest he is not seen. He is light and yet does not illuminate. He exists and yet is nowhere.

27 How many groups of inferences should I put forth by using the words 'He' and 'Who'? He does not answer to any mode of proof (i.e. He is beyond various proofs).

28 He is indescribable in words which become silent in his oneness that tolerates no duality.

29 The object of valid knowledge reveals itself when all kinds of Pramanas (means of valid knowledge) cease to exist. His liking for non-existence is wonderful.

30 If we wish to have a little glimpse of Him at any time, the seeing itself is a pollution in His Kingdom.

31 In these circumstances how can I enter His kingdom by praising or talking about Him? He has merged his name by assuming it.

32 The Atman (Shri Guru) does not proceed towards Himself. How can he recede also? However he does not give up the illusory screen of his name (i.e. Nivritti).

33 How can he destroy anything if there is nothing to be destroyed? How he can be called Nivritti?

34 When did the Sun perceive the darkness? Yet he is called the enemy of darkness.

35 That which is illusory becomes real, that which is inanimate becomes animate and impossible events become possible through his wonderful sport.

36 (Oh Shriguru), Thou showest the appearances through thy wonderful power and rejects them because they are mere appearances. Thou art beyond appearances and art not the object of any kind of perception.

37 Ah ! Sadguru ! How should I treat thee who art so mysterious ? Thou doest not allow thyself to be determined by any conception.

38 Thou hast raised so many names and forms and hast destroyed them through the force of thy power, yet thou art not satisfied.

39 Thou doest not allow thy friendly relation to any one without sacrificing his individuality. It is not proper to say that the servant loses himself and becomes a master.

40 If we try to give Him a particular designation he does not even bear the name Atman. As a matter of fact He does not like to become any particular object.

41 There is no night to the Sun; the salt is dissolved in water; sleep vanishes when the person wakes up.

42 The objects of camphor do not remain in the presence of fire. In the same way the name and form vanish in his presence.

43 When I try to bow him, he does not remain before me as the object of my salutation. He is not persuaded by any mode of difference.

44 The sun does not cause its own rising. So He does not become the object to my salutation.

45 By whatever means no one can place himself in front of him. In the same manner he has taken away his state of being the object of worship.

46 No reflection is seen in the mirror of the sky. In the same way he is not the object of salutation.

47 Let him not be an object of worship. Why should I feel it as something uncanny ? But he does not leave any trace of the person who goes to salute Him.

48 When the outer end of the hem of any garment is unloosened the inner hem is unloosened without any effort.

49 Or, as the reflection vanishes along with the relative objectivity of the original object, so the personality of one who salutes is taken away by him along with his own state of being the object of respect.

50 The sight is of no use where there is no form. We are placed in such a state by the grace of His feet.

51 The burning flame of a lamp is sustained by the combination of the wick and oil. It cannot be sustained by a piece of camphor.

52 As soon as the two (i.e. the camphor and the flame) are united both of them vanish simultaneously.

53 In the same way as soon as I see Him both the worshipper and the object of worship vanish like dreams in the state of waking.

54 In short, by using these words I have done away with the duality and paid the respectful homage to my dear companion in the form of Shri Guru.

55 Oh ! How wonderful is his friendship ! He has made conspicuous the duality of the master and the disciple where there is no room even for one-ness.

56 How is his intimate relation to himself without the existence of any other ? He is not and does not become different from Himself.

57 He becomes as great as the sky including within Himself the whole universe. He bears the night in the form of non-existence.

58 The ocean is the ground of fulfilment yet it is difficult to be fulfilled. So in the residence of Guru contradictions live happily.

59 There is no intimacy between light and darkness, yet both of them become one in the sun.

60 Difference arises even if we call it one. How can it be differentiated in various forms ? Will the contradictory things contradict themselves ?

61 Therefore, the words master and disciple mean but one Reality and the master alone lives in both the forms.

62 Both gold and an ornament abide in the same gold or the moon and its light abide in the same moon.

63 Or, the camphor and its fragrance are nothing but camphor, sugar and its sweetness are nothing but sugar.

64 So, though master and his disciple appear as two, the master alone enjoys himself under the guise of the two.

65 The face, knowing itself, recognizes that it alone is reflected in the miror and is itself the original object.

66 The person who is asleep in the place where there is no one else, is alone without any doubt. He is both the awakened and the awakener.

67 Just as, in the above instance, the awakener and the awakened one are the same, so in this case it is he who gets knowledge as well as he who imparts it. In this way he upholds the relation of the master and his disciple.

68 If without the aid of a mirror, the eye could enjoy its own meeting, I would be able to describe this sport of Guru.

69 Thus He is nourishing the deep intimacy without causing duality or disturbing unity.

70 Nivritti is His name; Nivritti is his splendour. Nivritti is the glory of His kingdom.

71 This Nivritti is not like the word Nivritti which is used in opposing the action and understanding the state of non-action.

72 The so called Nivritti is brought forth by Pravritti which sacrifices itself just as the night by sacrificing itself brings forth the daylight. He is not like this Nivritti.

73 He is pure and supreme sovereign and not like a jewel whose lustre shines with the help of the other substance.

74 When the moon pervades the whole sky by spreading its light, the beauty of her own disk is enhanced by herself.

75 So Nivritti Himself is the cause of his being Nivritti. He is like a flower turned into a nose to smell its fragrance.

76 Is it required to search for mirrors if the eyesight is able to turn back and see the fairness of the complexion ?

77 When the night is gone and the day comes to light is it necessary for the sun to try to become himself ?

78 He is not like an object of knowledge requiring various proofs. He is Guru without any doubt.

79 In this way I have paid my homage to the holy feet of Guru whose actionlessness is absolute without the slighest touch of action.

80 Now, Jnanadeva says that by this salutation to Shri Guru he has discharged the debts of four kinds of speech (Para, Pashyanti, Madhyama and Vaikhari).

CHAPTER III

Discharging the Debt of Speech

1 The sleep of the Atman is dispelled by their (i.e. of four kinds of speech) calling aloud, but the debt is not fully discharged because the waking itself is a kind of sleep.

2 As a matter of fact the four, i.e. Para and others, are useful for the salvation of the individual self. With the distruction of Avidya these also are destroyed.

3 As hands and feet disappear along with the death of the body or as the subtle senses depart along with the mind or as the rays disappear with the sun.

4 Or again as the dream vanishes before the sleep comes to an end, so these (four kinds of speech) disappear along with Avidya (with whom they are intimately connected).

5 The iron that is burnt lives as Rasayana or as the burnt fuel lives as fire.

6 Salt is dissolved in water but lives as taste, sleep is destroyed but lives in the form of wakefulness.

7 So, though the four kinds of speech are destroyed with Avidya, they come to life in the form of the knowledge of Reality.

8 These should light the lamp of knowledge by sacrificing themselves but this knowledge is a futile exertion.

9 The sleep, when it comes, shows dreams and when it is gone, makes the individual conscious of himself. It is sleep that causes both.

10 In the same way when living, Avidya is the cause of false knowledge and when dead, it arises in the form of real knowledge.

11 But whether living or dead this Avidya entangles the individual by binding him with the so called freedom or bondage.

12 If the freedom itself is a kind of bondage why the word freedom should be applied to it ?

13 A child is satisfied by the death of a bugbear. It does not even exist for others. So how should they believe in its death ?

14 Can we call him wise who deplores the loss of breaking the jar which does not exist ?

15 Therefore, if the bondage is unreal, how can freedom arise ? But Avidya makes room for it by its self-destruction.

16 And Sadashiva, in his Shiva-sutras, has said that knowledge itself is a bondage.

17 It is not that we accept this because it is said by Shiva or Shrivallabha (Krishna). It can be understood even if they had not said it.

18 The wise one of Vaikunth i.e. Shri Krishna has elaborately explained how the quality of Satwa binds one with the bonds of knowledge.

19 If the Atman, which is pure knowledge itself, requires the help of another knowledge, would it not be like the Sun thinking about the help of the other light ?

20 The Atman's state of being knowledge itself becomes meaningless if its greatness is due to the knowledge other than itself. If one lamp desires another lamp to enlighten it, it is as if it has lost itself.

21 Would it happen that a person ignorant of his own presence, would wander over various countries in search of himself ?

22 How can a person say that he was very glad to remember himself after so many days ?

23 So if the Atman, who is pure knowledge himself, thinks that He has real knowledge of himself and says, "I am He". it would be a bondage.

24 Such knowledge. which is bondage, is very undesirable because the original knowledge itself is merged and gives rise to the so called freedom.

25 Therefore the four kinds of speech, which are ornaments of four bodies, vanish along with the Avidya when the egoism of the individual self is destroyed.

26 When Avidya, being dejected, enters the fire of knowledge along with her organs, the ashes of understanding only remain.

27 When the camphor is dissolved in water it is not visible but remains as the fragrance in water.

28 When the ashes are besmeared on the body its particles are brushed away but it remains in the form of a white lustre.

29 The waters of a stream that has ceased to flow does not remain in the form of a current but it exists in the form of the moisture in the soil.

30 At the noontime the shadow of a person is not visible but it remains under his feet.

31 So the understanding, that swallows every thing other than itself, is merged in the Ultimate Reality but remains in its own form.

32 The four kinds of speech are unable to discharge this debt fully even by their self-sacrifice. I have discharged it by bowing my head to the sacred feet of Guru.

33 When the Para, Pashyanti, Madhyama and Bharati — the four kinds of speech are destroyed, they cling to the knowledge which is a kind of ignorance.

CHAPTER IV

Knowledge and Ignorance

1 Now by destroying the ignorance, knowledge reigns supreme like the wakefulness that destroys sleep.

2 Or a face enjoys the knowledge of its own identity which was already in existence but was due to its looking into a mirror.

3 In the same way the knowledge causes the understanding of the identity of the world and the self. But it is like piercing the knife with another knife.

4 Just as a person who on entering a cottage, sets it on fire and burns himself along with the cottage or as a thief who enters into a sack and fastens himself in it, gets bound himself.

5 Or as the fire in its effort to burn camphor burns itself, so the knowledge attains the same condition by destroying the ignorance.

6 When the support of ignorance goes away the knowledge spreads itself to the extent of destroying itself.

7 When the wick of a lamp is almost burnt to the end, the flame is seen more bright. But this brightness is nothing but the extinction of the light.

8 Who knows whether there is the rise or fall of the breast of a woman or whether it is the blooming

or fading of a jasmine bud ? (They are so instantaneous).

9 The rise of a ripple is but its calming down, the flash of lightning is its disappearing.

10 In the same way knowledge drinks the water of ignorance and grows large to the extent of its own complete annihilation.

11 Just as the deluge of Pralaya engulfs both space and water and does not allow anything to remain aloof.

12 Or when the disk of the sun becomes larger than the universe the darkness and light are turned into pure light.

13 Or after destroying the sleep the wakefulness destroys itself and remains in its pure form (where there is no consciousness of wakefulness).

14 In the same way knowledge that shines by ignorance, is swallowed up by the Absolute knowledge.

15 At that time the Absolute knowledge is like the moon whose seventeenth digit remains constant without its light being enhanced by the full moon night or lessened by the dark night.

16 The sun alone, who is never thrown into background by any other lustrous body and who can never be covered by darkness, bears comparison with it.

17 It is the Pure knowledge itself that is not enlightened by any other knowledge or darkened by ignorance.

18 But can the Pure Consciousness be conscious of itself ? Can the eye ball perceive itself ?

19 Can the sky enter into itself ? Can the fire burn itself ? Can any person climb upon his own head ?

20 Will the eye sight be able to see itself ? Can the taste have its own taste ? Can the sound listen to its own noise ?

21 Can the sun enlighten himself ? Can a fruit grow upon the fruit ? Can a fragrance smell itself ?

22 Therefore, that which is Pure Consciousness itself without the quality of being conscious, is not conscious of itself.

23 If the knowledge requires the aid of another knowledge, it is nothing but ignorance.

24 What is light is not darkness. But is it a light to itself ?

25 (As in the above instance the light is neither darkness nor light). So He neither exists nor non-exists. Now by saying this He appears as non-existing.

26 Then if the situation is this that nothing exists, who knows that there is nothing ?

27 But on what ground is the theory of Nilihism proved ? It is an unjust imputation to the Ultimate Substance.

28 If the extinguisher of a light is extinguished along with the light, who knows that there is no light ?

29 Or if a person gives up his life as soon as he gets a sleep, then who will know that sleep is nice ?

30 A pot appears as apot. If it is broken the condition of breaking also appears. But if it does not exist at all who would say unnecessarily that it is not ?

31 Therefore, he who perceives that nothing exists, does not himeslf, become nothing. The Atman has a unique existence, beyond existence and non-existence.

32 The Ultimate Substance is neither an object to itself nor an object to any other. Is it the cause of regarding it as not existing ?

33 A person asleep in a lonely forest was not perceived by any other. He was also not conscious of himself.

34 Still he does not become lifeless. Pure existence (of the Substance) is like this. It does not bear the discussion of existence or non-existence.

35 When the sight is turned inward, the state of its peceiving the objects does not remain, but it does not cease to exist and knows what happens.

36 A person of a dark colour stands in pitchy darkness. Neither he himself nor others are able to perceive him. But he knows himself perfectly well without any doubt.

37 His existence or non-existence is not like that of a person. He exists in Himself in His own way.

38 The sky being clear (without any cloud) the appearance of its form disappears. No form is seen by an observer but the sky stands as it is.

39 The water in a tank, being crystal clear, looks as if it has disappeared. Though it appears in this way to others it exists perfectly as it is.

40 Thus the Absolute exists in itself and is beyond the ordinary conceptions of existence and non-existence.

41 It is like the wakefulness where there is no trace of the consciousness of the sleep that has vanished and the consciousness of its own existence.

42 When a jar is placed upon the ground it is called the ground with a jar, and when it is taken away it is called the ground without a jar.

43 But when both these conditions do not exist, the ground exists in its pure state. The existence of the Absolute is a pure existence like this.

CHAPTER V

Existence, Knowledge and Bliss

1 The three attributes, existence, knowledge and bliss are incapable of exhaustively determining the Ultimate Reality. A poison being itself a poison is not poison to itself.

2 Lustre, hardness and yellowness together constitute gold ; Viscosity, sweetness and mellifluity together constitute nectar.

3 Whiteness, fragrance and softness, these three without being three separate things are only camphor.

4 The colour of camphor is white ; that which is white is soft ; or it is not these two, but the fragrance only.

5 Just as the three qualities mean but one thing like camphor and do not point to the existence of the triad, similarly the three i.e., existence and others, are merged in one Reality.

6 As a matter of fact the three words existence, knowledge and bliss are different. But the triad is merged in one Bliss.

7 Existence is bliss and knowledge, or is knowledge existence and bliss ? This cannot be distinguished like the sweetness of a nectar.

8 The sixteen Kalas of the moon appear as increasing night after night in the first fortnight, but the moon is as it is in itself, perfect at all times.

9 When the water is falling in the form of drops, we can count them. But we cannot do so when there is all water, without separate drops, on the ground upon which it falls.

10 In the same way the Shruti calls It existence in order to ward off Its non-existence. It is called knowledge to keep it away from materiality.

11 The breath of the Lord i.e. the Vedas declare It to be bliss because there is a complete annihilation of pain.

12 Non-existence and others are counter-correlatives to existence and others. The latter are used to differentiate It from the former.

13 Thus the word Satchidananda applied to Atman, does not denote Its nature but differentiates It from its opposites.

14 Will the material objects that are enlightened by the Sun, be able to enlighten the Sun himself ?

15 So, how the organ of speech will enlighten that by the light of which the organ itself knows its objects ?

16 What means of valid knowledge will be useful to the self-illuminating Atman who is not an object to any one and has no knowability ?

17 The means of valid knowledge is limited by the object of knowledge. It is of no use in the case of the Substance which is self-evident.

18 Thus if we try to know the Substance the knowledge itself is, as a matter of fact, the Substance. Then how can the knowledge and the known remain different ?

19 So the words, existence, knowledge and bliss do not denote the Substance, but they are the residues of our thought.

20 Thus those well-known words, knowledge, existence and bliss become current, but when they are united harmoniously to the knower —

21 — they vanish at that time like the clouds that shower rain, or like the streams that flow into the sea or the paths that reach the goal.

22 A flower fades after giving rise to a fruit or a fruit is lost after giving its juice and the juice itself does not remain after giving satisfaction.

23 Or the hand of a sacrifice is drawn back after offering oblations ; or a melody ends after giving rise to a pleasurable sensation.

24 Or a mirror disappears after showing the face its own reflection or a person goes away after awakening one who was asleep.

25 Similarly the three terms knowledge, existence and bliss after causing the Seer to see Himself, become lost in silence.

26 He is not that whatever we may speak about Him. It is not possible to speak about His real nature as

it is impossible to measure the height of one who measures, by the length of his shadow.

27 But when the person who measures becomes conscious of himself he feels abashed and gives up the act of measuring his shadow.

28 Existence naturally cannot be non-existence. Then can that existence be even called existence ?

29 And can that which has become intelligence by destroying the non-intelligence be even called intelligence ?

30 When there is complete wakefulness, then it is no sleep or awakening. So there is no intelligence in the Pure Intelligence.

31 Being bliss itself there is no feeling of unhappiness. So can that be even called bliss ?

32 Therefore, existence has vanished along with the non-existence, the intelligence along with the non-intelligence and bliss along with the misery. Nothing remains at last.

33 Now, renouncing the curtain of duality and pairs of opposite conceptions, it remains alone in its own blessedness.

34 If it is counted as "One" it becomes the other than one who counts. So it is one absolutely though not numerically.

35 One who remains outside the bliss can enjoy the bliss. Being bliss itself how can it enjoy itself ?

36 At the beating of the drum of the Goddess, she enters the body of her worshipper. But when there is no worshipper she does not enter the sound of the beating itself.

37 In the same manner He, being bliss himself, cannot experience His bliss and for the same reason, He does not know that He cannot.

38 Without looking into a mirror the face is neither in front of it nor behind it. In the same way He is not happiness or misery but pure bliss itself.

39 Giving up all the so-called illuminating theories like irrelevant talk in a dream, He conceals Himself even from His own understanding.

40 Before a sugar-plant is planted the juice exists (in its own pure state) but its sweetness is known to that juice itself.

41 Or before the The Vina (musical instrument with strings) is struck, the sound is dumb (i.e. inaudible). It is only audible to itself in that state.

42 Or before entering the interior part of a flower, the fragrance has to act as a bee to appreciate its smell.

43 The flavour of a food which is not cooked as yet, cannot be known to others except to the flavour itself.

44 So can that, which is bashful to enjoy by manifesting its blissfulness, be tasted or experienced by others ?

45 When the moon is in the sky at noonday her presence is known only to herself.

46 It is like beauty that has not yet assumed any form, youth without the birth of the body, religious merit before the performance of any ritual.

47 It would happen if the mind, before the springing of its sprout, would be intoxicated by sexual desire in that condition.

48 Or the talk about the sound of the musical instruments that are not constructed as yet and so invisible, would be understood by that sound only.

49 Or the fire, utterly avoiding the contact with any fuel, has the contact of itself only.

50 Those only would understand the secret of the self-evident Reality, who are able to perceive their face without the help of a mirror.

51 Talking in this way is as plain as talking about the harvest in a storage without even sowing its seeds.

52 So the Pure Intelligence transcends generality and particularity, ever enjoying itself.

53 Now after this that talk is wise which has drunk deep the draught of silence.

54 In this way the various modes of proof have accepted their own inability to prove and analogies have solemnly declared their inability to illustrate the Reality.

55 The various arguments have dissolved themselves because of their own invalidity. The assemblage of definitions has also dispersed.

56 The various means have gone away becoming futile. The experience has given up its object.

57 Here the thought along with the decision is extinct like a couragious warrior in the cause of his master.

58 And the understanding, being ashamed of its quality of knowing, caused its own destruction and there the experience being left alone became as if crippled.

59 If the crust of a piece of a talc is peeled off the talc itself disappears.

60 Or if the inner core of a plantain tree gives up the coverings because it is troubled by heat, how can it be made to stand erect ?

61 The experience is there because of the existence of its object and the subject. When both of them vanish can the experience alone experience itself ?

62 Are words of any use where the experience dissolves itself in this way ?

63 How can words describe the Reality where the supreme speech itself disappears and no trace is found of any sound ?

64 Why should there be any talk about waking a person who is already awakened ? Does any one

try to cook his food when he is satisfied by taking his meals ?

65 When the sun rises the light of lamps fade. Do they use plough in the field when there is the harvest ?

66 There is no cause of bondage and freedom. Nothing is left to be accomplished. There is only the pleasure of expounding.

67 When a thing is lost to us or to others in forgetfulness, it is regained by the word that reminds it.

68 If the word thus glorifies itself as a reminder, it has no other merit beyond this.

CHAPTER VI

Inefficacy of the Word

1 Indeed, the word, wellknown as a reminder, is a useful thing. Is it not a mirror that reflects the formless ?

2 It is no wonder that the visible is seen in a mirror; but, that which is invisible is seen in this mirror of the word.

3 It (the word) is like a rising sun in the family of the descendants of the great Avyakta (the unmanifested Reality). The sky comes to be what it is through the quality of the word.

4 It (the word) itself is the flower of the sky, but it is the cause of the fruit in the form of the universe. There is nothing that cannot be measured by the word.

5 It is like a torch-bearer that lights the path of right and wrong actions. It is a judge that decides between bondage and freedom.

6 When it sides with Avidya the unreal appears as real, and the real becomes worthless.

7 Like an exerciser this word makes the finite selfhood enter into the body of Pure Shiva.

8 The word sets free the finite self entangled in the body. The Atman meets Himself by means of the word.

9 When the sun causes the break of day, he becomes the enemy of night. Therefore we cannot compare the word with the sun.

10 The path of action and actionlessness, though opposite are supported at the same time by the word.

11 It sacrifices itself to help the knowledge of the Atman. How should I describe the different merits of this word ?

12 In short, the word is wellknown as a reminder. But here it can have no relation.

13 The word is absolutely useless in the case of the Atman that is self-luminous and stands in no need of any obligation.

14 There is no other thing besides the One Substance. Therefore it cannot be the object of remembering or forgetting.

15 How can one remind or forget oneself ? Can the tongue taste itself ?

16 There is no sleep to one who is awake. But is there even awaking ? In the same way there is no remembrance or forgetfulness to the Absolute.

17 The Sun does not know the night. How can he be conscious of the day ? In the same way the Substance is without memory or forgetfulness.

18 What is the use of the reminder when there is no memory or forgetfulness ? So the word is of no use in the case of the Absolute Reality.

19 Another good result is obtained by means of the word. But I am afraid to think about it.

20 It is foolish to say that Avidya is destroyed by the word and then the Atman became conscious of itself.

21 The Sun will first destroy the night and then will rise. These false words would be unworthy to be uttered in the assembly of the wise.

22 Where is that sleep by which the awakened one is offered ? Is there awaking that tries to wake up one who is already awake ?

23 So there is no Avidya even for the sake of being destroyed. There is no Atman that wants to enter its own state.

24 Avidya is non-existent like the son of a barren woman. Then what should the axe of right thinking cut into pieces ?

25 If the rainbow were real as it seems what archer would not have applied a string to it ?

26 I would beat Avidya by logical thinking if the water in the mirage would quench the thirst of the sage Agasti.

27 If Avidya were such a thing as to be destroyed by the word then why should not fire easily burn the imaginary city in the sky ?

28 Darkness does not tolerate contact with a lamp. But is there really anything to be destroyed before the lamp ?

29 It is futile to light a lamp in order to see the day.

30 The shadow is not there where it does not fall. It is equally not really there where it falls.

31 It is known in the waking state that the dream which was seen was false. So Avidya does not exist even though it appears to exist.

32 What is gained by storing in a house the ornaments created by the spell of a magician or by plundering a person who is naked ?

33 If the person were to eat imaginary dishes for a hundred thousand times, it is nothing more than fasting.

34 The soil on which a mirage does not appear is dry. But is the soil moistened where it appears ?

35 If it (Avidya) were real as it seems, men would have been drenched by the rain painted in a picture ; fields would have been moistened and tanks filled by it.

35 What necessity would there be to prepare the ink if one were able to write by mixing up darkness ?

37 Does not the sky appear as blue to the eyes ? (but it is not really blue). In the same way, you should know that the appearance of Avidya is false.

38 The Avidya itself naturally declares by its very name that it does not exist.

39 And its indefinableness implies its imaginary nature. Avidya proves its own non-existence in this way.

40 If it really exists why does it not tolerate the determination of its nature by thought ? The earth appears to be marked if the jar really exists upon it.

41 It is not a right apprehension if it be said that the Atman is revealed after the destruction of Avidya. It is like the knowledge of darkness residing in the sun (that is revealed after its destruction).

42 This Avidya is illusive but it conceals its illusive nature. It proves its own absence.

43 Thus, as it has been shown in various ways, Avidya is by its very nature non-existence. Then whom should the word destroy.

44 The ground only is struck if the shadow is vehemently struck. Nothing but the arm is damaged by slapping the void.

45 - 46 If with a great thrill a person is ready to drink the water of a mirage, or to embrace the sky, or to kiss his reflection, all his efforts become vain. The logic that tries to destroy Avidya is in the same situation.

47 One who yet entertains a desire to destrpy this Avidya, may leisurely take off the skin of the sky.

48 Or milk the nipple of a he-goat or perceive by means of the knees, or form a tablet of an evening by drying it.

49 Or by crushing a yawn he may take out the juice from it, and mixing it with indolence, pour it into the throat of a headless body.

50 He may turn the direction of the flow of a stream, turn over the shadow on the ground or prepare a rope of the wind.

51 He may beat a bug bear, bind his own reflection in a garment, or happily comb the hairs on his palm.

52 He may destroy the non-existence of a jar, pluck the flowers of the sky or break with ease the horn of a hare.

53 He may prepare ink from camphor, gather soot from the lamp of a jewel, or happily marry the child of a barren woman.

54 He may nourish the Chakor Birds by the nectar-like rays of the dark moon, and may catch with ease the aquatic animals in a mirage.

55 What more need be said ? Avidya is made up of non-existence. Then what should this word destroy ?

56 The word cannot be a pramana by destroying that which does not exist, as the darkness cannot determine the nature of the darkness.

57 Avidya is never born. So arguing about its non-existence is like lighting a lamp at noon in a courtyard.

58 Those who go to gather the harvest without sowing the field gain nothing but shame.

59 He, who has resorted to a naked ascetic, is as if sitting in his house without doing anything (i.e. his resorting is futile).

60 What is the use of waters showering upon waters ? In the same way the illumination of the word is of no use in destroying Avidya.

61 A measure may glorify itself as a measure so long as it does not try to measure the sky. The birth of a light is futile if it can perceive darkness.

62 If the tongue can be able to taste the dish of sky, its name 'Rasana' (that which is the cause of tasting a flavour) becomes meaningless.

63 Will the ornaments of a woman whose husband is alive, be fit to be worn by her when he is no more ? To eat the interior core of a plantain tree is to eat nothing.

64 What object is there — small or great — that is not illuminated by the sun ? But even he is of no use in the case of night.

65 What is there that is not perceived by the eyesight ? But it cannot perceive the sleep that does not exist in a person who is wakeful.

66 If the Chakora bird will try to search for the moon at day time, its effort will be utterly vain.

67 The reader of a blank paper becomes dumb. The person walking in the void becomes lame.

68 In the same way if words are ready to destroy Avidya, they become a meaningless prattle.

69 Does not the moon that is present on the new moon day spread darkness ? The thought in trying to destroy Avidya is in the same situation.

70 It is nothing but a fast to partake of the food that is yet to be prepared. The person looking with eyes that have lost its sight is blind.

71 In fact, the word would destroy itself if it tries to explain the meaning of a thing that does not exist.

72 Now should I, indeed, say that Avidya does not exist ? Nothing remains of the word that tries to destroy it.

73 If the thought stands in front of Avidya, it destroys itself along with it (Avidya).

74 So this Avidya by its own non-existence prevents the word to be a pramana by destroying Avidya.

75 And that the word should rise to greatness by showing the Atman, is quite contradictory.

76 Is there any country where a person has married himself ? Is there any eclipse where the sun has eclipsed himself ?

77 Will the sky set to meet itself ? Will the ocean flow into itself ? Will the palm touch itself ?

78 Does the sun illumine himself ? Does the fruit bear a fruit ? Can a fragrance smell itself ?

79 We can enable all the animate and inanimate objects to drink water in a moment. But can we enable the water to drink itself ?

80 Is there a single day among three hundred and sixty days that would cause the sun to see with his own eyes ?

81 If the God of destruction is angry he will burn the three worlds. But will he burn the fire itself ?

82 Is it possible even for the Creator to stand in front of Himself without a mirror ?

83 It is certainly impossible for the eye-sight to see itself, for the taste to taste its own flavour, or for any one to awaken a person who is wakeful.

84 How is it possible for the sandal paste to smear itself, for a colour to colour itself, or for a pearl to adorn itself by another pearl ?

85 Can gold be its own touchstone, a lamp its own illumination ? Can a flavour enjoy its own sweetness ?

86 The Almighty God Shankar held the moon on his head. But can the moon herself perch on her own head ?

87 In the same way the glorious Atman is pure and perfect knowledge itself. So how can the knowledge embrace itself ?

88 Being knowledge itself He does not understand to know Himself. It is as difficult as the perception of the eye by itself.

89 The knowledge would be able to know itself if the mirror would be able to reflect its own image.

90 A knife would be able to pierce a thing that is beyond all quarters by running towards it. But can it pierce itself ?

91 The tip of a tongue is expert in tasting the different flowers. But can it taste itself ?

92 But does its existence as an organ of tasting cease on that account ? It is not so because the tasting is immanent in it ?

93 So the Atman, who is knowledge, existence and bliss is self-evident. Now how can the word offer him that which is already his own ?

94 The Ultimate Substance does not prove or disprove itself with the help of any means of knowledge. It is self-evident, self-existent and beyond proof or disproof.

95 It is therefore groundless to believe that the word can gain greatness by enabling the Atman to experience himself.

96 The lamp lit up at midday neither dispels darkness nor spreads light. The condition of the word is the same (as it neither destroys Avidya nor illumines the Atman.)

97 Now Avidya, being non-existent, there is no destruction of it, and when Atamn is self evident what is there to be proved by any means ?

98 Thus being futile both ways, the word disappears like a stream that is lost in the waters of the deluge.

99 Now right thinking reveals that the word has no entrance howsoever to the Atman.

100 As it is meaningless to say that a bug-bear has come or the sky is hanging on the palm.

101 So the word with all its associates becomes a meaningless prattle like a picture with unnatural colours.

102 Now the knowledge and ignorance whose very life pitiably depends upon the word, are as real as the forests in a picture.

103 As a cloudy day vanishes when the clouds pass away, so when the word vanishes in deluge it vanishes along with both the knowledge and ignorance.

CHAPTER VII

Refutation of Ajnanavada

1 But for the help of knowledge the very word ignorance would have concealed itself under the ear i.e would never have been heard.

2 A firefly shines by entering into darkness (i.e. it has no real illumination) so the so called beginningless ignorance is utterly false.

3 The ignorance is great only in itself as a dream or darkness is great in itself.

4 The horses of mud cannot be harnessed ; or the magician's ornaments cannot be worn.

5 Though taken forcibly in the abode of knowledge the ignorance does nothing. Will there be any ripple of mirage in the moonlight ?

6 And what is called knowledge is nothing but ignorance either of the two can be shown by concealing the other (because they resemble each other).

7 Let us discontinue this preamble. Let us first make a search for ignorance. Then the falsity of knowledge will be understood by understanding the real nature of ignorance.

8 If the ignorance really lives in knowledge, why does it not turn its dwelling (i.e. knowledge) into ignorance ?

9 It is the inborn nature of ignorance to befool a thing in which it dwells.

10 Now if it be said that the sacred texts declare that the ignorance dwells in the Atman and envelops its resort.

11 (The objection can be answered thus). If the seed of ignorance dwells in the condition where there is no rise of duality then who knows that it exists ?

12 The ignorance, being non-intelligent, cannot know itself. Can it be a proof to its existence —

13 So, no sooner is it said that the ignorance would cause its understanding than the very contradiction would compel the speaker to keep silence.

14 If ignorance befools the knower (the Atman) who would say that this is ignorance ?

15 Would it not be shameful to call it ignorance if it cannot conceal the conciousness of its own existence ?

16 If the clouds really eclipsed the sun, who would enlighten them ? If a person is annihilated by sleep, who would experience it ?

17 Therefore, if the thing in which ignorance resides becomes ignorant, the ignorance being unable to know itself would vanish.

18 That by which the existence of ignorance is distinguished, can never be itself ignorance.

19 It is meaningless to say that there is cataract in the eye, yet the sight is not impaired.

20 If the fuel does not burn by its contact with the wild fire its power of burning will be futile.

21 If there is darkness in the house, yet it does not darken it, then it cannot be called darkness.

22 Who would call it a sleep that does not affect the wakefulness ? Can it be called night if it does not cause the daylight to disappear ?

23 The word ignorance becomes futile if the Atman is entirely pervaded by ignorance and yet it remains as it is.

24 Moreover it will be logically inconsistent to say that the ignorance resides in the Atman.

25 Ignorance is the gathering of darkness while Atman is the mine of effulgence. Now how can both of them be united ?

26 (They can be united) If wakefulness and dream, memory and forgetfulness, would go hand in hand.

27 If cold and heat can travel together to their resting place or a bundle of the sun's rays can be tied by the rope of darkness.

28 Or if night and day came to stay together at the same place, the Atman would continue to live with the help of ignorance.

29 If death and life can be intimate relatives, the Atman's existence will be dependent on ignorance.

30 Why should there be this contradictory talk that the ignorance that is dispelled by the Atman dwells happily with it ?

31 Oh, if the darkness gives up its nature and is turned into light, naturally it becomes the sun without any doubt.

32 If the fuel gives up its nature and is turned into a fire, the same fuel becomes the fire certainly.

33 Or no sooner a stream, giving up its separate existence, flows into the Ganges, than it turns into the Ganges itself.

34 In the same way there is no ignorance. It is entirely Atman. In fact the ignorance is turned into knowledge as soon as it comes into contact with it.

35 Ignorance, being contradictory to knowledge, cannot reside in it. Also it cannot exist independently.

36 If the fish of salt becomes alive, it can neither live in water nor outside the water.

37 "Atman shines where there is no ignorance" words like these should not be, therefore, listened to by the wise ones.

38 The illusory serpent, appearing on a rope, cannot be bound by it, much less can it be driven away.

14

39 Or the darkness, being afraid of daylight, turned to the full moon light but it was swallowed by the moon instantaneously.

40 Similarly the word ignorance becomes meaningless both the ways. The nature of the ignorance cannot be understood without logical inference.

41 Then what is the nature of ignorance ? Is it to be logically inferred from effect or is it directly apprehended ? Now let us search.

42 Oh, that which can be apprehended by the Pramanas like perception and others, is the creation of ignorance and not the ignorance itself.

43 The creeper with its strait sprout, looks charming. It is not a seed but the result of the seed.

44 Or the auspicious or inauspicious forms are seen in a dream. They are not sleep itself but the offspring of sleep.

45 Or, the moon is one but appears as two in the sky. It is not the defect of eyesight but the effect of that defect.

46 In the same way the triad of the subject, the object and the means of valid knowledge, are the results of ignorance and not ignorance itself.

47 Therefore, these Pramanas like perception, as the effect of ignorance, cannot certainly apprehend the ignorance.

48 If the effect of the ignorance is regarded as ignorance the senses by which it is apprehended, are themselves created by ignorance. (hence they are not reliable)

49 If that which appears in a dream is illusory then is the perceiver of the dream different ? (i.e. he is also not a real perceiver) So if the effect is nothing but ignorance, (the ignorance will be the cause of knowing ignorance).

50 It will be like the tasting of the raw sugar by itself, of the besmearing of collyirum by itself, or like the impaling of the stake by the stake itself.

51 In the same manner, if the effect being identical with the cause, is ignorance, then there will be all ignorance and who will know the existence of anything ?

52 In such a state one cannot think of the knower and the known. It would be like taking the evidence of a fish in a mirage.

53 So, oh dear friend, that which escapes the measuring of any proof, is not different from a sky-flower.

54 The ignorance does not allow any proof to exist. So who will begin to discuss about it ? The futility of ignorance should be known from this.

55 In this way ignorance is disproved by not being the object of perception or inference.

56 I am afraid to believe that the ignorance is real since it is neither the cause of anything nor the producer of its effect.

57 It can neither cause the Atman to dream nor put him to sleep in his own resting place.

58 Let it be so, (If the Ajnanvadin again says) the ignorance was in union with the Atman when he was in his pure state.

59 Fire exists in wood before two pieces of it are rubbed together.

60 (It can be replied that) The pure state of the Atman does not even tolerate the name Atman. So how can ignorance desire to find any room there ?

61 Should we remove the snuff before lighting a lamp or abandon the shade of the tree that has not yet grown ?

62 Or, besmear with an ointment the body that is not yet formed or cleanse the mirror that is not yet made ?

63 Or try to remove the cream of the milk that is yet in the udder ?

64 So, how can there be anything like ignorance in the Atman where there is even no room for the state of being called Atman ?

65 So naturally it becomes clear that even at that time ignorance does not exist. Now what is the propriety of even saying that it does not ?

66 Inspite of this, if one persists in saying that ignorance exists in the Atman that is beyond all being and non-being.

67 (It will be like saying that) The non-existence of a jar is broken into a hundred pieces, or death itself has been killed entirely.

68 Or like saying that sleep or fainting itself has fainted away, or darkness has fallen into a dark well.

69 Or non-existence got into troubles, or the interior part (i.e. void) of a plantain tree is broken, or the sky is turned into a whip and made the cracking Sound.

70 Or a poison was administered to a dead man, or the lips of a dumb man were silenced or the unwritten letters were erased.

71 So it is futile to say that ignorance remains (in the state of the Atman). Now it is said that it is identical with the Ultimate Substance.

72 See how can a barren woman give birth to a child ? Or can the seeds that are burnt, sprout ? Can darkness meet the sun ?

73 In this way, howsoever we search for ignorance in the Pure Intelligence, it will not be found out.

74 Desiring the cream if one were to shake the pot of milk, would it appear on the surface or be disintegrated ? It (the search for ignorance) would be like this.

75 Or if one wakes up hurriedly to catch the sleep, will it be caught hold of or be destroyed in vain ?

76 So why should one go mad in search of ignorance ? To search for it is naturally equal to not searching (because it does not exist).

77 The town of thought is not illuminated in any way by the existence of ignorance.

78 Can the eyes of thought be able to see the ignorance within or outside of Atman at any time ?

79 The face of decision is not anointed by ignorance (i.e. the ignorance does not even exist for the sake of thinking and taking a decision). It does not bear any proof even in a dream. Indeed the thought that tries to grasp it, loses itself.

80 With all this, do you think that you will find some way towards the ignorance ?

81 (To think like this would be) to erect a meeting hall using the horns of a hare as pillars, to illuminate it with the rays of the new moon.

82 And to enoy the festival by adorning the children of barren women with the sky flowers !

83 The desire (to search for ignorance) will be fulfilled if we can fill the measure glass of the sky with the ghee of a tortoise.

84 We have tried, in various ways, to search for ignorance. How many times should we repeat that it does not exist ?

85 So I would not utter the word ignorance even in a dream. But an idea occurs to me about it.

86 The Ultimate Reality is not such as would become the seer by seeing itself or any other object.

87 Then how is it that it presents before it the great visible world and assumes itself the function of a seer ?

88 The wide world rises and is also visible to us, in the state where even the name Atman cannot get access.

89 Though ignorance is not visible yet it exists without any doubt. It is proved by inference from the visible world.

90 The moon is one. But if it appears as two in the sky, should we not think that the eye-sight is impaired ?

91 The trees look fresh and green and it is not seen that they are sucking water from the source different from the ground on which they stand.

92 Still we cannot avoid inferring that their roots are certainly sucking water. So the ignorance also is known by inference from the visible world.

93 Sleep vanishes as soon as one awakes, it is not known to one who sleeps, but its existence can be inferred from the dreams.

94 So if there is the appearance of this vast world upon the Pure Substance, we can easily infer the existence of ignorance.

95 (To this we reply) How can we call this kind of knowledge ignorance ? Should we call the thing that causes daylight as darkness ?

96 Can it be called a collyrium (a dark thing) that makes an object look brighter and whiter than the moon ?

97 We can call this world the process of ignorance if water can perform the function of fire.

98 The knowledge will be worthy to be called ignorance if the full moon will be the cause of the dark night.

99 Will poison give out ambrosia with great love ? And if it does, can it be called a poison ?

100 Should we bring the flood of ignorance when all the becoming in front of us is enlightened with knowledge ?

101 If it is called ignorance, then what would be the nature of knowledge ? Is the Atman anything (knowledge or ignorance) ?

102 He does not become anything. He does not know what he is. All the means of knowledge become void.

103 He does not behave in such a way as to make us say that he exists. But there is no reason also to call him non-existent.

104 He exists without the existence of the other. He sees without being seen by anyone. If this is so why should he be regarded as lost ?

105 He silently endures the charge of the nihilists who regard him as nothing. He is not also disturbed by calling him of a particular nature. (i.e. as Sat, Chit and Ananda)

106 Does the Omniscient, who is the witness even of the deepest sleep, fail to understand this ? But he himself does not become visible.

107 The Veda says so much but it does not mention the name of the Atman. It only says 'Not this."

108 Whom does the sun not enlighten ? But has he enlightened the Atman ? Can the Substance (the Atman) be enveloped by the sky ?

109 The egoism thinking "It is I" embraces the physical body that is nothing but a bundle of bones, It leaves aside this Substance (i.e. Atman).

110 The understanding that grasps everything knowable, falters before this Substance. The mind imagines everything except the Atman.

1 The senses that rub their mouths on the barren land of sensual objects, cannot taste the sweetness in the Atman.

112 Is it possible to apprehend in all its totality the Atman who has filled his belly by eating all the existence along with non-existence ?

113 As the tongue cannot taste itself, the Atman cannot be its own object. How can he be the object to others ?

114 Let it be. As soon as Avidya, along with her innumerable names and forms, comes before the Atman, it vanishes with fear.

115 So how can any other thing find room where there is no desire to see one's own complexion ?

116 A person trying to put a stick into the puzzle of a string is troubled to find it outside the string when it is pulled. So any effort to decide the nature of the Atman becomes futile in the same way.

117 Or he who looks minutely his own shadow from head to foot and tries to jump over it fails to understand it.

118 So the person, who tries hard and decides that the Atman is like this, fails to grasp him.

119 Now, where the words cannot reach, tell me how can the intellect apprehend him as something other ?

120 How on the strength of that apprehension, can the eyelessness and the blindness of the Atman be dispelled and his vision be regained?

121 He cannot experience his state of being as an object of perception. So also his state of being a perceiver goes away. In such condition —

122 Who meets whom ? How can the eye-sight be opened where even the unity is dissolved.

123 He has opened the doors of light turning aside this great obstacle.

124 Innumerable forms and sights arise but one Pure Intelligence underlies all.

125 The underlying Supreme Intelligence is so intoxicated by the great glory of the vision that he does not see again the same mirror of the jewels in the form of objects.

126 He is so munificent that he causes his sight to wear every moment new apparels in the form of the objects of the world.

127 As the Atman regards the objects once created as stale and worn out, he presents to his vision ever fresh and new objects.

128 Also he becomes subject by wearing every moment new ornaments of apprehensions. (i.e. It is the Atman that himself appears as the knowing subjects, that vary with the variations of the objects that are known).

129 He felt uncomfortable in his original Atmanic dignity. So he girded up his loins to become many i.e. this manifold world.

130 This is the way of the Omniscient. The Pure intelligence is full up to the brim. But it is not known in any other house but in his own. (He knows Himself in the form of the visible world).

131 Thus the Pure Intelligence, where knowledge and ignorance embrace each other (i.e. vanish) opens His eyesight and meets himself in the form of visible objects.

132 As soon as He sees the visible world He enjoys it as its seer. The same enjoyment pervades the whole vision.

133 There goes on the process of giving and taking But the thread of unity does not break as the unity of the original face is not disturbed though it is reflected in a mirror.

134 Or as the standing posture of a noble horse which sleeps while standing, is not disturbed when it wakes up.

135 Just as water plays itself by assuming the form of waves, so the Ultimate Substance or Atman plays happily with Himself.

136 Is fire caught in the bondage of difference if it interweaves and wears garlands of flames ?

137 Can it be said that the sun is separate from his own rays that thickly surround him ?

138 Will the unity of the moon be disturbed if she is enveloped in her light ?

139 Though a lotus blossoms into a thousand petals it is one.

140 The king Sahasrarjuna has a thousand hands, but does he become one thousand and one ?

141 Even when there are spread on a loom a number of strips, there is to be found in them nothing but thread.

142 Though a crore of words meet in the residence of speech, all of them are nothing but speech.

143 Though there are foliages of visible objects and waves of different visions, they are not different from the seer.

144 If a lump of raw sugar is broken into pieces there is nothing but raw sugar.

145 So the Atman does not become the object of difference though he perceives the appearance or manifests himself in the form of the manifold objects.

146 The unity of the Atman is not lost even when he comes to fill the whole universe.

147 Though in a silken garment, having borders of two colours, there appear different shades of colour, all of them are threads only.

148 If the eye had been able to see the whole without opening its lids that are closed,

149 Or, if a Banyan tree has its full growth without the breaking of its seed, the expansion of the one Reality can be compared with it.

150 Then if he vehemently desires not to see himself, he rests in himself.

151 It is like the absorbing of the sight in itself when the eyelids are closed.

152 Or as the ocean is full in itself without the rising of the moon, or as a tortoise naturally draws its feet within itself.

153 Or as on the new moon day the moon (with all her sixteen kalas) enters the seventeenth digit.

154 So when the Atman withdraws the seer and the objects that are seen, he is falsely called a conqueror. It really is his resting in himself.

155 The Atman naturally is all that exists. Then who perceives what ? This state of not perceiving is his sleep.

156 He is naturally an object to himself if he says, "I don't desire this state of non-perception. I want to see myself."

157 The Atman is the eternal perceiver and the eternally perceived. Now what is there to be newly created?

158 Should the sky and the void, the air and touch, the light and brightness be newly related ?

159 The Atman shining as the universe, sees the universe. When there is no universe he sees its non-existence.

160 If by chance both the existence or non-existence of the world merged, he is the seer even of this state.

161 Is the coolness of the camphor due to the moon-light ? Is not the camphor anointed by itself (i.e. the coolness is due to its own nature) ? So the Atman is the Absolute seer in himself.

162 What more should be said ? The Atman is ever seeing himself in whatever condition he may be.

163 As a person imagines different countries of his liking and wanders through them with respect.

164 It is no wonder that when the eye is pressed it vibrates in the form of a pure shining star (that appears before the closed eyelids).

165 Therefore when the one Pure Intelligence is ever seeing itself what is the use of supposing any super-imposition.

166 Who else covers a jewel with the garment of lustre ? Does gold decorate itself by securing its golden quality ?

167 Does sandal wears the garment of some other scent ? Does the ambrosia serve itself ? Will the sugar taste itself ?

168 Or is the camphor smeared with white lustre or is the fire made hot by heating ?

169 Or that the creeper entwining itself with its own foliage should naturally create a bower for itself.

170 Or as a lamp is wholly filled up with light, the Pure Intelligence is filled with the spirit and vibrates (in the form of the seer and the seen).

171 Thus without any obligation He is observing himself naturally.

172 The seeing or the non-seeing is like this. Does the moon think about any difference due to darkness or light ?

173 Therefore if He desires that this (i.e. observing) should not be, he is already of that nature.

174 The Atman appears as the object of seeing for a short time. But when they meet each other both of them vanish.

175 There the object is filled with the seer, and the seeing is merged in the object. Both vanish, and their real essence remains.

176 Both of them come to embrace each other in any place and at any time melting their state of being seer and the seen.

177 Neither does the camphor enter fire nor does the fire enter the camphor. Both of them are destroyed at the same time.

178 When one is subtracted from one there remains only a zero, and its figure is rubbed out. A similar

thing happens when the seer and the seen merge into each other.

179 Or if any one tries to wrestle with his reflection, both the wrestling and the reflection vanish.

180 So when perception is gone, the perceiver and the perceived meet and are united.

181 The eastern and western seas are different so long as they do not mingle. But there is all water after their intermingling.

182 So many triads (of the perceiver, perception and the perceived) are naturally emerging. Do they require determining at every moment ?

183 The swallowing up of the two particulars, (the seer and seen) and emitting their opposites is like the opening and the closing of the eye of the Reality.

184 It is wonderful that as soon as the eyelids close the Atman assumes the form of a seer which vanishes as soon as the eye-lids open.

185 The natural condition of the Atman lies between the destruction of the seer and the seen and a new revival of them.

186 It is like the water remaining in its natural state when the wave that is arisen vanishes and a new one has not yet arisen.

187 Or like our condition when our sleep ends and yet we are not fully awake.

188 Or it can be imagined if we think about the eye-sight that has ceased to see one object and has not begun to see another, yet.

189 It is like the state of the sky when the day ends and the night is yet to come.

190 Or like the state of the Vital breath when one respiration is finished and the other is yet to be taken in.

191 Or like the state of an individual at the moment when all his senses are enjoying their objects simultaneously.

192 The ultimate nature of the Atman is like that. So can there be seeing or not seeing ?

193 Can it be said that a mirror can see its own cleanliness or not ?

194 Or by means of a mirror can a face be infront of or behind (the mirror) ? But can it be so to itself in the absence of the mirror ?

195 The Sun sees everything. But is it possible for him to witness the beauty of his own rising and setting?

196 Or can a juice drink itself ? Or does it hide its place on that account ? Both the things are impossible because it is a juice in itself.

197 Being the vision itself he does not know seeing and not-seeing. He himself is the cause of both.

198 Being the perception Himself he could not see himself. And so naturally he is the non-perception.

199 And how can the non-perception perceive itself ? Then again he is the perception himself.

200 These two dwell happily with each other and are destroyed by each other.

201 If the seeing is ever seeing itself, would this not be like not seeing ? So both seeing and not seeing do not touch Him. (who is pure Intelligence).

202 So if the Atman who conceals himself from seeing and not seeing, sees, then who has seen what ? (The Atman sees himself. So the seeing is like not seeing).

203 If the visible world appears, how can it be said that the seer has not perceived it ? (the answer to this objection is) His seeing is not due to the appearance.

204 Indeed, the appearance is seen. But in reality the appearance is nothing but the seer. So how can the non-existent be seen ?

205 Let the complexion be seen in a mirror. But it exists as a complexion in its own place. So the experience (of seeing it in a mirror) is futile.

206 This perception is like one's own perception in a dream when one is asleep.

207 If the person who is asleep is carried away in his dream in a comfortable carriage to the other place, is he really in that condition ?

208 Or is it really so if a headless couple of beggars appear (in a dream) to be ruling a kingdom?

209 A person in a dream, without being changed, is in the same condition in which he was in the absence of the sleep.

210 The distress of a thirsty person who has not seen the mirage is the same when he sees it. Because what has he gained (by seeing the mirage)?

211 Or if a person made friendship with his shadow, his behaviour is of no use.

212 So the seer, by becoming the seen and showing it to himself, has made futile the act of showing.

213 Because if the seen is nothing but the seer how can it tolerate the act of showing? Is he absent to himself if it is not shown?

214 Does the face become futile if it does not see itself in a mirror? It exists in itself as it is, even without the mirror.

215 So the Atman does not become futile if he is not shown to himself by the appearance. The act of not showing is of no use.

216 So the Atman is in his own state without making himself a seer. Now why should he, who is in such a state, be made an object of seeing?

217 It becomes redundant if it is said that what already existed was shown again. The showing becomes futile by also saying this.

218 It is the rope that really exists when there is the appearance of a snake on it. So it is the seer that really exists when there is the appearance of the seen upon the seer.

219 When there is a mirror before the face it appears unmistakably in the mirror. But as a matter of fact the face is in its own place and not in the mirror.

220 So among the seer and the seen, the seer really exists. So the seen is futile though it is seen.

221 Indeed, it is futile. But it does appear. So if by saying this its existence seems to be proved.

222 (It is not so) If some one sees the other and becomes the seer we can regard that he has seen it.

223 But here (in the case of the Atman) does the Atman see anything other than himself, though he may see or not see, though he may remain one or become many ?

224 The face has seen itself, though a mirror has shown it. The face is as it is in itself, though it is not shown by the mirror.

225 So if he is not shown, he is as he is in himself, or if he is shown, he is also the same.

226 Though revealed by wakefulness or concealed by sleep the person is the same in himself.

227 Or a king is as he is, though he is made conscious of his position by saying "You are a king"

228 Or is there any loss to his dignity if he is not reminded of his kingship?

229 So he (the Atman) may be shown or not shown, he does not reach a higher or a lower position. He is naturally in his own state of existence.

230 So what other thing is there that is mad after showing the Atman to himself? If there is no seer who should see the mirrors?

231 Does a lamp create the person who lights it or does it exist on account of that person? So the existence of any cause is due to the Atman.

232 The flame enlightens the fire. But can it be considered different from the fire?

233 And the thing that we call a cause is manifested and shown by him. If he sees it, he is by his own nature the object that is seen.

234 So there is no other cause besides him for the self-illuminating Atman to see himself.

235 In whatever form the appearance may be, it appears through him. Here there is no other besides him.

236 It is the gold that shines in the form of an ornament or a solid piece, because there is nothing but gold.

237 There is nothing else but water in the current or its waves. So no other thing exists or is brought into existence.

238-239 There is nothing else in the camphor but itself, though it may be inferred by the sense of smell, or taken into one's palm or seen with one's eyes. So, in whatever way, it is He-the Atman that experiences himself.

240 Now let Him appear as the seen or let Him be the seer, nothing else is manifested without Him.

241 The Ganges may flow as the Ganges or may remain as the ocean by mingling with it. but we cannot see anything new and wonderful in its existence as water.

242 Whether liquid or frozen, the ghee does not become anything else. Such an inquiry is meaningless.

243 The fire and the flames are not regarded as two separate things because both of them constitute the fire and are not different from it.

244 So it may be the seer or the seen, both the states are futile, because really it is the one state of the Atman that pulsates everywhere.

245 There is nothing else besides pulsation if we look from the point of view of the pulsation. So does the Atman see though he sees ?

246 It is not that the appearance is spread before and the seer watches it remaining behind. It is his pulsation when he sees himself.

247 It is like ripples sprinkling themselves upon water, gold covering a piece of gold, eyesight remaining spell-bound with its own vision.

248 It is like uniting a tune with a tune, a fragrance with a fragrance or serving the dish of contentment to contentment.

249 Or as if the raw sugar is anointed with the raw sugar, Meru, the mountain of gold, is covered with gold or the fire is surrounded with flames.

250 What more should I say? It is like the sky resting on the couch of the sky. Then who should sleep? and who should wake?

251 He saw himself as if he did not see. And without seeing himself his seeing is natural.

252 Here no talk is tolerated, no knowledge can get entrance, no experience can be proud of its greatness.

253 So his seeing himself is like this. It is like no one seeing nothing.

254 In short, the Atman is illuminated by the Atman. He awakens himself without awaking.

255 On account of the desire to see himself, all the states (i.e. that of the seer and the seen) are manifested without disturbing his own condition.

256 If he wishes to remain without seeing, the not-seeing itself becomes seeing. And on account of this seeing both seeing and not-seeing go away.

257 Though he may evolve in any form, his unity is not lost. Or if he contracts he is as perfect as before.

258 The sun can never catch hold of darkness. Then why should he listen to the talk about light?

259 Let there be darkness or light. He is like the Sun that remains alone in his glory in any condition.

260 So he (the Atman) may assume any position, he does not miss his own self.

261 Though innumerable waves rise and fall the ocean does not give up its nature.

262 The richness of the Atman who is Pure Illumination cannot be compared to the Sun because his rays go out of himself.

263 There will be no cloth in the world if the cotton-fruit does not break. (So the Atman cannot be compared to it.)

264 If a piece of gold remains as it is, it cannot adorn the various organs of the body.

265 No individual can go from one quarter to another without crossing the intervening distance. So he cannot be compared to the Atman.

266 So the play of the Atman has no parallel. He can be compared only with himself.

267 He is devouring the mouthfuls of his own light. But neither is his food of light reduced in quantity nor is the size of his belly changed.

268 Thus the Atman is ruling his kingdom in his own place with his unparalleled sport.

269 If this is called ignorance, it means the end of all logical thinking. Can we tolerate the talk of one who speaks like this ?

270 If that which illumines is called ignorance, it is like calling the thing that enables a man to see an underground store of wealth, a collyrium (a dark substance).

271 Is not the idol of Ambika (the consort of Shiva), though made of gold and hence shining, is called Kalika (dark goddess) ? So to call the self-illumination of the Atman ignorance is like this.

272 In reality all the sorts of elements from the God Shiva to the earth are illumined by his rays.

273 It is on account of him that knowledge knows, sight sees, and the light enlightens.

274 Ah! who is the mean person that has pointed him out as ignorance ? Is it really not like binding the sun in a sack of darkness ?

275 To write the letter "A" before the word "Jnana" (knowledge) and to regard it as enhancing the greatness of that "Jnana" ! Is it not an extraordinary method of elucidating the meaning of a word ?

276 Why should one place fire inside a box made of lac ? It will reduce everything to fire.

277 Therefore it would be irrelevant to speak about the doctrine of ignorance when all the universe is the vibration of knowledge.

278 First it is like committing a sin by uttering the word 'killing of a cow" (because the animal cow is regarded as sacred) and secondly it is utter falsehood (hence another sin). So how can the knowledge be called ignorance ?

279 And the talk about ignorance is itself a vibration of knowledge (i.e. becomes intelligible through knowledge). So why should not knowledge be regarded as knowledge ?

280 Let it be, by the same illumination of his own the Atman is seeing himself in various forms.

281 How can ignorance that pales before searching thought get eye-sight and see itself in the form of the visible world in front of it ?

282 If the ignorance says that it gives birth to the world which is knowledge, and tries to establish its existence by means of ignorance,

283 Then the world itself has proved emphatically the non-existence of ignorance, because ignorance and knowledge cannot be related like a substance and its quality.

284 Knowledge would be the quality of ignorance if pearls are produced from water or a lamp is sustained by ashes.

285 Ignorance would emit the lustrous knowledge. if the moon emits burning flames or the sky is turned into a slab of stone.

286 It is astonishing that a deadly poison should come out of the ocean of milk. But how can there be pure nectar in the deadly poison ?

287 Or suppose that ignorance is produced from knowledge; the ignorance would vanish at its very birth (because it cannot remain with knowledge) Then knowledge only will remain and there will be no ignorance.

288 So the sun is as great as the sun, the moon is like the moon and the lamp is like the lamp.

289 Do not fail to know that the light (of knowledge) is nothing but the light. The whole world is nothing but the illumination of the Substance or Atman.

290 The Shruti (the Upanishadas) declares with contentment that all that exists is illuminated by His light. Is it purposeless ?

291 Therefore the light of the Substance or Atman is the cause of the manifestation of the Atman's beauty that is enjoyed by the Atman himself.

292 But discarding this, to regard ignorance as the cause of the Atman's self-illumination, is utterly unreasonable.

293 Therefore the existence of ignorance is not found out in any way. It becomes futile though we try to search for ignorance.

294 The sun would find no existence of darkness though he visited the residence of night.

295 If a person tries to put sleep into a bag, he cannot even catch hold of wakefulness and remains alone as he is in himself.

CHAPTER VIII

Refutation of Knowledge

1 As for ourselves, we have neither ignorance nor knowledge. Our spiritual teacher has made us realize what we really are.

2 If we try to see how we are to ourselves the seeing itself is ashamed. So what should we do?

3 Happily our spiritual teacher has made us so great that we cannot contain ourselves within ourselves.

4 We are not limited by the state of being Atman. We are not disturbed by self-cognition. There is no change in us even by the contact of final emancipation.

5 No word that can describe us, has yet come into existence. No sight that is able to see us is possible.

6 Who can enjoy or perceive us making us an object of enjoyment? We are not even able to perceive ourselves.

7 It is no wonder that we can remain neither concealed nor manifest. But oh! how difficult it is for us even to exist!

8 In short, how can we describe by words the condition in which we are placed by Shri Nivritti?

9 Then, how can ignorance dare to come before us? How can Maya come into existence after her death?

10 Who can know any talk about knowledge when ignorance cannot get entrance ?

11 We have to light the lamps because there is night. The efforts of doing so are of no use when there is the sun.

12 So knowledge also disappears when there is no ignorance. Now both of them vanish.

13 Really speaking the words knowledge and ignorance are destroyed in the process of giving them separate meaning (The supposition of ignorance leads to the supposition of knowledge. But the word ignorance itself is illuminated by knowledge. So there is no ignorance that is taken for granted, hence no knowledge based upon this conception of ignorance.)

14 If a husband and a wife exchange their heads cutting each other's throat, both of them would lose their lives without exchanging their positions.

14 The lamp that is lighted behind a person is of no use to him. If the eye-sight can perceive in darkness, that darkness becomes futile (i.e. there is no difference between light and darkness)

15 So the utter non-cognition is called ignorance. How can that be the ignorance by means of which everything is comprehended ?

16 In this way knowledge became ignorance and ignorance disappeared on account of ignorance. Both of them become futile through each other.

17 Now he who knows does not know, and he, who does not know, knows. So where should knowledge and ignorance live ?

18 In this way, swallowing both the night of ignorance and the day of knowledge, the Sun of Pure Intelligence has arisen in the sky of Pure Consciousness.

CHAPTER IX

The Secret of Natural Devotion

1 Now fragrance became the nose, ears emerged out of the tune and mirrors evolved out of the eyes.

2 The fans become the blowing breezes. The heads assuming the form of Champaka flowers, give out sweet fragrance.

8 The tongue is turned into the flavour, the lotus opens in the form of the sun, the Chakor birds became the moon.

4 The flowers assumed the form of the bee, the damsel became a youth, or the sleeping person became his own couch.

5 The blossoms of the mango-tree became the cuckoo, the body itself became the breezes of winds coming from the Malaya mountain (where sandal trees grow), the flavours themselves became the tongues.

6 Or as a piece of pure gold made out of itself engraved ornaments for the sake of charming appearance.

7 So the enjoyer and the object of enjoyment, the seer and the object of sight, become one in the unity which is an unbroken whole.

8 A Shevanti flower blossoms into a thousand petals without coming out of its own state of being a Shevanti flower.

9 So, though the auspicious drums of new experiences are beating they are not heard in the town of inactivity.

10 Therefore the multitudes of senses simultaneously run to their objects in front of them.

11 But as soon as the eye-sight touches a mirror, the sight meets the sight (giving up the mirror). The same thing happens in the case of the running of the desires. (senses) (The object of the senses is no other than the seer and no sooner do they meet their object, than the seer is united with his own self).

12 Though there are three different things like a serpentlike ornament, an ear-ring, and a bangle, their purchaser purchases nothing but gold.

13 If the hand is stretched out to gather the ripples it gets nothing but water.

14-15 Though camphor presents itself as touch to the hand, as a nice object to the eye, or as a fragrant thing to the tongue, it presents itself as nothing but fragrance. So Atman alone vibrates in the form of the sensible manifold.

16 So when the hands, in the form of various senses like the ear and others, are ready to catch the object like words,

17 Then as soon as there is a contact between the object and the senses, the object does not remain as an object of sense. There is no other contact because everything is the Atman.

18 The parts that appear in a sugarcane are all contained in the juice or the full moon has all her lustre.

19 The meeting of the senses and their objects is like the moon light falling on the moon. or waters showering on the sea.

20 Though he may speak anything he likes, his silent meditation is not disturbed.

21 His actionless condition is not affected even though he performs countless actions.

22 Stretching the arms of desires the eye-sight embraces her objects but really she gains nothing (because both the sight and its object are nothing but the Atman).

23 As the sun, stretching the thousand arms of his rays to take hold of darkness, remains alone as he is,

24 As a person, getting up to meet the sport of a dream, finds himself alone,

25 So when there are objects of the senses before him the person who has attained the spiritual wisdom appears to become an enjoyer of that object, but we do not know whether he enjoys it or not.

26 If the moon tried to gather the moon-light then who has gathered what?. It is like a futile imagination without any result.

27 The yoga that is attained by the yogis through the means like restraining the senses is as lustreless before this path (of the wise one) as the moon is by day.

28 There is no action or inaction, and everything goes on as the experience of the Atman.

29 The non-dual one enters of his own accord the courtyard of duality. And the unity deepens along with the growth of difference.

30 The enjoyment of the objects of senses becomes sweeter than the bliss of final emancipation, and in the home of loving devotion the devotee and his God experience their sweet union.

31 Though he may walk in a street or sit still, he is always in his own house.

32 He has no goal to attain though he may perform any action. And it is not that without doing anything he does not achieve his object.

33 He does not allow any room to the memory or forgetfulness. In this condition his behaviour is uncommon.

34 His own sweet will becomes the moral discipline, any kind of behaviour is his meditation. The glory of the final emancipation serves as a sitting carpet to this condition.

35 The God himself becomes the devotee. The destination itself becomes the path, and the whole universe becomes one solitude.

36 He may be a god or a devotee at any time. He is enjoying the kingdom of inaction in his own condition.

37 The temple is merged in God pervading everything. The process of time and the expanse of space vanish.

38 The God contains his own being within himself. Then how can the Goddess find room there? So also there would be no attendants.

39 In such a condition if a faithful desire for the relation of the master and the servant arises, he has to employ God alone for this purpose.

40 All the means of devotion like the silent repetition of the name of God, meditation, a staunch belief, are not different from God.

41 Now God should worship God with God in the form of any kind of offering.

42 The idol of God, the temple and God's attendants, all of them are carved out of the same mountain-rock. So in the same manner why should there not be the performance of the acts of devotion (though there is nothing but God everywhere)?

43 A tree has no other object besides it though it spreads in the form of its foliage, flowers and fruits.

44 There is nothing wonderful if a dumb person observes the vow of silence or does not observe. So the wise one remains in his divinity whether he worships or not.

45 The Goddess formed of rice, though she is not worshipped, is already worshipped by the grains of rice. Should she be now worshipped by the grains of rice ?

46 Will the flame of a lamp remain uncovered (i.e. without light) if we do not ask her to wear the garment of light ?

47. Is not the moon entirely covered with her light though we do not ask her to wear the moon light ?

48 The fire has its heat naturally. Why should we think of heating or not heating it ?

49 The wise one is naturally the God Shiva himself. So not only he worships while worshipping but also does the same while not worshipping.

50 Now the lights of action and inaction are put out and devotion and non-devotion sitting in the same row have the same dish before them (i.e. they occupy the same position).

51 In this condition the sacred texts of the Upanishadas become a censure, and censure itself becomes charming hymns.

52 In fact both praise and censure are reduced to silence. Though there is any talk it is silence.

53 It is a pilgrimage to God Shiva though he (the wise one) wanders at any place. If he goes to the Shiva, the going is like not going.

54 It is wonderful that in this condition both walking and sitting in one place become the same thing.

55 If his eye-sight sees any object at any time in any way he experiences the joy of seeing the God Shiva.

56 Or though God Shiva is seen before him, he has, as if seen nothing. God and his devotee are on the same plain.

57 A ball falls down of its own accord, strikes itself, rebounds and is enraptured in its own bliss.

58 If at any time it would be possible to see such a play of a ball, we would be able to speak about the natural behaviour of the wise one.

59 Neither can the hand of action touch it nor the knowledge get entrance in it. Spontaneous devotion goes on in this way.

60 It has no end. It is resounding in itself. What bliss can be compared to this ?

61 This is the wonderful secret of natural devotion. This is the place where meditation and knowledge merge themselves.

62 Hari and Hara (God Shiva and Vishnu) are really identical. But the difference in their names and forms are also merged.

63 Oh ! Shiva and Shakti, that were swallowing each other, are both of them swallowed simultaneously.

64 Here Para (the highest kind of speech) eating all objects and drinking all other kinds of speech, took rest in sleep.

65 Oh Blessed and mighty Lord! you have made us the sole sovereign of the kingdom of the supreme bliss.

66 It is wonderful that you have awakened the wakeful, laid down to sleep those who have already slept and made us realize ourselves!

67 We are all in all yours. Out of love you call us your own. It is becoming to your greatness.

68 You do not take anything from anyone. You do not give your own to anyone. We do not know how you enjoy your greatness (the state of being Guru).

69 You are supreme as a Guru (a spiritual teacher). You are laghu (a light object) because you help one to escape from drowning in the waters of the worldly life. (The word Guru means both great and heavy. The word Laghu means both mean and light in weight). Both these qualities of yours are understood by one who is favoured by your grace.

70 If your unity had been disturbed while sharing it with your disciple, why should the sacred works have extolled you?

71 Oh Noble one, you are happy to become our kith and kin by taking away our feeling of difference from you.

CHAPTER X

Blessings to the World

1 Oh, Shri Nivrittinath! you have blessed me with this supreme bliss. Should I enjoy it within myself?

2 The Great God has endowed the sun with the fountain of light that illumines the whole world.

3 Was it for the moon's sake that the nectar was given to her? Or did the sea grant water to the clouds for their own use?

4 The light of the lamp is for illuminating the whole house. The expanse of sky is for the sake of the whole world.

5 There is the swelling of tides on the unfathomable sea. It is not due to the power of the moon? It is the spring that enables the trees to offer their blossom and fruits.

6 So it is an open secret that all this is the gift of your blessed divinity. There is nothing that is mine.

7 But why should I explain myself in this way? It is like obstructing the expansion of my master's glory.

8 What we have spoken is self-evident. Should words illumine the self-luminous?

9 Or if we had kept silence would not a Person have soon seen another Person ?

10 When a Person sees another person it reveals naturally the self-evident truth that, without any change the seer becomes the object of sight. (A person looking at another individual is also seen by him. So he is both the seer and object of sight).

11 There is no other secret about the nature of Pure Intelligence than this. This is evident even before its statement.

12 If it is said that in these circumstances the occasion to begin this work does not arise, we can reply that we are describing what is self-evident only out of love for it.

13 It may be the same thing that is dear to us, but there is a fresh flavour in tasting it again. So there is propriety in describing what is self-evident.

14 So it is not that I have spoken out a secret. It is self-luminous.

15 We are enveloped by perfect egoism. We have pervaded everything. We are not concealed or revealed by anything.

16 What can we offer to ourselves in the form of any exposition ? Is it lost by remaining silent?

17 Therefore my speech has become the deepest silence. It is like drawing the picture of a crocodile on the surface of water.

18 In this way even the ten Upanishadas cannot approach it. The understanding has merged itself.

19 Jnanadeva says that this is the rich nectar of spiritual experience. Let even the emancipated should take its draught.

20 The state of emancipation is nice, but the nectar of spiritual experience is so pure and sweet that even the eternal state of emancipation will eagerly desire to taste its sweetness.

21 Should I, who have got the vision of the sun say that every night there is moon but it is so peculiarly bright on the full moon night ?

22 The bloom of youth resides in a damsel, but it blossoms forth when she is united with her beloved.

23 With the advent of spring the trees begin to kiss the sky with their twigs bearing fruits and flowers.

24 Therefore I have served the dish of my spiritual experience in the form of this talk which is Anubhavamrit (i.e. the present work).

25 The difference between souls that are emancipated, or eager for emancipation or in bondage, remains so long as all of them have not tasted the sweetness of this nectar of experience.

26 As the waters (streams) coming to dip themselves in the Ganges become the Ganges, or as the darkness, meeting the sun becomes itself the light of the sun,

27 As we can talk of different qualities of metals so long as they have no contact with the philosopher's stone. All of them are turned into pure gold by that contact.

28 Those who enter the inner sanctorum of these words are like rivers mingling with the ocean.

29 As all the fifty letters — and others — meet in the letter 'Om', so there is nothing else besides the Atman in all the movable and the immovables in the world.

39 There is no other thing that can be pointed out besides God. In fact everything is pervaded by Shiva.

31 "Therefore" says Jnanadeva, "Let the whole universe enjoy the festival of this nectar of spiritual experience"

APPENDIX B

THE AMṚTĀNUBHAVA
(Sanskrit Version)

श्रीप्रह्लादमहाराजकृत अमृतानुभवस्य संस्कृतानुवादः ।।

प्रथमोऽध्यायः

(शिवशक्तिसमावेशनमनम्)

एवं यज्जगतां मूलं जनकं निरुपाधिकम् ।
शिवशक्त्यात्मकं द्वंद्वं वंदितं तन्मया मुदा ।।१।।
यः प्रियः स प्रिया भूत्वा प्रीत्या स्वसुखलिप्सया ।
चारुस्थल्यामेकपंक्तौ एकाङ्गे संभृतावुभौ ।।२।।
प्रीतिप्रवाहवेगेन निमीलन्तौ परस्परम् ।
किन्नु द्वैतस्य च व्याजादुद्गिलन्तौ न निश्चयः ।।३।।
यदेकं न भवेत्तत्र द्वयोर्दित्वं कुतस्तराम् ।
साकारौ वा निराकारौ न जानीमः स्वरूपतः ।।४।।
कथं स्वसुखलब्धौ तौ द्वैतभावेन मीलितौ ।
कौतुकेनापि नैकत्वं ददतौ स्फुटितुं मिथः ।।५।।
इत्थं वियोगभीरू तौ सुवाते बालकं जगत् ।
अद्यापि द्वैतभावोऽयं जगत्यस्मिन्न खंड्यते ।।६।।
चराचरस्य संसारः स्वांगे संदर्शितः खलु ।
न दत्तो हि तृतीयस्य स्पर्शं भवितुमप्यणुम् ।।७।।
एकसत्ताप्रकाशाभ्यामासनं भासनं द्वयोः ।
अनाद्येकत्वभावेन दम्पती नन्दतः स्वयम् ।।८।।
निमज्ज्यैकरसे प्रीत्या भेदस्तस्मात्स्वलज्जया ।
बहिः स्वानन्दभोगाय द्वैतमादाय निर्ययौ ।।९।।
देवेन देवी सम्पूर्णा तां विना स दिगंबरः ।
किंबहुनैकजीव्यौ तौ दंपती मिथस्तराम् ।।१०।।
कथं मेलापकः प्रीत्या तयोरासीत्परस्परम् ।
जगत्त्रये न मात्वा यौ विरेजतुरणुष्वपि ।।११।।

एकमेकं विना याभ्यां निर्ममे न तृणादिकम् ।
प्राणादपि च प्रेयांसावन्योन्यं दंपती च तौ ॥१२॥
गृहकृत्येऽतिनिपुणौ यदा स्वपिति पूरुषः ।
तदा दाम्पत्यभावेन जागर्ति गृहिणी स्वयम् ॥१३॥
ययोर्द्वयोरेकतरत् निद्रातो यदि जागृयात् ।
ग्रसित्वा सगृहं सर्वं न किंचिदवशेषयेत् ॥१४॥
विलोप्यांगद्वयं याभ्यां एकभावेन संस्थितम् ।
पुनरर्धार्धभागेन भेदवन्तौ बभूवतुः ॥१५॥
आश्रयश्चैकमेकस्य विषयश्च परस्परम् ।
अन्योन्यौ सुखिनौ तद्वदन्योन्याभ्यां निरंतरम् ॥१६॥
स्त्रीपुन्नामप्रभेदेन नंदत्येकः शिवः स्वयम् ।
ययोरर्धार्धभागेन भाति वै सकलं जगत् ॥१७॥
दण्डद्वये श्रुतिश्चैका गन्धश्च सुमनोर्द्वये ।
दीपद्वये यथैवैका दीप्तिः संराजतेतराम् ॥१८॥
ओष्ठद्वये यथैवैका गोष्टिर्दृष्टिश्च नेत्रयोः ।
द्वाभ्यां तथा जीवसृष्टिरेकैवेति श्रुतिर्जगौ ॥१९॥
अनादिमिथुनं चैतत्प्रकृतिप्रत्ययात्मकम् ।
एकत्वैकरसं भुंक्ते द्वैतं संदर्श्य चात्मनः ॥२०॥
स्वामिसत्तां विना स्थातुं न शक्नोति पतिव्रता ।
यां विना सर्वकर्तापि नैव किंचित्करोति सः ॥२१॥
भर्तुर्यद्दर्शनं यस्या भर्ता चैवासनं किल ।
न ज्ञायते च यद्द्वंद्वं निर्णेतुं तत्स्वरूपतः ॥२२॥
यथा गुडस्तथा स्वादः कर्पूरस्तस्य सौरभम् ।
पृथक्त्वेऽपि हि निर्णेतुं विवेकः पंगुतां व्रजेत् ॥२३॥
दीप्तौ तु गृह्यमाणायां हस्ते चायाति दीपकः ।
तद्वद्यस्या विचारे तु लभ्यते शिव एकलः ॥२४॥
प्रभया राजते सूर्यः प्रभागर्भगतो रविः ।
तद्वद्भेदं ग्रसित्वा तु प्रभैवैका विराजते ॥२५॥
द्योतकं प्रतिबिम्बस्य बिम्बं बिम्बानुमापकम् ।

प्रतिबिंबं तथा द्वैतव्याजेनैकं विराजते ॥२६॥
सर्वशून्यस्य निष्कर्षः स कृतः पुरुषो यया ।
येन भर्त्रा स्वसत्ताया विशेषः शक्तिरुत्कृता ॥२७॥
न शक्नोति शिवे स्थातुं शिवत्वं यां प्रियां विना ।
सैवात्मना शिवेनैव घटिता हि स्वलीलया ॥२८॥
ऐश्वर्येण सहेशस्य सृष्टिः स्वांगे कृता यया ।
स्वकीयस्योद्भवस्यापि या हेतुः स्वयमेव हि ॥२९॥
अरूपं स्वपतिं वीक्ष्य भूत्वा प्रत्यङ्मुखी ह्रिया ।
अलंचक्रे जगन्मात्रैर्नामरूपादिभूषणैः ॥३०॥
यत्रैकत्वस्य दुष्कालस्तत्र बाहुल्यसंभ्रमः ।
या सौभाग्यवती तस्या लीलया तस्य दर्शितः ॥३१॥
स्वांगस्यैवोपससंहृत्या यया कान्तः प्रकाशितः ।
येन कृत्वा स्वसंकोचं प्रियैवाग्रे प्ररोहिता ॥३२॥
यस्या दर्शनलोभेन क्षुब्धो द्रष्टृत्वमाप्नुयात् ।
यामपश्यन्हि यस्तिष्ठन्निजांगं त्यजति क्षणात् ॥३३॥
कान्तामर्यादया नूनं संजातो यो जगन्मितः ।
तत्त्वेनालोचिते यस्मिन्नभावो नामरूपयोः ॥३४॥
एतावन्मंदरूपेण विस्तृतः सन् विलुप्यति ।
यस्या विभवतो जातः स एव विश्वरूपकः ॥३५॥
यया भोजयितो भर्ता वेद्यान्नं बहुलं च तत् ।
भोजयित्री तया सार्धं भुक्त्वा तृप्तः स चाभवत् ॥३६॥
निद्रिते भर्तरि स्वीये प्रसूते या चराचरम् ।
यस्यां विश्रम्यमाणायां पुरुषत्वं विलुंपति ॥३७॥
यः कान्तो लोप्तुमिच्छेत्तद्दृशा दर्शितो हि सः ।
तावुभावुभयोर्यस्माद्दर्शकौ मुकुरौ समौ ॥३८॥
खादत्यात्मानमानन्दो यस्या एवांगसंगतः ।
सर्वभोक्तापि गृह्णाति न किंचिदपि यां विना ॥३९॥
या वै यस्य प्रियस्यांगं यस्याः सौभाग्यकं प्रियः ।
कालयित्वा द्वयं भागं जेमन्तौ तावुभावपि ॥४०॥

यथा गतिः समीरेण सहिता तत्स्वरूपिणी ।
कान्तिः स्वर्णात्मिका तद्वच्छिवेन सकला शिवा ॥४१॥
गन्धात्मिकैव कस्तूरी उष्मणा सहितोऽनलः ।
यथा शक्तिस्वरूपेण भाति वै सकलः शिवः ॥४२॥
अहोरात्रं स्वरूपेण मृषा स्यात् सूर्यसंगतम् ।
तथा सत्यस्वरूपे स्वे मिथ्याभूतावुभावपि ॥४३॥
बहुनोक्तेन किं तौ द्वौ शब्दमात्रस्वरूपिणौ ।
प्रणवाक्षररूढाया दशा तस्यास्तु वैरिणी ॥४४॥
अस्त्वेतन्नामभेदं वै ग्रसत्येकार्थता द्वयोः ।
नौमि तौ दंपती साक्षात् ज्ञानदेवोऽब्रवीदिदम् ॥४५॥
ययोरालिंगने चोभौ विशीर्णौ स्वस्वरूपतः ।
रजन्यामागतायां तु दृष्टिः शीर्णा यथा भवेत् ॥४६॥
ययोः स्वरूपनिर्धारे सपरा वैखरी गता ।
सिन्धुना सहिता गंगा यथा मग्ना लयांबुनि ॥४७॥
चांचल्यसहितो वायुर्जीर्णो व्योमोदरे यथा ।
यथा वा सप्रभो भानुर्लुप्तः प्रलयतेजसि ॥४८॥
ययोरालोचने तादृक् सदृक् दर्शनकं गतम् ।
भूयस्तौ दम्पती साक्षान्नतौ विश्वकुटुंबिनौ ॥४९॥
ययोः प्रवाहे वेद्यस्य वेदको नोदकं पिबेत् ।
नेदं कुतूहलं किं तु निजांगं त्यजति क्षणात् ॥५०॥
तत्राहं नमनं कर्तुं यदि शिष्ये द्वितीयकः ।
तदा परो लिंगभेदस्त्वेतस्मादधिकोऽस्ति किम् ॥५१॥
हिरण्मयं हिरण्यं हि यथा भिन्नतया भजेत् ।
इदं चापि तथैवास्ति सर्वदा वंदनं मम ॥५२॥
वाचयैवोच्यमानायां वाचायामेतयोर्द्वयोः ।
वाच्यवाचकयोर्भेदस्पर्शोऽस्ति किं मिथो वद ॥५३॥
स्त्रीपुन्नामप्रभेदेन गंगासागरसंगतिः ।
संविभाति तथाप्यस्ति पानीये द्वैतता किमु ॥५४॥
भास्य भासकताद्वैतं स्वस्मिन्संदर्शयन् रविः ।

अथापि सविता स्वस्य किमेकत्वं भिनत्ति हि ॥५५॥
चन्द्रोपरि भवेद्यद्वच्चन्द्रिकाया विकीर्णता ।
दीप्तिं विनोपलब्धिः स्यात्किमु दीपस्य कुत्रचित् ॥५६॥
मौक्तिकस्य प्रभा यद्वन्मुक्तोपरि समुल्लसेत् ।
अधिकं निर्मलत्वेन भ्राजते मौक्तिकं तया ॥५७॥
मात्राभिस्तिसृभिर्भिन्नो भिन्नाभिः प्रणवः किमु ।
रेखाभिस्तिसृभिः किंवा णकारो भेदमाप्तवान् ॥५८॥
न चलेदैक्यमूलं चेत्सुषमाप्यधिका भवेत् ।
निजोर्मिमुकुलान् कस्मात्तदा कं नावतंसतु ॥५९॥
एवं भवानीभूतेशो यावभिन्नावनादितः ।
प्रवृत्तोऽहं नमस्कर्तुमकृत्वा भिन्नभावनाम् ॥६०॥
प्रतिबिम्बं विशेद् बिम्बे दर्पणत्यागमात्रतः ।
रुद्धे वायौ तरंगेण यथांभसि विलीयते ॥६१॥
आत्मनः स्थानमाप्नोति गतनिद्रस्तु तत्क्षणे ।
तद्वन्मया मतित्यागाद्देवीदेवौ नमस्कृतौ ॥६२॥
त्यक्त्वा लोभमहंतायाः सैंधवं सिंधुतामियात् ।
तथैवाहं मतित्यागादभवं सांबशंभुभाक् ॥६३॥
रंभागर्भो यथाकाशो प्रविष्टो यां दशामियात् ।
शिवशक्तिसमावेशान्मया तद्वन्नमस्कृतम् ॥६४॥

॥ इति प्रथमोऽध्यायः ॥

द्वितीयोऽध्यायः

(सद्गुरुवन्दनम्)

अधुनोपायविपिने वसंतो यो विराजते ।
सौभाग्यतंतुर्विद्यायाः मूर्तिमान् करुणारसः ॥१॥
अनाद्यविद्याविपिने जीवभावेन यद्भ्रमत् ।
चैतन्यं तत्समुद्धर्तुं कृपया योऽभिधावति ॥२॥
मायेभमुपसंहृत्य मुक्तिमुक्ताफलोदनम् ।
भोजयेत्सद्गुरुर्यस्तं निवृत्तिं प्रणमाम्यहम् ॥३॥
यत्कृपापांगपातेन बन्धो मोक्षत्वमाप्नुयात् ।
ज्ञाता ज्ञातारमन्वेति यस्य सन्निधिमात्रतः ॥४॥
कैवल्यहेमदाने यो नोत्तमाधममीक्षते ।
द्रष्टुश्च दर्शने यो वै समर्थः संप्रकीर्तितः ॥५॥
स्वसामर्थ्यप्रभावाद्यो गुरुत्वेन शिवं जयेत् ।
पश्येदादर्शके यस्मिन्नात्मापि ह्यात्मनः सुखम् ॥६॥
बोधचंद्रकला या या विकीर्णास्तत्र तत्र हि ।
करोत्येकत्र ताः सर्वा यत्कृपापूर्णिमातिथिः ॥७॥
समाप्तं स्यादुपायानां धावनं यस्य दर्शनात् ।
प्रवृत्तिलक्षणा गंगा स्थिरा स्याद्यत्र सागरे ॥८॥
यस्यानवसरे द्रष्टा मूढः सन् याति दृश्यताम् ।
बहुरूपमिदं सर्वं विनश्येद्यस्य सेवनात् ॥९॥
स्वाज्ञानमंधतामिस्रं स्वबोधसुदिनेन तत् ।
यत्प्रसादार्कसंपर्काद्याति स्वच्छप्रकाशताम् ॥१०॥
यत्कृपासलिले स्नातः शुद्धो जीव इयान् भवेत् ।
यच्छिवत्वमप्यशुचि नांगे लापयति स्वके ॥११॥
रक्ष्यमाणे स्वके शिष्ये गुरुत्वं हारितं स्थितम् ।
तथापि सहसा यं वै गुरुत्वं न विमुंचति ॥१२॥

एकत्वं न सुखायातो गुरुशिष्यमिषेण च ।
पश्यदेवात्मनो रूपं पश्यतीति द्विधाभवत् ॥१३॥
यस्य कृपातुषारेण परीत्याविद्यकं विषम् ।
परिणमत्यपारेण बोधाख्येनामृतेन तु ॥१४॥
दृष्टे वेद्ये वेद्यमाने उदरे याति वेदकम् ।
तथापि दृष्टिरुच्छिष्टा न भवत्यात्मतां गता ॥१५॥
यत्सहायतया नूनं जीवो ब्रह्मत्वमश्नुते ।
औदासीन्येन यस्याशु ब्रह्मापि तृणतामियात् ॥१६॥
यस्योपास्तेरुपायाः स्युः फलभारे सुसंभृताः ।
परिपक्वदशामेत्य संस्थिता यदनुज्ञया ॥१७॥
यस्य दृष्टिवसंतो नो प्रविशेन्नैगमे वने ।
तावदात्मफलं तस्य हस्ते नायाति कर्हिचित् ॥१८॥
पुरो दृष्टिप्रसारेण पश्चान्नश्यति भौतिकम् ।
एतावंतं तु विजयं नैव गृह्णाति चात्मनि ॥१९॥
लघुत्वमूलरूपेण निवसन् गौरवे पदे ।
यन्नास्ति तन्नाशयित्वा सर्वदा भाग्यवान् हि यः ॥२०॥
निर्जले मज्यते येन घनीभूतेन तीर्यते ।
तीर्णेन नावशिष्येत येन कुत्रापि वा स्थले ॥२१॥
सावयवोऽयमाकाशो न बिभर्त्यवकाशताम् ।
अस्तु चैवं कश्चिदेकः संभृताकाश एव यः ॥२२॥
चंद्रादीनि सुशीतानि यन्मेलप्रभवानि वै ।
यच्छायया हि सूर्योऽपि सोज्वलत्वेन भासते ॥२३॥
शिवोऽपि जीवभावेन त्रसित्वा स्वदशां पुनः ।
आयातुं सुमुहूर्तं वै दैवज्ञं पृच्छति स्वयम् ॥२४॥
स्वप्रभाचन्द्रिकाद्वैतद्विगुणं प्रावृतोऽपि च ।
तथापि यस्य चंद्रस्य प्राकट्यं न व्रजेत्किल ॥२५॥
योऽभिव्यक्तोऽपि नाभाति प्रकाशोप्यप्रकाशवत् ।
अस्तित्वेनैव नास्तीति भासते यत्र कुत्रचित् ॥२६॥
अधुना यः स शब्दाभ्यां प्रमाणं किं करोम्यहम् ।

प्रमाणस्याप्यविषयः स कस्य विषयो भवेत् ॥२७॥
यत्र शब्दो निवर्तेत तेन साकं ब्रवीत्यसौ ।
द्वितीयस्य तु रोषेण स्वैकत्वस्यापि कुप्यति ॥२८॥
तदा भाति प्रमेयेन प्रमाणं प्रसरेद्यदा ।
आश्चर्यमस्य धुर्यस्य नास्तित्वस्य च लाघवम् ॥२९॥
किंचित्कदाचित्समये पश्यामि द्वैतभावनः ।
यद्ग्रामे दर्शनं तत्तु व्यलीकं सुविनिश्चितम् ॥३०॥
तत्र नत्याथ स्तुत्या वा क्व चाहं निदधे पदम् ।
अंगाभावेप्यनंगेन येन नाम्नैव वंचितम् ॥३१॥
आत्मन्यात्मप्रवृत्तिर्नो निवृत्तिस्तत्र वै क्व च ।
अथापि नामावरणं व्यलीकं न जहाति च ॥३२॥
निवर्त्यमेव नास्त्यादौ निवर्तयति किं पुनः ।
उपविष्टः कथं तर्हि निवृत्तिर्नामके पदे ॥३३॥
अंधकारस्वरूपेण कदाचित् गोचरो रवेः ।
तथापि तमारिरिति प्रसिद्धिस्तस्य चागता ॥३४॥
जडं प्रकाशते येन मिथ्याभूतं विरोहति ।
न घटते तद् घटते यस्य मायाविलासतः ॥३५॥
मायातो दर्शयस्यंगं मायिकं तं निषेधसे ।
अमायिकस्वरूपस्त्वं कस्याप्यविषयः खलु ॥३६॥
शिव शिव गुरो स्वामिन् गूढ त्वां किं करोम्यहम् ।
एकं हि निश्चयं कर्तुं न ददासि कथंचन ॥३७॥
बहुशो नामरूपाणि व्युत्पाद्योद्वसितानि च ।
परन्तु निजसत्तायास्तुष्टोऽस्यावेशतो न किम् ॥३८॥
सख्यं कर्तुं न जानासि जीवितग्रहणं विना ।
स्वामिभावेन शिष्येत शिष्यो नेदं तथा भवेत् ॥३९॥
विशेषस्याभिधानेन नात्मत्वं यत्सहेत्खलु ।
किं बहुनास्य नाभाव्यं केनाप्येतद्विनिश्चितम् ॥४०॥
यथैव रजनी सूर्ये न तिष्ठेल्लवणं जले ।
नावशिष्येद्यथा निद्रा जागरे स्वस्वरूपतः ॥४१॥

कर्पूरव्यक्तिलावण्यमग्निश्चापि न तिष्ठति ।
नामरूपं तथैवास्य न किंचिदपि तिष्ठति ॥४२॥
वंदनाय भवाम्यग्रे वंद्यत्वेन न तिष्ठति ।
वंद्यवंदकभेदोऽयमेतस्मिन्नेव तिष्ठति ॥४३॥
न करोत्युदयं भानुरात्मानं प्रति कर्हिचित् ।
वंदनाय तथैवायं वंद्यो वै न भवेद् ध्रुवम् ॥४४॥
किंचात्मनः सन्मुखत्वं न प्राप्येत कदाचन ।
तथैवानेन वंद्यत्वं हत्वा निष्काशितं बहिः ॥४५॥
आकाशस्य यथादर्शे नोत्तिष्ठेत् प्रतिबिंबकम् ।
नमस्काराय वंद्योऽसौ न भवेदिति कौतुकम् ॥४६॥
न भवेच्चेन्न भवत्वत्र गृह्णीयाद् वक्रतां कुतः ।
वंदकस्यापि यत्स्थानं न ददात्यवशेषितुम् ॥४७॥
बहिस्थे पल्लवे चैके स्फेलिते सति सत्वरम् ।
न स्फेलितोऽपि स्फिटति पल्लवश्चांतरस्थितः ॥४८॥
गृहीत्वा सहितं बिंबं प्रतिबिंबं विनश्यति ।
नीतं वंद्यत्वमेतेन वंदकेन सहैव हि ॥४९॥
तत्रास्ति दृष्टेः किं कार्यं यत्र रूपं न विद्यते ।
अस्माकं फलितौ श्रीमत्पादौ तौ दर्शयेद्दृशा ॥५०॥
प्रज्ज्वलेद्दीपकलिका गुणस्नेहाग्निसंगता ।
कर्पूरपुलिका तां तु नाप्नुयात्संगमात्रतः ५१॥
अन्योन्यं न द्वयोर्यावत्किंचिदालिंगनो भवेत् ।
उभयोस्तत्क्षणेनैव स्वरूपं चैवशिष्यते ॥५२॥
न पश्येयमिमं यावद्गतौ वंद्यत्ववंदकौ ।
यथा जाग्रद्दशायां तु स्वप्नकान्तौ न तिष्ठतः ॥५३॥
किमनेन बहूक्तेन द्वैतरूपं निरस्य वै ।
स्वसखा सद्गुरुः साक्षान्निवृत्तिर्वंदितो मया ॥५४॥
आश्चर्यमस्य सख्यस्य स्वांगेनैकत्वमप्युत ।
गुरुशिष्यात्मकद्वैतविस्तारो बहुशः कृतः ॥५५॥
कथं द्वैतं विना सख्यं कृत्वा चात्मानमात्मना ।

विलक्षणः स्वयं स्वस्मात्तद्भिन्नास्तीति नो भवेत् ॥५६॥
यस्योदरे जगत् सर्वं याति यद्गगनोपमम् ।
तदेव हि नास्तिभावनिष्कर्षं सहते पुनः ॥५७॥
यथा सिन्धुः पूर्णताया आश्रयोऽप्यथ दुर्भरः ।
विरुद्धधर्मयोर्यस्य गृहे प्राघुणिकं तथा ॥५८॥
तेजसस्तमसश्चैव सदा वैरं परस्परम् ।
परन्तु ते उभे सूर्ये सूर्यरूपेण तिष्ठतः ॥५९॥
यदेकं भण्यते तच्च भिन्नं नानेव नंदति ।
परस्परं विरुद्धं यद्विरुद्धं तं न चात्मनः ॥६०॥
अतः शिष्यो गुरुश्चेति शब्दयोरनयोर्द्वयोः ।
एकोऽर्थः श्रीगुरुः साक्षात् द्विधारूपेण संस्थितः ॥६१॥
सुवर्णं चाप्यलंकारः सुवर्णत्वेन तिष्ठतः ।
चंद्रश्च चंद्रिका चैव मिलित्वा चंद्र एकलः ॥६२॥
कर्पूरस्तस्य चामोदः कर्पूरः केवलः स्वयम् ।
स्वादश्च शर्करा द्वाभ्यां शर्करैका विराजते ॥६३॥
गुरुशिष्यस्वरूपेण दृश्यते यद्यपि द्विधा ।
तथापि श्रीगुरुः साक्षादेक एव समुल्लसेत् ॥६४॥
आदर्शेऽप्यथवा स्वास्ये दृश्योऽहमिति नान्यथा ।
इत्यात्मनः प्रतीतिस्तां मुखं जानात्यसंशयम् ॥६५॥
निरंजने निद्रितो यो निर्विवादं स एकलः ।
परं चेता चेतयितेत्येतदासीत् स्वयं द्वयम् ॥६६॥
स्वयं चेतेच्चेतयेच्च वेत्ति चावेदयेदसौ ।
इत्थं च यद्गुरुत्वं च शिष्यत्वं नंदयत्यसौ ॥६७॥
विनादर्शं यदा दृष्टिः स्वात्मदर्शनसंभ्रमम् ।
लभेत तर्हि लीलेयं कथनीया भवेन्मम ॥६८॥
अदत्त्वा स्फुरितं द्वैतमैक्यं चापि विघाटितुम् ।
सख्यस्य चाप्यतिशयं पुष्णातीत्यतिकौतुकम् ॥६९॥
निवृत्तिर्नाम यस्यैव निवृत्तिर्यस्य सौभगम् ।
यस्यैश्वर्यं निवृत्तिश्च निवृत्तिः सैव केवलः ॥७०॥

प्रवृत्तेश्च विरोधेन निवृत्तेश्च बोधनात् ।
आनीयते तथा शब्दान्निवृत्तिर्न भवेद् ध्रुवम् ।।७१।।
दत्त्वात्मानं यथा रात्रिर्दिनमुन्नतिमानयेत् ।
अन्यस्यापेक्षया चासौ निवृत्तिर्न भवेद् ध्रुवम् ।।७२।।
उद्वर्तनबलेनैव रत्नं सोज्ज्वलतामियात् ।
तदिदं न भवेद्रत्नं चक्रवर्तिस्वराडयम् ।।७३।।
प्रवेश्य स्वोदरे व्योम चंद्रः पुष्टया विवर्धते ।
तदा तच्चन्द्रिका चन्द्रे पतित्वा तत्र लुंठति ।।७४।।
यथा निवृत्तिभावस्य कारणं स्वयमेव हि ।
स्वामोदग्रहणायैव पुष्पं घ्राणमभूत्स्वयम् ।।७५।।
दृष्टिः स्वमुखलावण्यं दृष्टया कृत्वा तदाप्नुयात् ।
किमर्थं मुकुरायासः कर्तव्यः सूक्ष्मदर्शिभि : ।।७६।।
किं गतायां त्रियामायां दिवसे च समागते ।
पश्चात्स्वस्योदयं सूर्यः किं कुर्यात्स्वप्रकाशकः ।।७७।।
अतो बोधेन बोध्येन प्रमाणैः साध्यतेऽथवा ।
तथासौ न भवेत्किंतु स्वतः सिद्धप्रकाशकः ।।७८।।
एवं क्रियां विनैवेदं निवृत्तित्वं स्वयं भवेत् ।
तस्य श्रीचरणद्वंद्वमैक्यभावेन वंदितम् ।।७९।।
इति श्रीज्ञानदेवेन श्रीगुरोः पादपंकजम् ।
प्रणामे ऋणनिर्मुक्तं कृतं वाचाचतुष्टयम् ।।८०।।

तृतीयोऽध्यायः

(वाचाऋणशेषपरिहारः)

यासां कोलाहले आत्मा गतनिद्रो भवत्ययम् ।
वाचोऽनृणा न चैव स्युर्जागृतिः सुप्तिरेव सा ॥१॥
परादिकाश्चतस्रस्तु जीवमोक्षप्रयोजने ।
अविद्यासहिताःस्वांगैर्व्यंयं संप्राप्नुवन्ति हि ॥२॥
हस्तांघ्रयश्च देहेनेंद्रियाणि मनसा सह ।
यथा यथैव निर्यान्ति रविणा सह रश्मयः ॥३॥
निद्रावसानात्प्रथमं नश्यन्ति स्वप्नदृष्टयः ।
तथैवाविद्यया सार्धं नश्यंत्येता परादयः ॥४॥
रसरूपेण जीवन्ति मृतलोहादिधातवः ।
दग्धं धनानि संयांति यथा वह्निदशां पुनः ॥५॥
जले विधृत्य लवणं स्वादरूपेण शिष्यते ।
यथा जाग्रत्स्वरूपेण गता निद्रावशिष्यते ॥६॥
तथैवाविद्यया सार्धं चतस्रस्त्यक्तजीविताः ।
तत्त्वज्ञानस्य नाम्ना या व्युत्तिष्ठन्ति स्वयं पुनः ॥७॥
स्वयं मृत्वा लापनीयस्तत्त्वज्ञानप्रदीपकः ।
अयं तर्हि श्रमो लेयो बोधरूपेण तात्त्विकः ॥८॥
आगत्य मेलयेत्स्वप्नं गतात्मानं च दर्शयेत् ।
द्वयं दृष्ट्या नन्दयति यथा निद्रा हि देहिनाम् ॥९॥
एवमविद्या जीवन्ति ह्यन्यथा बोधकारिणी ।
तदेवोपरता सा च यथाबोधेन तिष्ठति ॥१०॥
अमृता वा मृता वापि ह्यविद्या न विमुंचति ।
बन्धमोक्षे न क्षिपति जीवं बद्ध्वा सुदारुणा ॥११॥
मोक्षोऽपि बंधरूपः स्यात्तदा मोक्षाभिधा कथम् ।

अज्ञानिनां गृहे तावत्प्रसिद्धिरनयोर्वृथा ॥१२॥
मृतं बागुलकं श्रुत्वा यथा हृष्यति बालकः ।
इतरस्य स नास्त्येव तन्मृत्युः केन मन्यताम् ॥१३॥
स्फुटितं घटनास्तित्वमिति मत्वानुशोचति ।
यः पुमान् स परिज्ञाता इति तं भण्यतां कथम् ॥१४॥
अविद्यकौ मोक्षबन्धौ अज्ञानजनमोहकौ ।
अविद्यया कृतं स्थानं मृत्वा तस्यापि निश्चितम् ॥१५॥
शिवसूत्रमिषेणेदं ज्ञानं बंधकरं त्विति ।
प्रोक्तं सदाशिवेनापि तस्माद् बंधकरं ध्रुवम् ॥१६॥
ज्ञानं बन्धकरं सत्त्वं गुणपाशेन निश्चितम् ।
प्रोक्तं भगवताप्येतद् गीतायामर्जुनं प्रति ॥१७॥
शिवकृष्णावुभावेतत् प्रोक्तवंतावतो वयम् ।
न स्वीकुर्मस्तथैवास्ते नोचतुर्यदि तावुभौ ॥१८॥
ज्ञानस्वरूप आत्मापि लिप्सेत् ज्ञानबलं यदि ।
सूर्यश्चितयति प्रातस्तथा किं न भवेदिदं ॥१९॥
ज्ञानेन श्लाघते ह्यात्मा तदा ज्ञानं वृथा गतम् ।
दीपश्चापेक्षते दीपं भ्रांतमंगं तदा निजम् ॥२०॥
स्थितं समीपमात्मानं न ज्ञात्वा मोहितः पुमान् ।
गवेषयति चान्यत्र स्वात्मानं किमिदं भवेत् ॥२१॥
कदाचिद् बहुकालेन स्मृतमात्मानमात्मना ।
अद्यात्मस्मरणेनाहं हृष्येयं मनुते नु किम् ॥२२॥
आत्मा ज्ञानात्मकस्तद्वज्ज्ञानेनैवात्मनः प्रभाम् ।
करोमि सोहमस्मीति बोधोऽयमपि बन्धकः ॥२३॥
स्वयं मज्जति ज्ञानेन भारभूतमतोऽप्रियम् ।
निवृत्तेनैव ज्ञानेन मोक्षमाप्नोति निश्चितम् ॥२४॥
तस्मात्परादिका वाचश्चत्वारोंगविभूषणाः ।
जीवभावस्य संत्यागे वीताः सार्धमविद्यया ॥२५॥
निजांगेंधनसंभूते ज्ञानाग्नौ प्रविशेद्यथा ।
तत्र दग्धो भस्मलेशो बोधस्यैवावशिष्यते ॥२६॥

यथा जले जलाद्भिन्नः कर्पूरो नैव दृश्यते ।
तथापि तत्पृथक्त्वेन सौगंध्यमुपलभ्यते ॥२७॥
चर्चितांगविभूतेस्तु नश्यंति परमाणवः ।
परंतु पाण्डुरत्वेन या कान्तिः सा स्थिरायते ॥२८॥
यथा जलं स्वरूपेण नासीद्भूमौ तथापि हि ।
आर्द्रताव्याजतस्तस्यां तदस्तीत्यवगम्यते ॥२९॥
न दृश्यते पृथक् छाया मध्याह्ने स्वतनोः परम् ।
पादमूले प्रविश्यासौ गुप्ता संतिष्ठते यथा ॥३०॥
ग्रसित्वा हि तथा द्वैतं स्वरूपे तत्प्रकारतः ।
केवलात्मत्वमात्रेण यो बोधः सोऽवशिष्यते ॥३१॥
ऋणशेषं विस्तरितुं वाचो मृत्वा न शक्नुयुः ।
मया तन्मोचितं नूनं पतित्वा गुरुपादयो : ॥३२॥
अतः परादयो वाचः समर्था नात्मदर्शने ।
आसां निस्तरणं तावज्ज्ञानाज्ञाने सुनिश्चितम् ॥३३॥

चतुर्थोऽध्यायः

(ज्ञानसत्तासिद्धिकथनम्)

अधुनाऽज्ञाननाशेन ज्ञानं तिष्ठत्यभेदतः ।
सस्वप्ननिद्रानाशेन यथा नंदति जागृतिः ॥१॥
दर्पणे निर्गते चैक्यबोधं प्राथमिकं स्वकम् ।
स्वयं मुखं प्रभुंजीत पुनर्निःसंशयं यथा ॥२॥
तथैव जगदात्म्यैक्यं करोति ज्ञानमंजसा ।
एवं चेच्छूरिकां विध्येच्छूरिकैव तथा भवेत् ॥३॥
स दहेदात्मना सार्धं योऽतः स्थित्वा दहेत् कुटीम् ।
आत्मना सह बद्ध्वा वा यथा चौरेण मौटिका ॥४॥
कर्पूरस्य मिषेणाग्निरात्मानं नाशयेद्यथा ।
ज्ञानस्यापि हि संजातं तथैवाज्ञाननाशनात् ॥५॥
अज्ञानस्याश्रयाभावे ज्ञानाधिक्यं यदा भवेत् ।
तदा ज्ञानं विनश्येत विनाशे विपरीतता ॥६॥
दशाहीनस्य दीपस्य प्रकाशो योऽधिको भवेत् ।
ज्ञेयः स विबुधैः सम्यक् तस्य नाशाय केवलम् ॥७॥
उत्थानं पतनं किंवा कुचभारस्य वेत्ति कः ।
विकाशो म्लानभावो वा जातेः पुष्पस्य वै यथा ॥८॥
उत्पत्तिर्या तरंगस्य सैव नाशाभिधा भवेत् ।
विद्युतो ह्युदयो यस्तु स एवास्तो न संशयः ॥९॥
तथा समग्रमज्ञानं पीत्वा ज्ञानविवर्धने ।
आत्मनो निधनं यावन्निःशेषं साधयेत्किल ॥१०॥
कल्पांते जलसंपूरो यथा स्थलजलद्वयम् ।
निमज्जितुं विना नार्वाक् स्थातुं जानाति सर्वथा ॥११॥
विश्वाधिकं विवर्धेत यदा सूर्यस्य मंडलम् ।
तदा तेजस्तमश्चेतत्तदेव भवति द्वयम् ॥१२॥

यथा निद्रां निरस्यादौ हृत्वा जागरणं स्वयम् ।
तिष्ठेच्च जागरो भूत्वा स्वरूपेणैव जागरः ॥१३॥
संहृत्यैव यथाऽज्ञानं ज्ञानं यच्च विवर्धते ।
ज्ञानाऽज्ञाने ग्रसीत्वैतज्ज्ञानमात्रेण तिष्ठते ॥१४॥
पूर्णिमायां न पुष्णाति नामायामपसर्पति ।
कला सप्तदशी चान्द्री शेषीभूता विधौ यथा ॥१५॥
तेजांतरेण नाक्रामेन्न बिभ्येत्तमसापि वा ।
तत्सादृश्येनोपमितु द्वितीयः सूर्य एकलः ॥१६॥
अज्ञानेन भवेदंधं ज्ञानेन च समुज्ज्वलेत् ।
तथा तन्न भवेत्किंतु ज्ञप्तिमात्रैकलक्षणम् ॥१७॥
निष्कलं ज्ञप्तिमात्रं तज्ज्ञायते तेन तद्यदि ।
चक्षुषा दृश्यते चक्षुस्तथेदं न भवेत्किमु ॥१८॥
विशेदाकाश आकाशं किमग्निः स्वतनु दहेत् ।
लोकेस्मिन्पुरुषः को वाप्यारोहेन्निजमस्तके ॥१९॥
दृष्टिः पश्येत्किमात्मानं स्वादः स्वादति किं स्वयम् ।
एवं कुत्रापि घटते नादः श्रोष्यति नादताम् ॥२०॥
सूर्यः प्रकाशते सूर्यं किं फलः फलति स्वयम् ।
घ्रियते किमु गंधेन गंधश्चेति वृथा यथा ॥२१॥
तथैव चात्मनः स्वीयं वेदनं न भवेद् ध्रुवम् ।
ज्ञानत्वेन विना तस्माच्चिन्मात्रं ज्ञप्तिरूपकम् ॥२२॥
यज्ज्ञानं ज्ञानसंबंधं ज्ञानत्वेन सहेत चेत् ।
तदज्ञानं नु कथं तर्हि न भवेज्ज्ञानभावतः ॥२३॥
यथा यच्चैव तेजोऽस्ति तत्तमो न भवेत्किल ।
मास्तु तेजस्तमस्तर्हि किं स्यात्तेजश्च तेजसः ॥२४॥
तद्वदस्तित्वनास्तित्वे निवर्तेते उभे यतः ।
अर्थादागतमेवास्य मिथ्यात्वं वस्तुतः स्वयम् ॥२५॥
तर्हि किंचित्स्वरूपेण नास्ति चेदिति मन्यते ।
प्रत्ययस्तर्हि नास्तीति कस्य स्यादिति भण्यताम् ॥२६॥
शून्यसिद्धान्तबोधोऽयं सिद्धः स्यात् सत्तया कया ।

स नास्तीत्यपवादोऽयं वस्तुनो यदि भण्यते ॥२७॥
यथा निर्वाणिते दीपे नश्येन्निर्वाणिता तदा ।
नास्ति दीप इति ख्यातिः कस्य स्यादिति मे वद ॥२८॥
प्राप्तायामपि निद्रायामप्राणो निद्रितो भवेत् ।
तदा जाग्रद्दशायां तु कस्य सुप्तिसुखस्मृतिः ॥२९॥
कुंभत्वात् दृश्यते कुंभो भंगात्तद्भंगभासनम् ।
सर्वथैव यदा नास्ति तदा नास्तीति को वद ॥३०॥
किंचिन्नास्तीति बोधोऽसौ किमु बोधाद्भिना भवेत् ।
अस्तित्वेन विनैवास्ते बोद्धा यः सर्वसाक्षिकः ॥३१॥
अन्यस्य चात्मनश्चापि विषयी न भवेदयम् ।
अतो नास्तित्वभावस्य कारणं तु भवेदिदम् ॥३२॥
निर्जने निद्रितो यो ना जनैर्नान्यैः स दृश्यते ।
स्वस्यापि विस्मृतिस्तस्य जीवितं तु न नश्यति ॥३३॥
तद्वस्तुशुद्धस्वरूपेण यदस्तित्वेन वर्तते ।
अस्ति नास्तीति शब्दोऽपि सहते न कदापि तत् ॥३४॥
दृष्टिः परावृता स्वस्मिन्दृष्टित्वमपि हीयते ।
परन्तु स्वस्वरूपेण नास्तीति न भवेत्स्वयम् ॥३५॥
न ज्ञायते तमिस्रायां कृष्णः स्वेनेतरेण वा ।
अथापि वै समग्रोऽहं स्वयमस्मीति वेत्ति सः ॥३६॥
आसनं नासनं चास्य मानुष्यसदृशं न हि ।
सन्मात्रैकस्वरूपेण केवलं चित्प्रकाशकम् ॥३७॥
यथा स्वनिर्मलत्वेन संस्थितोऽकाशसंचयः ।
स स्वस्य स्वयमेवास्ति नान्यस्य दृष्टिगोचरः ॥३८॥
यथा शुष्केऽपि सरसि पानीयं नान्यगोचरम् ।
तथाप्यन्तस्वरूपेण स्वस्थं संपूर्णमस्ति तत् ॥३९॥
तद्वदस्तित्वभावेन यद् वस्त्वस्ति तदस्ति वै ।
'अहमस्मि' इति त्यक्त्वा सन्मात्रं चित्सुखात्मकम् ॥४०॥
यथा जाग्रत्सुप्तिसंधौ यो भावः समुपद्यते ।
वृत्त्यंकुरं विना कश्चिद्वाचा वक्तुमगोचरः ॥४१॥

भूमिसंस्थापिते कुंभे सकुंभा साऽभिगद्यते ।
अपनीते तथा कुंभे ह्यकुंभा सैव भण्यते ।।४२।।
परंत्वेतत् द्वयं भूमेरंगे न स्पृशति स्वयम् ।
तद्वच्छुद्धतमं शान्तं स्वयं ज्योतिस्वरूपकम् ।।४३।।

पंचमोऽध्यायः

(सच्चिदानंदपदत्रयविवरणम्)

सत्ता चैव प्रकाशश्च सुखं चैतत्त्रिकं विना ।
लक्ष्यं यथा त्रिबत्वेन बिबस्य बिबता न हि ॥१॥
कांतिकाठिन्यकनकैः कनकं गम्यते त्रिभिः ।
द्रवत्वस्वादपीयूषैरेकं पीयूषमुच्यते ॥२॥
मार्दवत्वं सुगंधत्वं उज्ज्वलत्वमिति त्रयम् ।
एकस्मिन्नेव कर्पूरे भासते तत्त्रयं यथा ॥३॥
अंगेन चोज्ज्वलः सन् यो मदुत्वेनापि संस्थितः ।
नोज्ज्वलो न मृदुश्चापि सौगंध्यात्मक एव सः ॥४॥
यथा कर्पूर एकस्मिन् त्रितयं त्रितयं विना ।
तथा सत्तादिकं चापि ह्यू ह्यते सत्स्वरूपके ॥५॥
एवं सदादिभेदेन प्रवृत्तं यत्पदत्रयम् ।
परन्तु न्यूनितं चैतदानंदेनैव केवलम् ॥६॥
सत्तैव किं प्रकाशश्च प्रकाशः किमु सत्सुखम् ।
यत्तद्विवेक्तुं नायाति मृष्टांशश्चामृते यथा ॥७॥
शुक्ले प्रतिदिनं चंद्रे वर्धंते षट् कला दश ।
चन्द्रस्तु निजरूपेण संपूर्णस्तिष्ठति स्वयम् ॥८॥
पृथक्त्वेन विभाव्यन्ते पतंतो जलबिंदवः ।
परन्तु पतनस्थाने किमप्यस्ति जलं विना ॥९॥
तथैवासन्निरासाय श्रुत्या प्रोक्तं सदात्मकम् ।
जडस्यैव निवृत्त्यर्थं प्रोक्तं चिद्रूपसंज्ञकम् ॥१०॥
दुःखस्यैव विनाशेन स्थितं तत्सुखसंज्ञकम् ।
प्रभोनिश्वासभूतैस्तु वेदैर्निगदितं खलु ॥११॥
असदादित्रयं चैव सदादिप्रतियोगिकम् ।
व्यावर्तनात्त्रयस्यास्य जातं सत्त्वादिकं त्रयम् ॥१२॥

एवं सदादयः शब्दाः न भवंत्यात्मवाचकाः ।
अन्यव्यावर्तनात्सिद्धा इति ब्रूते श्रुतिः स्वयम् ॥१३॥
यथा सूर्यप्रकाशेन जडमाभासते च यत् ।
तज्जडं किमु सूर्यस्य भासकं भवति स्वयम् ॥१४॥
तथा यत्तेजसा वाचा वाच्यं वक्तुं प्रवर्तते ।
सैव वाक् किमु चिद्रूपं वस्तुतत्त्वं प्रकाशयेत् ॥१५॥
नास्ति यस्य प्रमेयत्वं स कस्य विषयो भवेत् ।
तस्य च स्वप्रकाशस्य प्रमाणं किं भविष्यति ॥१६॥
प्रमेयस्य परिच्छेदात्प्रमाणत्वं हि नंदति ।
तेन किं प्रतिपाद्येत स्वतःसिद्धं च वस्तु यत् ॥१७॥
एवं वस्तुपरिज्ञाने कर्तव्ये सति तत्त्वतः ।
ज्ञानस्वरूपं वस्त्वेव ज्ञाता ज्ञानं च तत्र किम् ॥१८॥
अतः सदादयः शब्दा न भवंत्यात्मवाचकाः ।
किन्तु विचारशेषास्ते श्रुतिभिः परिभाषिताः ॥१९॥
एवं यानि प्रसिद्धानि सच्चित्सुखपदानि च ।
प्रवृत्तानि स्वसंवादाद् द्रष्टारं मीलितं तदा ॥२०॥
तदा वृष्टेः सरेन्मेघो यथैवोघः समुद्रगः ।
दर्शयित्वा गतं वस्तु मार्गस्तिष्ठति वा यथा ॥२१॥
पुष्पं फलस्वरूपेण फलं च रसरूपतः ।
रसोऽपि तृप्तिदानेन तिष्ठत्येव ह्यनुक्रमात् ॥२२॥
किंचाग्नावाहुतिं हुत्वा पश्चादपसरेत्करः ।
सुखयित्वाऽथवा गीतं तूष्णीं भूत्वैवतिष्ठति ॥२३॥
मुखं मुखाय संदर्श्य निर्याति मुकुरं यथा ।
प्रबोध्य निद्रितं वाऽथ निर्याति च विबोधकः ॥२४॥
एवं सच्चित्सुखादीनि पदानि गणितानि वै ।
संदर्श्य द्रष्ट्रे द्रष्टारं मौनमार्गेण यांति च ॥२५॥
यद्यदुच्येत तत्तन्न यद्भूवेत्तन्न चोच्यते ।
छायया न मीयेत परिमाता यथा हि वै ॥२६॥
पश्चादात्मस्वरूपस्य स्मृतिर्मातुर्यदा भवेत् ।

तदा लज्जा मापयित्री संकोचं भजते क्षणात् ॥२७॥
स्वभावेन या सत्ता सैवासत्ता तु नो भवेत् ।
सत्ताया अपि सत्तात्वं तथैव प्रभवेत् किमु ॥२८॥
तथैवाचिन्निरासेन चिन्मात्रत्वं समागतम् ।
चिन्मात्रस्य तथैवास्य चिन्मात्रत्वं च किं भवेत् ॥२९॥
प्रबोधे नास्ति वै निद्रा न तिष्ठेत् तत्र जागरः ।
तद्वच्चिन्मात्रकं सैव चिन्मात्रे किमु वै भवेत् ॥३०॥
तथैवेदं सुखत्वेन दुःखं च न भवेत् किल ।
सुखस्वरूपकस्यास्य सुखमित्युच्यतां किमु ॥३१॥
असत्त्वेन गतं सत्त्वं अचित्त्वेन च चिद्गतम् ।
असुखेन सुखं तद्वच्छिष्टं किमपि सत्सुखम् ॥३२॥
अधुना सत्सुखं तुच्छं त्यक्त्वा तद्द्वंद्वकंचुकम् ।
सुखमात्रस्वरूपेण स्वयमास्ते च केवलम् ॥३३॥
एकत्वेन तु यद्गण्यं द्वितीयं गणकेन तत् ।
अत एकमगण्यं यत्तदिदं त्वेव मे फलम् ॥३४॥
अनुभूय सुखं पश्चात्तत्सुखी तत्सुखेन च ।
सुखमात्रमिदं त्वेकं को नु किं त्वनुभूयताम् ॥३५॥
तदैवावतरेत् देवी यदा डंका निनादती ।
डंकामात्रस्वरूपेण डंकैवावतरत्किमु ॥३६॥
तथैवात्मसुखत्वेन यस्य नास्ति सुखज्ञता ।
अथवा यत्सुखेनाहमस्मीत्यपि न विद्यते ॥३७॥
विनादर्शं मुखं स्वीय विमुखं नापि संमुखम् ।
तथैव सुखमात्रं यत्सुखासुखवर्जितम् ॥३८॥
विहाय सर्वसिद्धान्तपदवीः परिपूर्णताः ।
मुषित्वात्मानमपि यज्ज्ञप्तिमात्रं स्वयं स्थितम् ॥३९॥
वापं विना यथैवेक्षुरसो यत्र च तिष्ठति ।
तत्रैव तद्रसस्वादः खाद्यते तेन केवलम् ॥४०॥
वीणा न सज्जिता यावत् तस्या नादोऽस्ति यः स्वयम् ।
स एव तस्य नादस्य वेत्तान्यो नास्ति तं विना ॥४१॥

पुष्पोद्गमात्पूर्वमेव पुष्पसारोऽस्ति यस्तदा ।
स एव भ्रमरस्तत्र गंधं जिघ्रति नान्यथा ॥४२॥
यथा वा पाकनिष्पत्तेः पूर्वं तत्कालिकी रुचिः ।
तथैव सा स्वादनीया नान्ययोग्या हि सा भवेत् ॥४३॥
तथैव सुखमात्रत्वात्स्वस्यापि विषयं नयेत् ।
तत्सुखं किमु नान्यस्य विषयं स्याच्च कर्हिचित् ॥४४॥
यथा व्योमगतश्चंद्रो मध्याह्ने नोपलभ्यते ।
तथापि तस्य सद्भावः तेन कृत्वैव बुध्यते ॥४५॥
रूपाभावे तु लावण्यमंगाभावे च यौवनम् ।
सत्क्रियानुदये पुण्यं यत्स्वरूपेण वर्तते ॥४६॥
मनोवृत्त्यंकुरो नासीद्यदा तत्पूर्वकालिके ।
तत्रत्येनैव कामेन माद्यते तर्हि तद् घटेत् ॥४७॥
किंवा वाद्यविशेषाणां सृष्टिर्नो दृष्टिगोचरा ।
तदा न तस्य नादस्य श्रोता नादः स एव हि ॥४८॥
काष्ठस्पर्शो यदा न स्यादनलस्य तु सर्वथा ।
तदाज्वलनमग्नेस्तु तस्य तेनैव केवलम् ॥४९॥
दर्पणेन विना चास्यं दृष्टिगोचरतामियात् ।
वर्माणीमानि विद्यंते स्वतः सिद्धे च वस्तुनि ॥५०॥
क्षेत्रवापं विना सस्यलाभः स्याद्बीजसंग्रहे ।
एवंरीत्या व्यक्तमिदं चिदव्यक्तं निरुपितम् ॥५१॥
एवं विशेषसामान्ये चैतन्यं न स्पृशेत्खलु ।
तस्योपभोगस्तेनैव कर्तव्योऽनन्यभावनात् ॥५२॥
अथ यद्भाषणं तत्तु विचक्षणमनेन वै ।
मौनस्यापि च यन्मौनं पीत्वा निःशेषमास्थितम् ॥५३॥
अप्रमाण्यं प्रमाणैस्तैरंगीकृतमथात्मसु ।
दृष्टान्तैः स्वीयरूपस्य दर्शने शपथः कृतः ॥५४॥
अंगस्यानुपपत्तेस्तु संकोचं युक्तयो गताः ।
तत्रोत्थिताः पंक्तयस्तु लक्षणानामलक्षके ॥५५॥
उपायाः पलितास्तत्र ब्रह्मणि व्यर्थतां गताः ।

प्रतीत्या सूचना त्यक्ता प्रत्ययं कर्तुमात्मनः ॥५६॥
स निश्चयो विचारोऽपि यत्र नैधन्यमागतः ।
स्वामिकार्ये यथा शूरः स्वनाशं साधयेत् स्वयम् ॥५७॥
साधयित्वात्मनो नाशं बुद्ध्या बोधः सुलज्जितः ।
अनुभाव्यं विनैवासौ तुष्णीमनुभवः स्थितः ॥५८॥
अभ्रकंचुकपुंजस्य एकैक शकले क्रमात् ।
निरस्यमाने निःशेषं न किंचिदवशिष्यते ॥५९॥
रंभागर्भस्त्यजेदंगात्प्रावारानुष्मसंकुलः ।
यदि चेत् स कथं तर्हि स्वयं तिष्ठेत्स्वरूपतः ॥६०॥
अनुभाव्य तथैवेकं द्वितीयमनुभावकम् ।
एताभ्यामनुभूतिर्वै तद्विना कस्य सा भवेत् ॥६१॥
एतावत्स्थानपर्यन्तं नानुभूतेरवस्थितिः ।
तत्र चाक्षरपंक्तिः सा वहेन्नामात्मिकां किमु ॥६२॥
परा न प्रचरेद्यत्र नादस्योद्भवनं कुतः ।
तत्रोष्टपुटसंघाते वैखरी प्रसरेत् किमु ॥६३॥
प्रबोधानंतरं व्यर्थाः प्रबोध्यमिति चोक्तयः ।
तृप्तः किं पाककार्येषु तत्परो भवति क्वचित् ॥६४॥
प्रभया भांति किं दीपा उदिते च दिवस्पतौ ।
क्षेत्रे वा सस्यसंपन्ने किं स्याल्लांगलकर्षणम् ॥६५॥
न बंधमोक्षयोर्व्याजं न वा कार्यं न किंचन ।
इतःपरं तु शब्देन कर्तव्यं किं निरूपणम् ॥६६॥
आत्मनश्च परस्यापि हृता यद्वस्तुविस्मृतिः ।
पश्चाल्लब्ध्वा स्मृतिं शब्दात्तद्वस्तु प्राप्यते पुनः ॥६७॥
एतस्मादपरं शब्दे वैभवं नैव विद्यते ।
स्वकीर्तिः स्मारकत्वेन जगत्यस्मिन्प्रसारिता ॥६८॥

षष्ठोऽध्यायः

(शब्दखंडनम्)

बहूपयोगी शब्दोऽयं नादोऽपि धृतिमान्यतः ।
विशदो मूर्त आदर्शः किमु नामूर्तवस्तुनः ॥१॥
पश्यत्पश्यति चादर्शं आश्चर्यं तत्र नो भवेत् ।
अदृश्यं दृश्यते यत्र वस्त्वस्मिन्शब्ददर्पणे ॥२॥
महदव्यक्तवंशेस्मिन्नुदितः किमसौ रविः ।
अनेनैकगुणेनैव व्योम्नि व्योमत्वमागतम् ॥३॥
स्वयं खपुष्पवच्चास्ते जगद्रूपं फलं ददत् ।
शब्दस्य मापकं मानं किमस्ति जगतीत्रये ॥४॥
निषेधविधिमार्गस्य दर्शनेऽसौ प्रदीपकः ।
कलिलापनदक्षोऽसौ शुभयोर्बंधमोक्षयोः ॥५॥
असौ पतेदविद्यांगे तदाऽसदिति रूढति ।
कपर्दिकात्रयं वापि न लभेत्सत्यवस्तु तत् ॥६॥
शुद्धो शिवशरीरेऽस्मिन्नंदनो जीवभावभृत ।
मंत्रज्ञ इव शब्दोऽयं बंधमोक्षविधायकः ॥७॥
उद्विग्नो देहबन्धेन जीवः शब्देन मोचितः ।
आत्मापि चात्मनः शब्दादैक्यभावेन मीलितः ॥८॥
उदयं दिवसे यातस्तावन्निट्द्रोह आगतः ।
अतः सूर्योऽपि शब्दस्य नोपमानं लभेद् ध्रुवम् ॥९॥
प्रवृत्तिश्च निवृत्तिश्च विरुद्धेऽपि परस्परम् ।
शब्देनैकेन द्वंद्वं तच्चाल्यते तत्करग्रहात् ॥१०॥
स्वयं नश्यन्नात्मविद्यासाहाय्यं यः करोति वै ।
वर्णयामि किमेतस्य शब्दस्यैकैक गौरवम् ॥११॥
किमयं बहुना शब्दः प्रसिद्धः स्मृतिदानतः ।
अथाप्यात्मनि शब्दस्य प्रवृत्तिर्नोपपद्यते ॥१२॥

न किमप्युपयोगित्वं शब्दस्यात्मनि वास्तवम् ।
स्वसंवेद्यस्य कस्यास्ति नोपकारस्तु कस्यचित् ॥१३॥
प्रवर्तेद्विषयत्वेन यः स्मृतेर्विस्मृतेरपि ।
तर्हि यद्वस्तुनो वस्तु द्वितीयं न हि तिष्ठति ॥१४॥
कश्चिदप्यात्मनात्मानं स्मरेद्वा विस्मरेदपि ।
किं जिह्वा स्वयमात्मानं स्वादते स्वादते न वा ॥१५॥
जागरे न हि निद्रास्ति जागरे जागरोऽस्ति किम् ।
तथा वस्तुस्वरूपे स्वे स्मरणास्मरणे न हि ॥१६॥
रविर्निशां न जानाति किंवा जानाति वासरम् ।
स्मरणास्मरणे तद्वद्ध्यमात्मैव केवलम् ॥१७॥
नैवं स्मृत्यस्मृती यत्र स्मारकः किं करिष्यति ।
अतः संवित्स्वरूपेऽस्मिन् शब्दसंचरणं कुतः ॥१८॥
अन्यदेकं परं कार्यं शब्देनानेन सिध्यति ।
परंत्वत्र विचारोऽसौ न बध्नाति च साहसम् ॥१९॥
नश्यत्यविद्या शब्देन पश्चात्स्वेनात्मभासनम् ।
इत्युच्यमाने मूढत्वमागतं खलु वक्तरि ॥२०॥
रात्रिं हन्याद्रविः पश्चात्करिष्यति निजोदयम् ।
व्यलीका किमिमे शब्दा राजेरन्बुधसंसदि ॥२१॥
निद्रायै जागृतं रुष्येदीदृङ् निद्रा क्व तिष्ठति ।
किंवा तज्जागृतं येन जागर्तव्यं भवेत् पुनः ॥२२॥
अतोऽविद्या स्वरूपेण नाशार्हा नहि निश्चितम् ।
आत्मानात्मस्थितिं लब्धुं इच्छेदित्यपि नोचितम् ॥२३॥
अविद्या तु स्वरूपेण वंध्याशावकसंनिभा ।
अतस्तर्काख्यखड्गेन किंवा शब्दस्तु खंडयेत् ॥२४॥
दृश्यमानं शक्रधनुर्यदि सत्यं तथास्ति च ।
को वा धनुर्धरस्तस्मिन्न करोति गुणार्पणम् ॥२५॥
यद्यगस्तितृषायास्तु पूर्णता स्यां मृगांभसा ।
विनाशयेत्तदाऽविद्यां तर्कः कर्कशशब्दभाक् ॥२६॥
शब्दनाशसहाविद्या यदि स्याज्जगतीतले ।

कुलस्तर्हि दहेन्नाग्निर्गंधर्वनगराणि च ॥२७॥
न तिष्ठति क्षणमपि दीपस्याभिमुखं तमः ।
परन्तु किमु तत्रास्ति नाशार्हे वस्तु वास्तवम् ॥२८॥
अथवा वासरं द्रष्टुं क्रियते वर्तिसंचयः ।
लावानपि विमूढस्य एष उद्वस उद्यमः ॥२९॥
यत्र नोत्पततिच्छाया तत्र नास्त्येव सा यथा ।
पतितापि तथा यत्र सा तत्रापि न विद्यते ॥३०॥
दृष्टः स्वप्नोऽस्ति मिथ्येति जागरे ज्ञायते यथा ।
तद्वदविद्याकालेऽपि तस्याः सत्त्वं न विद्यते ॥३१॥
सद्मसंभृतलब्धानि शैलूषाभरणानि तैः ।
किंवा नग्नीकृतं नग्नं को विशेषोऽस्ति तेन च ॥३२॥
मनोरथसदन्नानि भुंजंति बहुवासरम् ।
उपवासादृते नान्यद्युक्तमस्यातिरिच्यते ॥३३॥
मृगांबु यत्र नो भाति तत्रास्त्येव हि शुष्कता ।
अथवा भासने यत्र तत्रास्ति किमु सार्द्रता ॥३४॥
यदि दृश्यमिदं सत्यं तर्हि चित्रघनांबुभिः ।
सिंचंतु मनुजा मूलमारामवनभूरुहाम् ॥३५॥
खलित्वा तमसः पुंजं लिख्यन्तेऽक्षरपंक्तयः ।
तर्हि किं मषिनिर्माणे कर्तव्यः श्रमसंभ्रमः ॥३६॥
नेत्राणि किमु नो सत्यं पश्यंत्याकाशनीलताम् ।
तद्वदविद्यामिथ्यात्वं ज्ञातव्यं किल कोविदैः ॥३७॥
अविद्या निजनाम्नैव नास्ति मे विद्यमानता ।
इति सा स्वमुखेनैव स्वाभावं वक्ति भीरुकान् ॥३८॥
अनिर्वाच्या ह्यविद्या तु स्वाभावविषये पुनः ।
दिव्यं गृह्णाति सा नित्यं तदनिर्वाच्यलक्षणम् ॥३९॥
अस्ति किंचित्स्वतस्तर्हि निश्चयं सहते न किम् ।
यथा घटस्य सद्भावाद्दृश्यते भूमिरंकिता ॥४०॥
अविद्यानाशने तादृङ्न प्रमोदय आत्मनि ।
यथा दिनकरस्यांगे नोदेति तमसोऽस्तिता ॥४१॥

मायाविनी त्वविद्येयं मायात्वं च विलुंपति ।
अभावेनैव स्वीयेन मृषा सत्यत्वमागता ॥४२॥
इत्थं बाहुल्यभावेन नास्त्यविद्या स्वरूपतः ।
कस्योपर्यधुना शब्दः तर्कख्यश्चालयेत् करः ॥४३॥
सबलैस्ताडचमानायां छायायां भूश्च भिद्यते ।
अंतराले हते किंवा हस्तो भवति कुंठितः ॥४४॥
व्यर्थं मृगांबुनः पानं गगनालिंगनं वृथा ।
चुंबनं प्रतिबिंबस्य तद्वत्तर्कविचेष्टितम् ॥४५॥
वृथैव स्यात्तथात्रापि ह्यविद्यानाशने ध्रुवम् ।
प्रवृत्तस्य हि तर्कस्य वेगः शून्यत्वमाप्नुयात् ॥४६॥
अविद्येयं नाशनीया इति यो भावयेद्यदि ।
तेन बुद्धिमता युक्त्या निष्कास्या गगनत्वचा ॥४७॥
गलेऽजा दुह्यतां तेन जानुनेत्रेण दृश्यताम् ।
शुष्कयित्वा संधिवेलां कुर्यात्काचरिकां च सः ॥४८॥
तेन जृंभा पेषणीया निष्पीडच बहु तद्रसम् ।
कालयित्वाऽलसेनैव पाययेद् गोलकं मृदः ॥४९॥
निवर्तयतु कुल्यांबु छायामुद्यातु स स्वकाम् ।
तथैव मरुतस्तन्तून्वेष्टयत्वपि मूढधीः ॥५०॥
स वै बागुलकं हन्तुं प्रतिबिंबं बिभर्तु वा ।
किंवा पाणितले केशान्विनेतुं स प्रवर्तताम् ॥५१॥
घटाभावं स्फोटयतु खपुष्पाण्यवतंसतु ।
विषाणं शशकस्यापि विमोटयतु बालिशः ॥५२॥
कर्पूरस्य मसिं कृत्वा रत्नदीपे च कज्जलम् ।
वंध्यादुहितरं वापि सुखेनोद्वहतु स्वयम् ॥५३॥
सोऽमाचंद्रमसा नित्यं पुष्णात्वतलचक्रकान् ।
मृगांबुजालान्जंतून्वै स पालयतु सर्वदा ॥५४॥
अहो कियद्धि वक्तव्यं अविद्याभावरूपका ।
अधुनानेन शब्देन नाश्यतां कथमीदृशी ॥५५॥
नास्ति यत्तस्य नाशेन शब्दो नैति प्रमाणताम् ।

अंधकारेंऽधकारस्य स्वरूपं न भवेद्यथा ॥५६॥
अविद्या नास्ति जात्यैव पुनस्तद्बाधयुक्तयः ।
अजिरस्था यथा दीपा मध्याह्ने तद्वदास्थिताः ॥५७॥
बीजावापं विनैवादौ कर्तुं क्षेत्रनिकृन्तनम् ।
यान्ति ते बालिशास्तेषां लज्जैवास्ति न चापरा ॥५८॥
पिशाचांगं समारोढुं यश्चिकीर्षति मूढधीः ।
अकुर्वंस्तत्समारोहं तूष्णीं तिष्ठति सद्मनि ॥५९॥
को वा विशेषस्तत्रास्ति वर्षो वर्षन्जलोपरि ।
अविद्यानाशने तर्कसंकल्पस्तु तथा वृथा ॥६०॥
तावद्धि श्लाघते मानं यावदभ्रं न मापयेत् ।
तमो दिदृक्षोर्दीपस्य यथा जन्म निरर्थकम् ॥६१॥
आकाशरसनिष्पन्नमन्नं यदि पिपासति ।
जिह्वा तर्हि रसस्यार्द्ररसनेत्युपनामिका ॥६२॥
अनूढाया वल्लभेन सौभाग्यं किमु शोभते ।
खादिताः कदलीगर्भा न गताः खादिता इव ॥६३॥
स्थूलसूक्ष्मपदार्थेषु कं वा नार्कः प्रकाशयेत् ।
परन्तु रात्रिविषये जात एवाप्रयोजकः ॥६४॥
किं किं न दृश्यते दृष्ट्या परं निद्रां न पश्यति ।
न पश्यति कुतो निद्रा जागृतौ सा न संभवेत् ॥६५॥
उद्यमश्चक्रवाकानां व्यर्थीभवितुमर्हति ।
यदि चंद्रमसं द्रष्टुं प्रवर्तंते दिवैव ते ॥६६॥
अवर्णपत्रसंघस्य वाचको याति मूकतान् ।
गतिमानप्यंतराले गच्छन्पंगुत्वमाप्नुयात् ॥६७॥
इत्थं तर्काभिदो जल्पः सिद्धस्य प्रतिषेधकः ।
अविद्यासंमुखस्तिष्ठन्सद्यो याति निरर्थताम् ॥६८॥
न कुर्यादंधकारं किं कुहूं प्राप्तः सुधाकरः ।
अविद्यानाशने तर्कस्तादृशीं गतिमाप्नुयात् ॥६९॥
अनिष्पन्नेन चान्नेन भोजनं तद्धि लंघनम् ।
दृष्ट्वैव नांधतां याति किं गते नयनद्वये ॥७०॥

नास्ति वस्तुस्वरूपेण शब्दार्थो भवितुं वसेत् ।
तेन कृत्वा निरर्थकत्वात्स्थितः शब्दोऽपि नश्यति ।।७१।।
अविद्या नास्ति नास्तीति कथं वच्मि पुनः पुनः ।
तन्नाशने प्रवृत्तत्वात्स्वयं शब्दोऽपि नश्यति ।।७२।।
अतो ह्यविद्याभिमुखो विचारो यः समुत्थितः ।
अविद्यासहितस्वांगं त्यक्त्वा तिष्ठति लज्जितः ।।७३।।
अतोऽविद्याविनाशेन शब्दः प्रामाण्यमाप्नुयात् ।
स्वनास्तित्वादविद्या न ददाति भवितुं त्विदम् ।।७४।।
आत्मना प्रति वात्मानं शब्दः संदर्श्य गौरवम् ।
यायादित्यपि संप्रोक्तुं विरुद्धं बहुधाचन ।।७५।।
स्वस्योद्वाहः स्वेन साकं भवतीति क्वचिच्छ्रुतम् ।
निजांगं ग्रसते सूर्यः किमेतद् ग्रहणं भवेत् ।।७६।।
किमाकाशो विशेत्स्वस्मिन् सिंधुः सिंधौ समाविशेत् ।
किंवा करतलं स्वस्मिन्नारोहेदतिकौतुकात् ।।७७।।
चराचरांस्तु पानीयं पातुमेति क्षणेन वै ।
पानीयस्य तु पानीयं पातुं कः शक्नुयात्किमु ।।७८।।
एकोऽपि दिवसोऽप्येवं षष्ठ्युत्तरशतत्रये ।
कदाचिदपि सूर्यस्य सूर्यं नेत्रेण दर्शयेत् ।।७९।।
त्रैलोक्यं प्रदहेज्जातु कृतान्तः कुपितो यदि ।
परन्तु वह्निना वह्निं प्रदग्धुं प्रभवेत् किमु ।।८०।।
दर्पणेन विना स्वस्य सम्मुखीभवितुं स्वयम् ।
ब्रह्मापि न हि शक्नोति यद्यपि स्याच्चतुर्मुखः ।।८१।।
परीत्य दृक् दृश्यं पश्येत्किं रुचिं स्वादयेद्रुचिः ।
जागृतं प्रतिभूयः किं जागरीक्रियते किमु ।।८२।।
चंदनश्चर्चयेत् स्वांगं रंगो रंगेन रज्यते ।
किमलंक्रियते मुक्तं मुक्तेनैव कदापि हि ।।८३।।
स्वर्णेन कर्ष्यते स्वर्णं दीपो दीपं प्रकाशयेत् ।
कुत्रापि श्रूयते चैतन्निमज्जेत रसो रसे ।।८४।।
स्वशेखरे शंकरेण चंद्रमा उपवेशितः ।

चंद्रस्य मस्तके चंद्रं किमायात्युपवेशितुम् ॥८५॥
आत्मराजस्तथा तावन्निबिडज्ञानमात्रकः ।
अत आलिंग्यते ज्ञानं ज्ञानेन कथमित्यहो ॥८६॥
ज्ञप्तिमात्रं तथात्मानं वेत्तुं नो वेत्ति यः स्वयम् ।
यथा नेत्रेण नेत्रस्य दुर्लभं स्वीयदर्शनम् ॥८७॥
यद्येव दर्पणः स्वांगे पश्येदात्मानमेकलम् ।
तर्ह्यात्मवेदनं तत्र स्वात्मानं वेत्तुमर्हति ॥८८॥
दिगंतरे स्थितं छिद्याद् धावित्वा छुरिका परम् ।
तथा कृत्वा तदंगं तु कथं भिद्येत कर्हिचित् ॥८९॥
रसान्वै स्वादितुं नाना जिह्वाग्रं चतुरं च यत् ।
परन्तु तन्न जानाति स्वात्मानं स्वादितुं किल ॥९०॥
रसात्मकरसज्ञाया स्वरसास्वादनं न हि ।
इति कृत्वा रसज्ञा सा न भवेदिति नो भवेत् ॥९१॥
स्वतःसिद्धस्तथैवात्मा सच्चिदानन्दरूपकः ।
एवं सत्यात्मकः शब्दः कथं स्यादुपकारकः ॥९२॥
केनचिद्वै प्रमाणेन गृह्यवे वस्तु वा न वा ।
यस्मान्नहि स्वयं स्वस्य वेदनं वाप्यवेदनम् ॥९३॥
आत्मात्मलाभेनात्मानं नंदयित्वा विशेषतः ।
महत्वं आप्य शब्दोयं शोभामेतीति नो भवेत् ॥९४॥
तमोनाशं प्रकाशं वा यथा मध्याह्नदीपिका ।
न करोति तथैव स्यादिह शब्दस्य नोभयम् ॥९५॥
अविद्यायास्तु नास्तित्वात्तस्मान्नाशो न संभवेत् ।
स्वसंवेद्यप्रकाशात्मा कस्तस्य स्यात्प्रकाशकः ॥९६॥
एवं उभयपक्षेऽपि शब्दो भूत्वा निरर्थकः ।
प्रलुप्तोऽभूद्यथा गंगाप्रवाहः प्रलयोदके ॥९७॥
अर्थतस्तर्हि नास्त्येव ययोरस्तित्वसंभवः ।
एवं चेत्तर्हि शब्देन कस्योपरि प्रवृत्तता ॥९८॥
यथा बागुल आयातो वाक्यमेतन्निरर्थकम् ।
यथा वा भूतले व्योम लंबेतेतिवचो वृथा ॥९९॥

रंगरंजितचित्राणि कृत्रिमाणि यथा तथा ।
निरर्थकानि शोभन्ते भूत्वा जल्पानि तान्यपि ॥१००॥
शब्दैकजीवने चैवं ज्ञानाज्ञाने हि फल्गुनी ।
सत्यत्वेन तथा भातश्चित्रार्पितवने यथा ॥१०१॥
विनाशं दुर्दिनं यायादभ्रेण सहितं यथा ।
शब्देनसहितस्तद्वन्महाप्रलयमात्मवान् ॥१०२॥

सप्तमोऽध्यायः

(अज्ञानखण्डनम्)

ज्ञानक्षोभो यदा नासीन्न ह्यज्ञानं तदापि हि ।
वर्णमात्रस्वरूपेण कर्णमूले निलीयते ।।१।।
तमस्यंतर्हितो भूत्वा खद्योतो दीप्तिमावहेत् ।
मृषात्वेन तथाऽज्ञानं भजेदिदमनादिताम् ।।२।।
स्वप्नस्य महिमा स्वप्ने तमसि तमसः प्रथा ।
अज्ञानगरिमा तद्वदज्ञानादितरत्र न ।।३।।
धारासु धर्तुं नायांति जातु कृत्रिमवाजिनः ।
बहुरूपविभूषाभिर्नैति कर्तुमलंक्रिया ।।४।।
वेदनात्मगृहे तावदज्ञानं नोपलभ्यते ।
उत्तिष्ठेत्किमु कौमुद्यां मृगांबुलहरीपयः ।।५।।
ज्ञानं यद्भण्यते साक्षादज्ञानं तद् द्वितीयकम् ।
एकं विलोप्य चैकंतु दर्शितव्यं तथा नु किम् ।।६।।
अस्तु तावत्प्रसंगोऽयं कुर्यामज्ञानशोधनम् ।
तन्निश्चये परिज्ञाते पश्चाज्ज्ञानविनिश्चयः ।।७।।
अज्ञानं तु स्वरूपेण ज्ञानांगे यदि जीवति ।
यत्रास्ति तर्हि तस्यापि नाज्ञानं कुरुते कुतः ।।८।।
अज्ञानेनास्यते यत्र तेनाप्यज्ञेन भूयताम् ।
ईदृग्जातिस्वभावोऽयमज्ञानस्यास्ति सर्वथा ।।९।।
शास्त्रस्य च मतं त्वेवं वसत्यज्ञानमात्मनि ।
तेनैव लभ्यते ह्यात्मा विषयाश्रयभावतः ।।१०।।
अनुत्थिते द्वितीये तु तदा ज्ञानं द्वितीयकम् ।
अस्तीति ज्ञायते केन यद्यज्ञानान्न चेतरत् ।।११।।
अज्ञानं तावदात्मानं न जानाति जडत्वतः ।
प्रमाणं च प्रमाणं तु जानीयात्कथमित्यपि ।।१२।।

एतस्माद्यदि स्वज्ञानं कुर्यादज्ञानमित्यपि ।
वचो वक्तुं विरुद्धत्वाद् वाग्भिर्मौनं समाश्रितम् ॥१३॥
अज्ञानं यदि चात्मानं वितनोति विमूढताम् ।
अज्ञानं ज्ञायते केन विनात्मानं तदा पुनः ॥१४॥
अहो येनात्मपर्याप्तः क्रियते ज्ञानविज्ञकः ।
अज्ञानं भणितुं तत्तु न किं लज्जेत कोविदः ॥१५॥
अभ्रेण ग्रस्यते भानुस्तर्ह्यभ्रं कः प्रकाशयेत् ।
सुषुप्तौ नास्ति सुप्तश्चेत्सैव केनानुभूयते ॥१६॥
आस्ते यत्र यदज्ञानं तदप्यज्ञानतामियात् ।
उभयोरपि तुल्यत्वान्न जानीते परस्परम् ॥१७॥
एकमज्ञानमस्तीति येन निश्चीयते स्वतः ।
कालत्रये तदज्ञानं न भवेदिति निश्चयः ॥१८॥
न भवत्यंधता नेत्रे पटले चागते सति ।
व्यर्थीभूतास्तदा शब्दाः सर्वे पटलवाचिनः ॥१९॥
ज्वलनेंधनसंयोगो न दहेदिंधनं यदि ।
तदग्नेर्दाहिकाशक्तिर्व्यर्थीभवितुमर्हति ॥२०॥
अंधकारं न कुर्याच्चेत्तमः सद्मनि संभृतम् ।
अंधकाराभिधा व्यर्था तदा भवति वाक्पथे ॥२१॥
दद्याज्जागरितुं निद्रा या तां निद्रेति को वदेत् ।
न कुर्याद्दिवसं न्यूनं तर्हि सा रजनी कथम् ॥२२॥
एवमात्मा न मूढः स्यादज्ञाने यदि सत्यपि ।
अज्ञानमिति शब्दस्य मृषात्वं चागतं तदा ॥२३॥
अन्यदपि यदज्ञानं समवस्थातुमात्मनि ।
प्रवक्तुं कारणं न्यायादपेतं वचनं भवेत् ॥२४॥
तमःस्वरूपमज्ञानमात्मा च स्वप्रकाशकः ।
एकत्र सहसंवासः कथं स्यात्तद्विरुद्धयोः ॥२५॥
स्वप्नश्च जागरश्चोभौ स्मरणास्मरणे तथा ।
युग्मे इमे एकपंक्त्या चलतां यदि संगते ॥२६॥
शीतातपौ मिथौ मैत्र्या वसेतामेकवेश्मनि ।

तमसा किमु बध्यंते प्रसह्य रविरश्मयः ॥२७॥
आयात्येकस्थले स्थातुं त्वहोरात्रं विमत्सरम् ।
तदाज्ञानस्य सामर्थ्याच्चिदात्माप्युपजीवतु ॥२८॥
जीवनं चापि मृत्युश्च मिथुनं शोभते यदि ।
तर्ह्यात्मना सहैवास्तामज्ञानं नेति को वदेत् ॥२९॥
आत्मना यच्च बाध्येत तन्नंदेदात्मना सह ।
किमिमानि विरुद्धानि गदिन्तुं वचनान्यहो ॥३०॥
अंधकारः प्रतिज्ञां स्वां हित्वा तेजो भवेद्यदा ।
तदा तेजस्वरूपत्वान्निभ्रान्तः सूर्य एव सः ॥३१॥
त्यक्तं काष्ठेन काष्ठत्वं वह्नित्वेन समाश्रितम् ।
तदा वह्निस्वरूपेण इंधनं तद्विराजते ॥३२॥
सत्यं चान्यप्रवाहत्वं वारिणा गंगया सह ।
समेत्य तत्क्षणेनैव गंगैवाभाति मुक्तिदा ॥३३॥
यद्यज्ञानं न चैवैतत्तर्ह्यात्मत्वेन तिष्ठतु ।
नोचेदज्ञानरूपेण स्थातव्यं स्वस्वरूपतः ॥३४॥
आत्मन्यज्ञानसंसर्गो विरुद्धत्वान्न युज्यते ।
भिन्नत्वेन तु तत्सिद्धिः कदाचिदपि नो भवेत् ॥३५॥
सजीवा सैंधवी मत्स्यी जले वाप्यथवा स्थले ।
न जीवति यथा तद्वत् तदज्ञानं न जीवति ॥३६॥
अज्ञानं यदि नश्येत भासेतात्मा तदैव तु ।
वचांस्येतानि विद्वद्भिः श्रोतव्यानि न तत्वतः ॥३७॥
यः सर्पो भासते रज्जौ स तया किं निबध्यते ।
अथवा न भवेत्तस्य दण्डेनाप्यपसर्पणम् ॥३८॥
तथैवोभयतः शब्दो गतश्चाज्ञानवाचकः ।
कुतर्केन विना वक्तुं नायात्येव स्वरूपतः ॥३९॥
राका तमोदिनभयात्क्षणदां शरणं ययौ ।
तत्रापि विधुना सर्वं ग्रसित्वा नास्तिसात्कृतम् ॥४०॥
प्रत्यक्षं नानुमेयं वा किमज्ञानं स्वरूपतः ।
इदानीमपि तत्च्छुद्धिं गृह्णीमस्तद्विचारतः ॥४१॥

प्रत्यक्षादिप्रमाणैः स्यादज्ञानग्रहणं यदि ।
तदप्यज्ञानकार्यं चेदज्ञानं न भवेत्किमु ॥४२॥
उल्लसंती दृश्यमाना सांकुरा सरला लता ।
तद्बीजं न भवेन्मुख्यं बीजकार्यं तु तद्भवेत् ॥४३॥
दृष्ट्यामारोपते स्वप्नः शुभाशुभस्वरूपतः ।
निद्रया जनितं कार्यं निद्रातुल्यं न तद्भवेत् ॥४४॥
एकचन्द्रे द्विचंद्रत्वं दृश्यते व्योमगे यदि ।
तिमिरस्यैव तत्कार्यं किं नु तत्तिमिरं भवेत् ॥४५॥
प्रमाणत्वं प्रमेयत्वं प्रमातृत्वमिदं त्रयम् ।
अज्ञानस्य च तत्कार्यं नाज्ञानसदृशं भवेत् ॥४६॥
प्रत्यक्षादिप्रमाणानां हेतुरज्ञानमेव च ।
तस्मादज्ञानजन्यत्वादज्ञानं तानि नान्यथा ॥४७॥
अज्ञानकार्यमज्ञानं मन्यते यदि चेद् बुधैः ।
तर्हि तस्य प्रमातापि कृतिस्तस्य न किं भवेत् ॥४८॥
स्वप्ने यद्भाति तत्स्वप्नः किमन्यः स्वप्नदृक् भवेत् ।
तथैवाज्ञानकार्यं चेदज्ञानं केवलं यदि ॥४९॥
अंजनेनांजनं दिग्धं गुडेनास्वादितो गुडः ।
विद्धः शूलश्च शूलेन यथेदमपि तत्तथा ॥५०॥
तथैव कारणाद्भिन्नं कार्यमज्ञानतां भजेत् ।
उभयोरेकरूपत्वात्तर्हि किं केन गृह्यते ॥५१॥
ग्राह्यग्राहकरूपोऽयं विचारो नैति मानसे ।
प्रमाणं च भवेत्तर्हि मृगांबुशफरोपमम् ॥५२॥
प्रत्क्षादिप्रमाणानां नास्ति यद्दृष्टिगोचरम् ।
तस्य चान्यत्खपुष्पस्य को विशेषोऽस्ति मे वद ॥५३॥
प्रमाणं नैति यत्तस्य केनास्तित्वं निरूप्यते ।
अनेनापि विजानीयादज्ञानाभावनिश्चयः ॥५४॥
प्रत्यक्षादिप्रमाणानां न यद्भाजनतां भजेत् ।
अप्रमाणिकमज्ञानं जातं तर्हि स्वभावतः ॥५५॥
नोत्पादयेत्स्वतः कार्यं न वा कारणतामियात् ।

अतो बिभेम्यहं वक्तुं सत्यमज्ञानमित्यपि ॥५६॥
स्वप्नं दर्शयितुं नालं निद्रा आत्मानमस्तु तत् ।
न शक्नोति स्वापयितुं स्वाश्रयं तर्हि सा वृथा ॥५७॥
इदमस्तु यदा ह्यात्मा सन्मात्रो निष्कलोऽमलः ।
यदि तस्मिंस्तदाज्ञानमस्ति चेत्तर्हि मृग्यताम् ॥५८॥
यथैव मथनात्पूर्वं काष्ठे तिष्ठेद् हुताशनः ।
तथैवात्म्यैकभावेन विद्यतेऽज्ञानमात्मनि ॥५९॥
तथैवात्मेति नामापि यदा नास्त्येव केवलम् ।
तदाप्यज्ञानसद्भावः किंनु साध्येत साधुभिः ॥६०॥
दीपं विनैव यत्पूर्वं कज्जली किं निरस्यते ।
अनुत्पन्नतरोश्छायामपनीयेत कर्हिचित् ॥६१॥
अनुत्पन्नतनौ किं स्यादुद्वर्तनविलेपनम् ।
आदर्शेऽघटिते किं तत्परिशुद्धिर्विधीयते ॥६२॥
पयस्यूधस्थिते मस्तु स्यादादौ यदि तद्बहु ।
प्रकाशनविधौ तावद् बुद्ध्या यत्नो विधीयताम् ॥६३॥
तद्वदात्मनि चात्मत्वं यदानास्त्येव केवलम् ।
विद्यते च तदाऽज्ञानं कथं कीदृक् तदुच्यताम् ॥६४॥
अतस्तदापि नाज्ञानमासीदिति विनिश्चितम् ।
इदानीं नास्ति नास्तीति कतिवारं ब्रवीम्यहम् ॥६५॥
ईदृगात्मा यदा स्वीयभावाभावौ न च स्पृशेत् ।
तदानीं विद्यतेऽज्ञानं कीदृक् तत्तु मयोच्यते ॥६६॥
स्फुटित्वा घटनास्तित्वं शतचूर्णं भवेद्यथा ।
किंवा सर्वात्मना यद्वन्मृत्युर्मरणमाप्तवान् ॥६७॥
किं निद्रामागता निद्रा मूर्च्छा मूर्च्छां समागता ।
किमंधकूपे पतिता विश्वस्याप्यंधकारिणी ॥६८॥
अभावः संवलितो रंभागर्भो भग्नोऽथवा किमु ।
किंवा विस्फालितश्चासीदंबरांबरपल्लवः ॥६९॥
मृतस्य गरलं दत्तं मुखं मूकस्य कीलितम् ।
विनापि लिखितं लेख्यं यथैव परिमार्जितम् ॥७०॥
अज्ञानं स्वीयमस्तित्वं क्षणं भुंक्ते तथा मृषा ।

इदानीं तर्हि वस्त्वेव भूत्वा अस्त्वेव केवलम् ॥७१॥
पश्य वंध्या प्रसूते किं भर्जं बीजं प्ररोहति ।
किंवा पश्येदंधकारं सहस्रांशुः स्वतेजसा ॥७२॥
तथैव शुद्धे चिन्मात्रे सर्वतोऽज्ञानशोधनम् ।
कृतं तथापि तत्सत्वं यत्र कुत्रापि न स्फुरेत् ॥७३॥
आलोडितं दुग्धभांडं यद्धि मस्तुविलिप्सया ।
कथं तस्योपलब्धिः स्याद्यदि तत् कलुषीभवेत् ॥७४॥
निद्रां दधामि हस्तेन प्रबुध्येति समुत्थितः ।
तेन सा लभ्यते किंवा स्वरूपेण विनश्यति ॥७५॥
तथैव द्रष्टुमज्ञानं पैशाच्यं ध्रियते कथम् ।
यदा द्रष्टुं प्रवर्तेत तदैवादर्शनं नु किम् ॥७६॥
एवं विचारनगरे युक्तिभिर्बहुशोधितम् ।
परं त्वज्ञानमस्तीति विचारं कोऽपि नावदेत् ॥७७॥
कस्मिंश्चित्समये आत्मन्यथवा भिन्नमात्मनः ।
विचारो निजनेत्राभ्यां पश्येदज्ञानमंजसा ॥७८॥
स्वप्ने न शृणुयान्मानं निर्धारास्यं न लिम्पति ।
अथवा निजशौर्येण निरुक्तिः क्रियते ह्यसौ ॥७९॥
एतावत्सु विभागेषु यद्येकं प्रतिपद्यते ।
तदा तस्यानुस्मरणाद्भवेदज्ञानमार्गणम् ॥८०॥
अमायाश्चंद्रबिंबेन गंधर्वनगरे सभा ।
शशशृंगकृतस्तंभा वंध्यापुत्रेण निर्मिता ॥८१॥
वियत्पुष्पमयी माला वायुतंतुविगुंफिता ।
अर्पिता निजकंठे सा वंध्यायास्तनयोत्सवे ॥८२॥
कच्छपीघृतमादाय वियन्मानेन मीयताम् ।
इत्येते कृतसंकल्पाः किमु सत्या भवन्त्यमी ॥८३॥
अस्माभिरधुना ज्ञानं बहुशः परिशोधितम् ।
सर्वथा नास्ति नास्तीति कति वच्मि पुनः पुनः ॥८४॥
अधुनाऽज्ञाननामापि न स्वप्नेऽपि वदाम्यहम् ।
अन्यदेकं परंत्वस्मिन्विषये स्फुरितं मम ॥८५॥

द्रष्टात्मानं स्वभिन्नं वा न हि द्रष्टृत्वमाप्नुयात् ।
इयदपि निजांगेन यद्वस्तु न लभेत्किल ॥८६॥
तद्वस्तु पुरतो भाति दृश्यं विश्वं सुविस्तृतम् ।
दृश्यत्वेन स्थितं विश्वं द्रष्टृत्वं भजते स्वयम् ॥८७॥
आत्मत्वं संकटं यत्र तत्रैतावत्समुत्थितम् ।
यदुत्थितं तत्प्रत्यक्षं पश्याम पुरतः स्वयम् ॥८८॥
यद्यप्यदृश्यमज्ञानं किं दृश्यमितरत् तथा ।
तस्मादज्ञानसद्भावे दृश्यमेवानुमापकम् ॥८९॥
व्योमगश्चन्द्र एकः सन् द्विगुणी दृश्यते यदा ।
तदा तिमिरमायातं स्वनेत्रे ज्ञायते न किम् ॥९०॥
फलपुष्पान्विता सन्तः पादपा भूमिसंच्छ्रिताः ।
पिबन्त्येव हि पानीयमदृष्टेषु मुखेष्वपि ॥९१॥
पादैः पिबन्ति पानीयं जानीयादिति निश्चितम् ।
तथैवाज्ञानसद्भावो दृश्यादेवानुमीयताम् ॥९२॥
जाग्रतेर्याति निद्रा तां न वेत्ति निद्रितः स्वयम् ।
परंतु स्वप्नतस्तस्या अस्तित्वमनुभूयते ॥९३॥
केवले वस्तुमात्रेऽस्मिन्नेतद् दृश्यं प्रकाशते ।
तदा ह्यज्ञानमस्तीति किं सुखेनैव उच्यताम् ॥९४॥
किमंगैतादृशं ज्ञानमज्ञानं भण्यते त्वया ।
दिवसः कुर्वतः का स्यादंधकारतया भिया ॥९५॥
येन यद्रंजितं वस्तु चन्द्रादपि समुज्ज्वलम् ।
कृतं सुधवलं तत्किं कज्जलं भण्यते बुधैः ॥९६॥
यदि मित्रतया वह्नेः कार्यं निष्पादयेज्जलम् ।
अज्ञानकार्यकं दृश्यं तदा मन्यामहे वयम् ॥९७॥
अमायाः पूर्णमासीव पूर्णं कुर्यां कलानिधिम् ।
ज्ञानमज्ञानमाप्नोति प्राप्नुयात्पात्रतां तदा ॥९८॥
यदि दैवाद् विषं स्वास्मात् प्रस्रवेदमृतं शुभम् ।
तदा तस्य विषं चेति केन वा समुदीर्यताम् ॥९९॥
व्यवहारः प्रवाहोऽयं तद्वज्ज्ञानविजृंभितः ।

आनीयते तत्र पुरः किमज्ञानमृगांबुनः ॥१००॥
अज्ञाननामकं चैतज्ज्ञानं तर्हि किमात्मकम् ।
किमन्यद्वास्तवं किंचिद्विद्यते सच्चिदात्मनि ॥१०१॥
येन किंचिन्न भूयेत भवेत्तद्वेत्ति न स्वतः ।
प्रमाणानां इदं भानशून्यं गंधर्वपत्तनम् ॥१०२॥
अस्तीति भणितुं योग्यं नाचरेद्यन्निजांगतः ।
नास्तीत्यपि वचो वक्तुं योजनीयमपार्थकम् ॥१०३॥
अन्यत्वेन विनैवास्ते भाति यच्चेतरं विना ।
इत्येवं यत्स्वरूपेण वस्तु तन्नास्तिता कथम् ॥१०४॥
सोढं शान्ततया येन मिथ्यावादफलं कृतम् ।
विशेषाणां च सर्वेषां दत्ता पृष्टिश्च सर्वशः ॥१०५॥
येन प्रतीयते निद्रा प्रतिक्रांतापि साक्षिणा ।
स किमेतन्न जानीयान्नाप्नुयाद्दृश्यतां पराम् ॥१०६॥
किं किं न निगमो ब्रूते परं यन्नाम नोदितम् ।
इति किमपि नास्तित्वं येन प्राप्तं समंततः ॥१०७॥
किं न प्रकाशयेत् सूर्यः परमात्मा न दर्शितः ।
वियद्व्याप्ति विना वस्तु किंचित्तिष्ठति किं क्षितौ ॥१०८॥
अहमिति यो गृह्णाति देहमस्थ्यादिसंचयम् ।
जहाति सोऽप्यहकारं पदार्थं स्वयमादरात् ॥१०९॥
बुद्धिर्या लोलुपा बोध्ये परमेनं न बुध्यति ।
एतद्विनान्यसकल्पा भवन्ति मनसोऽपि च ॥११०॥
मुखैरखंडं घर्षन्ति विषयानुखरोपमान् ।
एतान्यपि तदास्वादं न गृह्णान्तींद्रियाण्यतः ॥१११॥
नास्तित्वेन सहास्तित्वं खादित्वा पुरितोदरम् ।
कथं कस्यापि तद्वस्तु सकलं विषयं भवेत् ॥११२॥
स्वस्माप्यविषयं यत्तद् द्रष्टुं केन च शक्यते ।
स्वरसं स्वादितुं नैव शक्नुयाद्रसना यथा ॥११३॥
आस्तामेतदसंख्यानि नामरूपाणि वा पुरः ।
उद्भाव्य चागता विद्या यत्र बिभ्यति सान्वया ॥११४॥

तस्मात्स्वयं मुखं द्रष्टुं न तृप्तिं याति वै क्षुधा ।
अन्यत्किमाविशेत्तत्र केवले सच्चिदात्मनि ।।११५।।
अंतरेव बहिर्मुद्रं कटकं बहिर्निर्मितम् ।
दुरोदरो तथा तद्वन्निर्णयो याति शून्यताम् ।।११६।।
विलंघितुं स्वकां छायां मस्तकांतां य उद्यतः ।
यथा तस्य परिभ्रष्टा मतिर्भवति नान्यथा ।।११७।।
तथा वस्तुस्वरूपेऽस्मिन्ननेकाभिश्च युक्तिभिः ।
इदमित्थं च तच्चेति व्यवस्था सा वृथाश्रमः ।।११८।।
अधुना तत्कथं ब्रूयादत्र शब्दो निवर्तते ।
द्वितीयं दर्शनं तत्र दर्शयेत् किं स्ववैभवम् ।।११९।।
यद्दर्शनबलेनादावचक्षुरंधतां गतः ।
निरस्य पश्चात्किं वस्तु प्राप्नुयाद्दर्शनीयताम् ।।१२०।।
दृश्यत्वमात्मनश्चापि द्रष्टुं न लभते स्वयम् ।
तत्र दृश्यत्वनास्तित्वाद्द्रष्टृत्वमपि हीयते ।।१२१।।
तत्रापि किं कमन्वेति कुतो दृष्टिः परिस्फुरेत् ।
ऐक्येन सहितं सर्वं चिदाकाशे लयं गतम् ।।१२२।।
एतावत्संकटं येन निरस्यैकेन वस्तुना ।
प्रकाशस्य कपाटानि उद्घाटच निहितानि हि ।।१२३।।
सृष्टयो दृश्यजातेषु दर्शनानां समुत्थिताः ।
अधःस्थितं तु चिन्मात्रं समाश्रित्य स्थिताश्च ताः ।।१२४।।
बह्वीभिर्दर्शनर्द्धीभिश्चिच्छेषः संभृतोऽप्ययम् ।
आदर्शे वेद्यरत्नस्य नित्यनूतनमीक्षते ।।१२५।।
क्षणे क्षणे नवीनां च दृश्यबालककंचुकिम् ।
दृष्ट्वा कृत्वा वेष्टयते ह्युदारत्वेन संस्थितः ।।१२६।।
गतक्षणेषु चांगानि मत्वा पर्युषितानि च ।
संत्यज्य तानि वेगेन दृष्टिः पश्यति नूतनम् ।।१२७।।
प्रतिक्षणं तथैवं यो ज्ञातृत्वाभरणानि च ।
धृत्वा स्वचेतसि प्रीत्या स्वस्मिन्ज्ञातृत्वमुद्वहेत् १२८।।
यत्रात्मपदशेषस्य नावकाशोऽस्ति किंचन ।

तथा सत्यपि येनैवं कृतं कटिनिबंधनम् ॥१२९॥
चिन्मात्रमुखपर्यन्तं सर्वज्ञत्वस्थितं च यत् ।
परन्त्वन्यगृहे तत्तु ज्ञातुं नैव च शक्यते ॥१३०॥
तूष्णीमभूद्यत्र सर्वं ज्ञानं चाज्ञानमेव च ।
दृश्यत्वेन तदप्यात्मदृष्टिगोचरतामगात् ॥१३१॥
पश्यति प्रथमं दृश्यं द्रष्टृत्वेन वितुष्यति ।
तच्च दर्शनरूपेण स्थितं मध्ये प्रभासते ॥१३२॥
घटति ग्रहणं दानं त्वैक्यतंतुर्न त्रुट्यति ।
दर्पणेन कृतं भाति मुखं तद्द्वितीयं न हि ॥१३३॥
यथा स्वांगेषु स्वांगेन जाग्रतो निद्रितोऽपि वा ।
अभिन्नो न भवेत्तद्वद्ग्रह आदानमेव च ॥१३४॥
वीचिव्याजेन पानीयमात्मन्न्युल्लसते तथा ।
तद्वद्वस्तुनि वस्त्वैव खेलते स्वसुखेन च ॥१३५॥
गुंफिता ज्वालमाला च धृता यद्यपि वह्निना ।
तथापि भिन्नतां प्राप्ता किमसौ स्वस्वरूपतः ॥१३६॥
किं रश्मिपरिवारेण महता वेष्टितोऽप्यसौ ।
तथापि रश्मिसंघातैर्भिन्नः सूर्यः किमुच्यते ॥१३७॥
चंद्रकांत्या तु चंद्रोऽसौ वेष्टितो बहुशोऽप्यसौ ।
न्यूनत्वं चंद्रभावस्य किमायातं वदस्व नः ॥१३८॥
दलानां तु सहस्रेण पंकजं विस्तृतं भवेत् ।
तथापि पंकजे नास्ति द्वितीयो भासकश्च न ॥१३९॥
सहस्रं बाहवः सन्ति कार्तवीर्यशरीरिणि ।
तथापि किं विभक्तोऽभूदेकोत्तरसहस्रकः ॥१४०॥
प्रसृताः शंकुसंघेषु बहवः सूत्रपुंजकाः ।
परं तंतुं विना नास्ति द्वितीयो भाव एव हि ॥१४१॥
कोटिशः शब्दसंघाता वाङ्निकेतेन चागताः ।
वाग्जालेन विना किंचित्वर्तते न हि किंचन ॥१४२॥
दृश्यदर्शनका भेदास्तथोद्भूता ह्यनेकधा ।
द्रष्ट्रा विभक्तास्तैरेव द्रष्टैव त्रिविधः स्मृतः ॥१४३॥

गुडस्य गोठको यद्वत्स्फुटित्वा द्विविधाभवत् ।
तथापि गुडसंभिन्नो नो भवेद्गुड एव सः ॥१४४॥
यथेदं दृश्यजातं तु पश्यन्नानाविधोस्तु सः ।
परन्तु भिन्नतायाश्च विषयो नैव सैव सः ॥१४५॥
तस्यात्मनश्च शब्दस्य रेखासौ नापतद्वयी ।
यदि विश्वसमग्रेऽस्मिन्संभृतः समवस्थितः ॥१४६॥
द्विबंधे पट्टकूले तु रूपलावण्यसंपदः ।
नानाविधा हि दृश्यंते न ह्यनेके च तंतवः ॥१४७॥
अनुद्घाटच स्वपक्ष्माणि समग्रा दृष्टिरात्मनि ।
सावकाशतया सृष्टिं द्रष्टुं प्रलभते यदि ॥१४८॥
मध्ये बीजं त्वनास्फोटच वटो विस्तृततामियात् ।
तर्ह्यद्वैतविभागस्य संघटेदुपमा ह्यसौ ॥१४९॥
द्रष्टव्यो न मयात्मेत्येवमुद्वहते गृहम् ।
तर्हि स्वांगस्य शयने विश्रांतो भवति ध्रुवम् ॥१५०॥
पक्ष्मणां जायमाने च मीलने दृष्टिरात्मनः ।
उदरे विश्य चैवास्ते परज्ञानविवर्जिता ॥१५१॥
संभृतः सागरो यद्वन्नोद्गते च सुधाकरे ।
कमठी गिलते यद्वत्स्वांगविस्तारमात्मनि ॥१५२॥
अमावस्यातिथौ यद्वच्छशी सप्तदशांशके ।
प्रविश्य तिष्ठते स्वेन रूपेणान्यन्न दृश्यते ॥१५३॥
तथा दृश्यं गतो जेतुं द्रष्टा लभति जैतताम् ।
दृश्यतायाः प्रलापोऽपि वर्तते द्रष्टरि ध्रुवम् ॥१५४॥
सहजेनैव सर्वं च तर्हि कः किं प्रपश्यति ।
तद्धि दर्शनमेवास्ति स्वस्वरूपस्य निद्रता ॥१५५॥
अहमेवात्मनात्मानं पश्येयं नेतरद्बहु ।
तर्ह्यात्मनात्मविषयः सहजेनैव वर्तते ॥१५६॥
दृश्यं यत्तु पुराणेन दृश्यत्वेन ह्यनादिमत् ।
प्रस्तुतं किमिदं केन रचितुं गम्यते वद ॥१५७॥
गगनस्यावकाशेन स्यंदेन पवनस्य च ।

दीप्त्या च तपनस्यापि संबंधः क्रियते किमु ॥१५८॥
विश्वं पश्येत्पुरस्तर्हि चेद्विश्वत्वेन भासते ।
अथवा नास्ति चेत्तर्हि नास्तित्वमपि पश्यति ॥१५९॥
विश्वस्यास्तित्वनास्तित्वे निमग्ने यदि कालतः ।
तथाप्येतामपि दशां पश्यत्येव हि केवलाम् ॥१६०॥
कर्पूरस्यापि शुभ्रत्वं वर्तते न परंतु सः ।
तेन लिप्तस्तथैवेदं दर्शनं हि स्थले स्थलम् ॥१६१॥
बहुना किं प्रलापेन वाक्श्रमेणैव केवलम् ।
कस्यामपि दशायां वै वस्त्वात्मानं प्रपश्यति ॥१६२॥
देशान्तरं मनस्यैव कल्पयित्वा यथारुचि ।
ततस्तस्मिन्सादरोऽसावटते मानुषो यथा ॥१६३॥
नेत्रसंघटितो नेत्रः स्वस्मिन् चित्राकृति दधन् ।
स्फुरेच्छुद्धस्वरूपत्वाद्विस्मयःक इहोच्यताम् ॥१६४॥
अत एवैकचिद्रूपे स्वात्मनात्मानमीक्षते ।
आरोपेणात्र किं कार्यं वर्तते तद्वद स्वतः ॥१६५॥
कान्तेः प्रावरणं कोऽपि रत्नस्य कुरुते किमु ।
हेम्ना हेमत्वं मार्जित्वा स्वात्मालंक्रियते नु किम् ॥१६६॥
सौरभं चंदनं वेष्टि सुधा स्वं परिवेषयेत् ।
स्वादुतां वा गुडः स्वीयां स्वादयेदित्यमस्ति किम् ॥१६७॥
कर्पूरस्योज्ज्वलत्वं वा पुटतः साधितं किमु ।
वह्नि निरुष्णः कृतः किन्तु तापयित्वाथवा वद ॥१६८॥
यथा लता स्ववल्लीभिर्वेष्टिता स्वस्वभावतः ।
कुरुते भवनं दिव्यमनायासेन केवलम् ॥१६९॥
प्रभासमुद्भवे दीपप्रकाशः सहजो यथा ।
चैतन्येन गृहीतः सन् चिद्रूपः स्फुरते तथा ॥१७०॥
स्वयमेवात्मना स्वीयमीक्षणं कुरुते विभुः ।
परं कर्तव्यताहीनं केवलं स्वस्वभावतः ॥१७१॥
इत्येतद्दर्शनं चादर्शनं ज्योत्स्नातमाविव ।
न्यूनं चंद्रमसः किंनु द्वाभ्यां वा स्फुरते खलु ॥१७२॥
तस्मादिदं न भवतामिति चेत् कर्तुमुद्यतः ।

तर्ह्यसौ स्वस्वभावेन तथैवास्तेऽप्रयासतः ॥१७३॥
द्रष्टा दृश्यमिति द्वैतं किंचित्संदृश्यते यदि ।
परस्परप्रवेशेन न किंचिदपि तत्तदा ॥१७४॥
दृश्यं द्रष्टरि द्रष्टा च दृश्ये प्रविशते यदा ।
मध्ये द्वयं न भूत्वा तु शिष्येत् सत्यत्वमेतयोः ॥१७५॥
ततः कुत्र कदाचिद्वा मध्यस्थं द्रष्टृदृश्ययोः ।
मेलने कृतमात्रं स्यात्तदप्यद्वयमित्युत ॥१७६॥
कर्पूरेऽग्निः प्रविष्टः किं कर्पूरो वह्निमाविशत् ।
तथा न समसाम्येन व्ययो जातः किलैतयोः ॥१७७॥
एकैकयोर्व्ययो जातः शून्यं शून्येन मार्जितम् ।
यथा तथैव भवति मेलने द्रष्टृदृश्ययोः ॥१७८॥
बहुना किं स्वबिंबेन बाहुयुद्धे कृते नरः ।
प्रलीनो भवते युद्धसंरंभसहितो यथा ॥१७९॥
तथा रुष्टा यदा दृष्टिर्द्रष्टृदृश्ये मिथस्तराम् ।
स्वजेते हि द्वयोरैक्यं तदा संभवते खलु ॥१८०॥
तावत्पूर्वापरौ सिंधू यावन्नैकीबभूवतुः ।
यदैक्यभावमापन्नौ तदा नीरं यथैकलम् ॥१८१॥
बहुधैवं भवत्येव त्रिपुटी व्यवहारतः ।
सर्वदा चाप्रयासेन क्षणक्षणविलक्षणा ॥१८२॥
गिलित्वा तु विशेषौ नो निर्विशिष्टं निगीलितम् ।
मेषोन्मेषैकनेत्रे तु वस्त्वेवैतन्न संशयः ॥१८३॥
पक्ष्मणा मिलते पक्ष्म द्रष्टृत्वं द्रवते तदा ।
तयोरुन्मेषणे तत्तु यात्यस्तमिति विस्मयः ॥१८४॥
द्रष्टृदृश्ये यदा ग्रस्ते तदोल्लेखोऽस्ति योन्तरा ।
तस्य प्रकाशका योगभूमिका गर्जते गृहे ॥१८५॥
यत्रोत्थितस्तरंगस्तु तिष्ठन्नग्रेऽपि नो भवेत् ।
तत्र स्थले यथा नीरं स्वस्वरूपेण राजते ॥१८६॥
अथवा विगता निद्रा जागृतिर्नैव चागता ।
यदा तदा स्वकीया तु संस्थितिर्नु भवेद्यया ॥१८७॥

एकस्मादुत्थिता स्थानादन्यत्र न भवेत्स्थिता ।
तथेदं भाति वै दृष्टेः पश्यतो मे यथार्थतः ॥१८८॥
दिनस्त्वस्तं गतो रात्रिर्न करोति प्रसारताम् ।
गगनेन ह्यसौ भावः कथितः सायमित्युत ॥१८९॥
मग्नः श्वासो गृहीतः सन् नोत्थितः पुनरप्यसौ ।
द्वाभ्यां स्पृष्टस्तथार्थो यो न भवत्येव कर्हिचित् ॥१९०॥
समग्रैरिंद्रियैः कायविषयग्रहणं ननु ।
कृतमात्रे यथा तस्मिन्ननुभूतिस्तथा भवेत् ॥१९१॥
तेन तुल्यमिदं स्थानमयं निष्कर्षतः खलु ।
आत्मभावस्त्वनेनाथ द्रष्टुं चाद्रष्टुमाप्यते ॥१९२॥
आदर्शः स्वीयभूम्यां वा स्वात्मशोभानिरीक्षणम् ।
कर्तुमप्यथवाकर्तुं शक्तो भवति किं स्वयम् ॥१९३॥
संमुखं विमुखं वापि भवते मुखमात्मनः ।
यद्यादर्शो वर्ततेऽग्रे न चेन्नोभयसंभवः ॥१९४॥
रविः सर्वांगसंदृश्यः परं त्वेतद् घटेत किम् ।
उदयास्तरुचिं स्वीयां गृह्णीयाद्धि स्वयं कथम् ॥१९५॥
रसः प्राश्येत्किमात्मानं लापयित्वाथवा मुखम् ।
तिष्ठते किमु तस्येदं रसत्वेन यथा न हि ॥१९६॥
दर्शनादर्शने नैव दर्शनत्वेन वेत्त्यसौ ।
परं द्वयमनेनेदं स्वेनैवेहास्यते खलु ॥१९७॥
यस्माद्दर्शनमेवासौ दर्शनं स्वेन तस्य न ।
तस्माददर्शनं चासावनायासेन वर्तते ॥१९८॥
स्वदर्शनं कथमिति स्वेन द्रष्टुं यदि स्थितः ।
तर्हि दर्शनमेवास्ते स्वयमेव ह्यसौ पुनः ॥१९९॥
स्वयं परस्परेणेदं एकपंक्त्या च नंदति ।
एकमेकेन बाधित्वान्नास्त्यैतत् कृतमित्यहो ॥२००॥
दर्शनं दर्शनस्यास्ते तर्हि नोऽदर्शनं त्विदम् ।
तस्माद् अस्य प्रवृत्ति द्वे कदाप्यद्धा न बोधतः ॥२०१॥
दर्शनादर्शने मुष्ट्वा आसनं खल्विदं मतम् ।

अथवा पश्यते तर्हि केन किं वीक्षितं वद ॥२०२॥
दृष्टेन दृश्यभासेन दृष्टमित्युच्यतां न चेत् ।
तर्हि दृश्यादिदं दृश्येतेत्थं न भवति ध्रुवम् ॥२०३॥
दृश्यं दृश्ये भवेत्तत्तु सत्यं द्रष्टरि वर्तते ।
प्रस्तुतं नास्ति तद्दृष्टं कथमाकाशपुष्पवत् ॥२०४॥
दर्पणे पश्यतु मुखं मुखत्वेऽस्ति परंतु तत् ।
दर्पणस्था प्रतीतिः सा तर्हि जातैव किं वृथा ॥२०५॥
द्रष्टैवात्मानमायांत्या निद्रायाः पाणिना स्वयम् ।
तेन स्वप्नेन सदृशं वीक्षतेऽत्र न कर्हिचित् ॥२०६॥
निद्रितः शिबिकामध्ये वाह्यतेऽन्यैः स्ववाहकैः ।
परंत्वेतावतीं सत्यां दशामाप्नोत्यसौ किमु ॥२०७॥
विनैव शिरसा कश्चित्कश्चिद्रंकोऽपि भूपतिम् ।
स्वात्मानं पश्यति स्वप्ने तद्वत्सत्यं किमेतयोः ॥२०८॥
सैव निद्रा यदा नास्ति तदा यो यत्स्थले यथा ।
तथैवास्ते तदा स्वप्नैर्न किंचिदपि दर्श्यते ॥२०९॥
तृषार्तस्य यदा नास्ति मृगतोयसमागमः ।
श्रमस्तदा यदा लब्धं तदाप्तं केन किं वद ॥२१०॥
छायैवापादिता येन सहायार्थमथात्मनः ।
तस्य मूढस्य करणं खलु जातं वृथा यथा ॥२११॥
तथैवानेन दृश्येन द्रष्टारं दर्शनं हि तत् ।
दर्शयित्वा कृतं व्यर्थं दर्शितव्यमपि ध्रुवम् २१२॥
दृश्यमास्ते द्रष्टरि तद्दर्शितव्यं सहेत्कुतः ।
न दर्शितं हितस्येदं न भवेद्दर्शनं किमु ॥२१३॥
न दृष्टो मुकुरस्तर्हि मुखं किं स्यान्निरर्थकम् ।
न हि किन्तु विना तेनाप्यात्मन्येवास्ति सर्वदा ॥२१४॥
तथैव ह्यात्मनात्मानं माया नो दर्शयेद्यदि ।
तर्ह्यात्मैव तथा किंवा सैव मिथ्येति मे वद ॥२१५॥
द्रष्टा तु स्वयमेवास्ते न कृतोऽपि स्वदर्शकः ।
अधुना जात एवासौ किं कर्तव्यं स्वरूपदृक् ॥२१६॥

पुनरुक्तं तदा जातं पुनः संदर्शितं यदा ।
अनेनापि हि शब्देन दर्शितव्यं वृथागतम् ।।२१७।।
सत्यत्वेन यथा रज्जुराभासे रज्जुसर्पयोः ।
द्रष्टृदृश्योस्तथा भेदे द्रष्टा सच्छब्दभाक् ध्रुवम् ।।२१८।।
दर्पणेन मुखेनाथ मुखं संदृश्यते जनैः ।
परं मुखे मुखं सत्यं दर्पणे नास्ति सर्वथा ।।२१९।।
द्रष्टृदृश्यद्वये सत्यस्तथा द्रष्टैव केवलम् ।
तस्माद्दृष्टमपि दृश्यं व्यर्थमेव विभाति वै ।।२२०।।
व्यर्थं भवतु नामेदं परं त्वास्तेऽक्षिगोचरम् ।
अनेनाक्षेपवाक्येन दृश्यमस्तीति चेद्ब्रुवेत् ।।२२१।।
तर्ह्यन्यदन्यं संदृश्य भवते दर्शकं यदि ।
मंतुमायाति तर्ह्येदमस्माभिर्दृष्टमित्यहो ।।२२२।।
पश्यत्वत्र न वा पश्यत्वैकं नानात्वमस्तु वा ।
परंत्वसौ विना स्वेन किं पश्यति वदस्व नः ।।२२३।।
मुखेनैव मुखं दृष्टं यदप्यादर्शदर्शितम् ।
यदा न दर्शितं तेन तदपि स्यान्मुखे मुखम् ।।२२४।।
यदा दर्शयिता नास्ति तदाप्यात्मा स्वमात्मनि ।
यदा दर्शयिता चास्ते तदाप्यात्मनि वर्तते ।।२२५।।
जाग्रत्या दर्शितः स्वस्मिन्निद्रयापादितोऽथवा ।
पुरुषः पुरुषत्वे स्वे परं त्वास्ते यथैकलः ।।२२६।।
गद्यापि त्वं नृपोऽसीति प्रत्ययो नैव दर्शितः ।
तथापि नृपतिः स्वीये नृपत्वे राजतेतराम् ।।२२७।।
राजत्वमथवा राज्ञो नानीतं प्रत्ययाय चेत् ।
तथापि तस्मिन्न्यूनत्वं किमायातं वदस्व तत् ।२२८।।
तथायं दर्शितं नो वा दर्शितः स्वस्वरूपतः ।
न वर्धते हीयते वा किं त्वास्ते पूर्ववत्स्वयम् ।।२२९।।
निमित्तव्याजतस्तर्हि तिष्ठेद्दर्शयितुं स्वयम् ।
द्रष्टा नास्ति तदादर्शा द्रष्टव्याः केन भण्यताम् ।।२३०।।
दीपो दर्शयितारं किं दीपं दर्शयिताकरोत् ।

निमित्तमत्र सत्तायं स्यादनेनैव विनिश्चितम् ।।२३१।।
वह्निः ज्वालयते वह्नेः शिखैव खलु सद्भवा ।
असत्यग्नौ शिखाजन्मप्रत्ययो हि कथं भवेत् ।।२३२।।
वक्तव्यं यन्निमित्तं तदनेनादर्श्यते ध्रुवम् ।
दृष्टं तर्हि स्वभावेन दृश्यमप्ययमेव हि ।।२३३।।
तस्मादेनं स्वप्रकाशमात्मना द्रष्टुमंजसा ।
विनानेन निमित्तं वै नास्ति नास्त्येव कुत्रचित् ।।२३४।।
केनाप्यसौ प्रकारेण दृश्यमेवं सदर्शनः ।
विनानेन किमप्यत्र नास्तीति कति वच्मि वै ।।२३५।।
अलंकारः सुवर्णं च स्वर्णमेव विनिश्चितम् ।
यस्मात्तत्र द्वितीयं वै नास्त्यैवान्यत् सुवर्णतः ।।२३६।।
जलं विना तु नास्त्येव द्वयं जलतरंगयोः ।
तस्मादन्यत्किमप्यत्र नास्ति वा नो भवेद् ध्रुवम् ।।२३७।।
दृश्योऽनुमेयो ग्राह्यश्च दृष्टिघ्राणकरैः क्रमात् ।
भवतामथ केनापि प्रकारेणेंद्रियैर्ग्रहः ।।२३८।।
परंतु नास्ति कर्पूरे विना कर्पूरभावतः ।
तथा कयापि रीत्यासौ स्वस्यास्ते स्वयमेव हि ।।२३९।।
दृश्यतां दृश्यभावेन द्रष्टा भूत्वास्तु चाथवा ।
परं त्विमं निवाह्यात्र नास्त्येवातिशयः परः ।।२४०।।
गंगात्वेनावहग्दंगा सिंधुर्भूत्वाऽथवा स्थिता ।
पानीयत्वे तथाप्यापि पश्यामो नान्यथा वयम् ।।२४१।।
घनीभूतं द्रुतं वेदं सर्वमेवाप्रयोजकम् ।
घृतत्वं च भवत्येवाभिन्नं स्वघृतभावतः ।।२४२।।
ज्वालेयं ज्वलनश्चायम् इति द्वैतं न भाव्यते ।
यस्मादिदं द्वयं वह्निमात्रमेव न चान्यथा ।।२४३।।
तथा दृश्यं च द्रष्टेति वंध्यमेतद्दृशाद्वयम् ।
विचारेणेक्षमाणे तु स्फूर्तिमात्रः स एकलः ।।२४४।।
स्फूर्त्या न जातु नास्त्येव विना वै स्फूर्तिमात्रतः ।
विलोक्य तर्हि किं चान्यत्पश्यतीति वदाधुना ।।२४५।।

नाग्रे प्रसरते दृश्यं पश्चाद् द्रष्टा न पश्यति ।
विचारेणेक्षमाणे तु द्रष्टा दृश्यं स्वयं स्फुटम् ॥२४६॥
कल्लोलेन जलं क्षिप्तं स्वर्णं स्वर्णेन प्रावृतम् ।
दृष्टिरूपास्तदा पादा दृष्टैरेव विमिश्रिताः ॥२४७॥
श्रुतिः संमीलिता श्रुत्या दृत्या संमीलिता दृतिः ।
तृप्त्यैव सा तथा तृप्तिः केनापि परिवेषिता ॥२४८॥
स्वर्णेन मण्डितो मेरुर्गुडसत्कारितो गुडः ।
ज्वालाभिरथवा स्वाभिर्वेष्टितः पावको यथा ॥२४९॥
किमिदं बहु वक्तव्यं नभसः शयनं नभः ।
स्याच्चेत्केन प्रसुप्तव्यं केन वा जागृयादिह ॥२५०॥
दृष्टोऽप्यनेन भवति न दृष्ट इव वस्तुतः ।
अदृष्टोऽपि तथैवायं स्वयं दर्शनमेव यत् ॥२५१॥
वक्तृत्वं नात्र सहते नालं ज्ञातृत्वमत्र च ।
शक्नोत्यनुभवेनापि स्वांगं प्रख्यापितुं किल ॥२५२॥
तस्मादेनमनेनैव प्रकारेणावलोकयेत् ।
विलोक्य वापि केनापि न किंचिद्वै विलोकितम् ॥२५३॥
बहूक्तेन किमात्मैवमात्मनैव प्रकाशते ।
अचेताश्चेतयितुमातिष्ठते स्वस्य वै स्वयम् ॥२५४॥
स्वदर्शनविधाः सर्वाः गच्छन्त्येव विकाशताम् ।
परं निजात्मतत्त्वं हि भङ्क्त्वा न तु कदाचन ॥२५५॥
न दृष्ट्वा स्थातुमादर्शं चेदिच्छेत्तर्हि दर्शनम् ।
भवत्येव च पश्यंश्चेद्दर्शनादर्शने गते ॥२५६॥
विस्तृतः कथमप्यास्ते त्वेकत्वं न विमुञ्चति ।
अथवा संक्षिपेत् तर्ह्यप्ययमेवाखिलं भवेत् ॥२५७॥
सूर्यहस्तेऽन्धकारो वै नायात्येव कदाचन ।
प्रकाशस्य कथा तत्र शृणुते किमसौ रविः ॥२५८॥
प्रकाशोऽयं तमश्चेदमिति भावनया विना ।
एकाक्येव यथा सूर्यो यत्र कुत्राऽपि दृश्यते ॥२५९॥
यथासुखमयं भूमिमारूढोऽपि हि कौतुकात् ।

परं त्वेनमसौ नैवान्तरितः स्यात्कदाचन ॥२६०॥
सिंधुसीमा न संभग्ना पानीयत्वेऽपि नान्तरम् ।
पतन्तोऽपि हि संभग्नास्तरंगा वै सहस्रशः ॥२६१॥
रश्मयः सन्ति सूर्ये वै परं बिंबाद्बहिर्गताः ।
तस्मादुद्बोधसंपत्तेरुपमेया भवन्ति न ॥२६२॥
कार्पासस्य फलं यावद्विदीर्णं नैव जायते ।
तावन्न संभृयादेव जगत्पटविभावने ॥२६३॥
सुवर्णगोल एवैकोऽवयवेष्वखिलेषु वै ।
भूषणं न भवत्येव विनालंकारभावतः ॥२६४॥
नास्फालितान्तरायो हि दिगन्तान्न दिगन्तरम् ।
प्राप्तुं शक्नोत्यसौ वायुस्तस्मादुपमितो न सः ॥२६५॥
तस्मादत्रोपमेयं वै विद्यते नात्मलीलया ।
इदानीमयमेवास्योपमेयोऽनुभवेद् ध्रुवम् ॥२६६॥
स्वप्रकाशोदनग्रासैर्बहुधा जैमितोऽप्यसौ ।
व्ययो नान्तः परं कुक्षौ वलिर्न पततेतराम् ॥२६७॥
एवं निरुपमो ह्यात्मा स्वविलासैः स्वयं स्फुटम् ।
शास्त्यसौ स्वप्रकाशाख्यं राज्यमप्रतिबंधकम् ॥२६८॥
तदुच्यतेऽज्ञानमिति तर्हि नीतिर्गता वनम् ।
अधुनाभ्युपगच्छामो ज्ञानं तस्येति चेद्वचः ॥२६९॥
ज्ञापकं ह्यात्मनोऽज्ञानमिति चेद्भण्यते सुखम् ।
भण्यतां निधिमादर्शेत्तत्किं नाञ्जनमुच्यते ॥२७०॥
सुवर्णगौरा कालीति भण्यते नांबिका किमु ।
तथैवाज्ञानवादोऽयं स्वप्रकाशात्मनः खलु ॥२७१॥
याश्चाशिवात्पृथिव्यंतं तत्त्वनानात्वभावनाः ।
यस्य रश्मिभिरायांति सोज्वलत्वं हि सोज्वलैः ॥२७२॥
स ज्ञानमभवद् ज्ञानं दृङमात्रं दृष्टिभासवत् ।
प्रकाशस्य हि दीपं तु प्रकाशश्चापि पश्यति ॥२७३॥
तदेतत्केन विदुषाऽज्ञानांगुल्या प्रदर्शितम् ।
निबद्धः केन मूर्खेण तमसा रविरंशुमान् ॥२७४॥

ज्ञानाक्षरेष्वपूर्वेषु ज्ञानस्यैव महत्त्वता ।
शब्दार्थस्योज्ज्वलत्वं तु न भवेत्किमपूर्वकम् ।।२७५।।
लाक्षामंजूषमध्येऽग्नेर्निवेशः संभवेत्कथम् ।
प्रसृतोऽन्तर्बहिस्तस्य स्वसमं कुरुते क्षणात् ।।२७६।।
तस्माज्ज्ञानं जगद्रूपं भण्यतेऽज्ञानरूपतः ।
तर्ह्यंत्राणि विकीर्णानि वाचः कृत्वा विडंबनम् ।।२७७।।
अक्षरैर्गोवधो येन पुरोऽप्यनृतबाधता ।
सदोषोऽज्ञानवादोऽयं ज्ञाने किं क्रियतेतराम् ।।२७८।।
अज्ञानमिति चाभाषा स्फुरतेऽर्थतयैव हि ।
इदानीं ज्ञानमेवैतदिति नो केन मन्यते ।।२७९।।
अस्त्वेतदात्मभूपोऽयं स्वयमेव स्वतेजसा ।
वीक्षत आत्मानमेवेत्थं प्रकारैर्बहुलैरपि ।।२८०।।
निरुक्तं सानुमानं यत्तदेवाप्तं विलोचनैः ।
लोचनाग्रे मिलद्यच्च तदेवाप्तं हितस्य वै ।।२८१।।
इत्यस्ति यज्जगज्ज्ञानं तेनाज्ञानं प्रसूयते ।
चेदनेनानुमानेन ज्ञानास्तित्वं प्रतीयते ।।२८२।।
तर्ह्यज्ञानं तु नास्तीति जगतैव व्यवस्थितम् ।
यद्धर्मिधर्मभावोऽयं तयोर्नास्त्येव कर्हिचित् ।।२८३।।
प्रसूवीत जलं मुक्तां दीपः प्राणिति भस्मना ।
तर्हि ज्ञानं भवेद्धर्मो ह्यज्ञानस्य न चान्यथा ।।२८४।।
इंदोर्भवति चेज्ज्वाला आकाशं च भवेत् शिला ।
तर्ह्यज्ञानमिदं शुद्धं स्वरूपं ज्ञानमावहेत् ।।२८५।।
क्षीराब्धौ कालकूटं तु वर्तते कटुभावतः ।
सुधाभावो विषे यद्वज्ज्ञानाभावो तथा नरे ।।२८६।।
ज्ञानेऽज्ञाने जातमात्रे तदज्ञानं वृथा गतम् ।
पुनरप्येकलं ज्ञानमज्ञानं नास्ति सर्वथा ।।२८७।।
तस्मात्सूर्यसमः सूर्यश्चंद्रश्चंद्रसमस्तथा ।
दीपकस्योपमानं तु दीप एव न चेतरत् ।।२८८।।
प्रकाशो यः प्रकाश्यं स नान्यथेदं कदाचन ।

तस्माज्जगदिदं सर्वं वस्त्वाभासो न संशयः ॥२८९॥
यस्य भासा सर्वमिदं विभातीति वृथैव किम् ।
ददत्युद्गारमात्मीयं श्रुतयोऽनुभवामृतम् ॥२९०॥
तस्माद्वस्तुप्रकाशेन वस्त्वेव खलु शोभते ।
लाभाय चापितस्यैव भवते नेतरस्य वै ॥२९१॥
विनैव वस्तुनात्मानं प्रकाशयितुमंजसा ।
अज्ञानहेतवः सर्वे वृथा भूत्वा व्रजन्ति वै ॥२९२॥
तस्मादज्ञानसद्भावो न प्रकारेण केनचित् ।
लभ्यतेऽतः श्रमेणालं मार्गणं तस्य वै वृथा ॥२९३॥
अंधकारकलांशोऽपि लभ्यते न विवस्वता ।
गतेनाप्यालयं रात्रेस्तद्वदज्ञानमार्गणम् ॥२९४॥
वस्त्रांचले निबध्नामि निद्रामीत्युद्यमे कृते ।
जागृतिर्निर्गता पाणौ स्थितोऽयं प्रत्युतैकलः ॥२९५॥

अष्टमोऽध्यायः

(ज्ञानखण्डनम्)

तथास्मदभिधानेनाज्ञानस्य ज्ञानता नहि ।
अस्मासु वयमेव स्मः कृतं सद्गुरुणा खलु ॥१॥
वयं नः कथमित्थं वै द्रष्टुं गच्छामहे यदा ।
किं कर्तव्यं हि तत्स्थाने केवलं यत्तु लज्जते ॥२॥
एतावत्स्थानपर्यन्तं गुरुनाथेन नंदिताः ।
यत्स्वानुभूतिसंपूर्णा वयमस्मासु नो भृताः ॥३॥
मिमीमहे न चात्मत्वे स्वसंवित्त्या न धर्षिताः ।
कैवल्येनांगलग्नेन भेदभावं न चाप्नुमः ॥४॥
यास्मद्दृष्टिः समर्था सा वाक्सृष्टिर्न कदाप्यभूत् ।
याऽस्माकं पश्यते सा च दृष्टिरेव न संभवेत् ॥५॥
नास्माकं विषयीकृत्य भोक्तुं शक्तः परः क्षितौ ।
नैव चास्मत्प्रकारं वै पश्यामो न च कर्हिचित् ॥६॥
लोप्तुं प्रकटितं नैव लभामोऽत्र न विस्मयः ।
परं त्वस्मत्स्थितेर्नैव प्रकारं विद्महे वयम् ॥७॥
बहुना किं प्रजल्पेन यत्स्थितौ स्थापिता वयम् ।
श्रीमन्निवृत्तिनाथेन तद्वाग्हस्ते कथं ददे ॥८॥
सम्मुखीभावतु तत्राऽज्ञानशपितः कथं भवेत् ।
आस्तामज्ञानवार्तेयं मितं किं मीयते पुनः ॥९॥
अज्ञानस्य प्रवृत्तिर्वै यस्मिन्ग्रामे न विद्यते ।
तत्र ज्ञानकथां तर्हि की वेत्ति न हि कश्चन ॥१०॥
रात्रिर्यदा तदा दीपा लापितव्यास्तु नान्यदा ।
सति सूर्ये लापिताश्चेच्छ्रम एव हि केवलम् ॥११॥
नाज्ञानं विद्यते तस्माज्ज्ञानं तत्रैव तद्गतम् ।
अधुना संस्थितः पंथा निमिषोन्मेषयोर्द्वयोः ॥१२॥
अभिधानैर्यदप्येतैः ज्ञानाज्ञानपदार्थयोः ।

अर्थस्यान्योन्यभावेन विस्तृत्योक्तं मया किल ॥१३॥
दंपत्योः शिरसी छित्वा यथा संरोपिते मिथः ।
वैपरीत्यं न हि परं समाप्तं जीवितं द्वयोः ॥१४॥
पश्चात्संदर्शितो दीपः वृथा भूत्वैव गच्छति ।
दृष्टिः पश्येत्तमस्तर्हि दृष्टिः सैव वृथा यथा ॥१५॥
तथा न ज्ञायते यत्तदज्ञानमिति शब्द्यते ।
अखिलं ज्ञायते येन तदज्ञानं कथं भवेत् ॥१६॥
इत्यज्ञानमगाज्ज्ञानं ज्ञानमज्ञानमाव्रजेत् ।
एते उभेऽत्र संजाते वंध्ये वै नामरूपतः ॥१७॥
ज्ञातैवात्र न जानाति न ज्ञाता यः स बोधति ।
जीवनं वा तथेदानीम् अज्ञानज्ञानयोः कथम् ॥१८॥
ज्ञानाज्ञानद्वयं चैवं विधाय स्वोदरे दिवा ।
चिदाकाशे चिदादित्यः पूर्णत्वेनोदितः सदा ॥१९॥

नवमोऽध्यायः

(अकृत्रिमभक्तिवर्णनम्)

अधुनामोद एवासौ नासारूपोऽभवच्छ्रुतेः ।
निर्गताः श्रवणाश्चाथ मुकुरा लोचनोत्थिताः ॥१॥
स्वसमीरणभावेन विभांति व्यजनाः स्वयम् ।
शिरांसि चंपकत्वेन गंधवंति भवंति वै ॥२॥
जिह्वा गता हि रसतामब्जं सूर्यत्वेन विकासते ।
ज्योत्स्नादृशश्चकोराश्च जाताश्चंद्रमसः स्वयम् ॥३॥
पुष्पाण्येव षडंघ्रित्वं गतानि नरतां स्त्रियः ।
प्राप्ता चाथ स्वशय्यात्वं गता निद्रैव हि स्वयम् ॥४॥
चूतांकुराः कोकिलत्वं गताश्च मलयानिलाः ।
सांगा जातास्तथा सर्वे रसवंतः स्वयं रसाः ॥५॥
दृग्गोलः सुभगत्वस्य पात्रीभूतो भवत्विति ।
समुत्कृत्य नितांतो वै घटितो नैकधा यथा ॥६॥
तथा भोग्यं च भोक्ता च दृश्यं द्रष्टेति सर्वशः ।
समाप्तमस्मिन्नद्वैते भेदाभावविराजिते ॥७॥
शतपत्रैः सकाशान्नो निर्गमित्वैव तच्छदैः ।
आसहस्रमधोत्यर्थं विरतृतं भूयते यथा ॥८॥
नित्यनूतनैरनुभवैर्वादिनं निनदे सति ।
अक्रियानगरे नैव ज्ञायते तत्कदाचन ॥९॥
तस्मात्विषयतां तस्य नाममात्रेण केवलम् ।
इंद्रियाण्युपधावन्ति स्वैरं तद्ग्रहणेच्छया ॥१०॥
परं त्वादर्शसंस्पर्शे कृतमात्रे दृशो यथा ।
दृगेव लभते तद्वत्संजातं वृत्तिधावने ॥११॥
नागो मुद्रा कंकणंच त्रिभिर्लिंगैरिति त्रिधा ।
भेदैरुद्गृह्यते स्वर्णं तथापि स्वर्णमेव तत् ॥१२॥

नूनं विचिन्त्य कल्लोलानानयामीति चेत् करः ।
आमुक्तस्तर्हि तत्रापि लभ्यते केवलं जलम् ।।१३।।
हस्तयोः सुखसंस्पर्शः सुरूपश्चापि नेत्रयोः ।
रुचिप्रदश्च जिह्वायाः कर्पूरो यद्यपि पृथक् ।।१४।।
तथापि तस्य सौगंध्यादपरख्यापनं न हि ।
तथा बहुप्रकारेण स्फुरते यत्तदेव तत् ।।१५।।
तस्माच्छब्दादिविषयान्श्रोत्रादींद्रियपाणयः ।
ग्रहीतुमुपधावंति यच्च यत्र यदृच्छया ।।१६।।
तत्र संबंधमात्रे तन्नेंद्रियाणां हि किंचन ।
ततोऽस्ति यत्तदेवास्ते संबंधः केन कस्य न ।।१७।।
पर्वाणीक्षौ विदृश्यन्ते यानि तान्येकलं रसे ।
लभ्यंते च तथा सर्वे राकाचंद्रेंऽशवो यथा ।।१८।।
पतिता चंद्रिका चंद्रे वृष्टिर्जाता यथोदधौ ।
तथा विषयसंयोगः करणानां बभूव ह ।।१९।।
तस्मान्मुखागतं यत्तद्वाणी यद्यपि जल्पति ।
तथापि मौनमुद्रायाः समाधिर्न विघट्टिता ।।२०।।
व्यापाराणां सहस्राणि कृत्वा त्यक्तानि यद्यपि ।
तथापि नैव संभग्नमक्रियत्वं कदाचन ।।२१।।
प्रसार्य वृत्तिबाहू दृक् रूपमालिंगते मुदा ।
परं सत्याभिधानेन न किंचिल्लभते हि सा ।।२२।।
ध्वान्तं गृहीतुमुद्धृत्य रविः करसहस्रकम् ।
प्रवर्तते तथाप्यन्ते स्वस्यास्ते वै स्वयं यथा ।।२३।।
स्वप्नदृष्टविलासानां सुदृढं नु स्वजाम्यहम् ।
इत्याशयोच्छ्रितस्तर्हि यः स एव न चेतरत् ।।२४।।
उदितैर्विषयैरेवं ज्ञानी विषयितामियात् ।
तदा द्वयं न भूत्वा किं भवते तन्न विद्महे ।।२५।।
विचितुं चंद्रिकामिंदुर्गतश्चेद्विचितं नु किम् ।
प्रसूय वंध्यानि यथा भवंति स्मरणानि वा ।।२६।।
प्रत्याहारादिषु स्वांगं येनांगेषु विलापितम् ।

स योगः खलु मार्गेऽस्मिन्दिवा चंद्रमिवाभवत् ॥२७॥
द्वैतावस्थांगणेऽद्वैतं स्वयमागच्छते मुदा ।
भेदो यदा यदाऽभेदद्वैगुण्यं च तदा तदा ॥२८॥
कैवल्यारोहमकरोत्स्वैरं विषयसेवनम् ।
संजातं भक्तभज्यैकं भक्तेर्वेश्मनि सर्वदा ॥२९॥
संस्थितः स्वगृहे एवं मार्गं चलति यद्यपि ।
अथवा तिष्ठते तर्ह्यप्यध्वानं च निगच्छति ॥३०॥
तथा किमप्यसौ कुर्वन्निह किंचिदपेक्षितम् ।
वर्तते इति मत्वापि तदकृत्वा न तिष्ठते ॥३१॥
स्मरणास्मरणे नैवं प्रसर्तुं ददतेतराम् ।
दशाया व्यवहारोऽयमसाधारण इत्यहो ॥३२॥
स्वैरं विधिर्बभूवाथ समाधिः स्वेच्छयाभवत् ।
दशामिमामधिष्ठाय मोक्षसिद्धिर्भवेद्ध्रुवम् ॥३३॥
देव एवाभवद्भक्तः स्थलमेवाध्वतामगात् ।
संस्थितं विश्वमेवैतद्भूत्वैकांततया स्वयम् ॥३४॥
यस्य कस्यापि देवस्य भक्तः कोऽपि भवत्यलम् ।
संस्थितो यत्र कुत्रापि तत्रैवायमकृत्रिमः ॥३५॥
देवसंघटनाद्देवालयस्याभूच्च पूर्णता ।
देशकालादि नायाति विभागाय कथंचन ॥३६॥
देवे देवो न संमाति तत्र देव्यन्वयः कुतः ।
परं त्वघटमानैव प्रायशः परिवारता ॥३७॥
स्वामीसेवकसंबंधायेत्थं श्रद्धा यदोत्थिता ।
देव एव तदेकाकी सर्वतस्तेन साधितः ॥३८॥
उपचारजपध्याननिर्धारेष्वखिलेष्वपि ।
नान्यत्समर्पणं देवात्सर्वं देवमयं यतः ॥३९॥
देवमेवाय देवेन यावद्देवं भजेन्मुदा ।
अर्पणस्याभिधानेन यस्य कस्याप्यहर्निशम् ॥४०॥
देवालयं परीवारो देवश्चोत्कृत्य पर्वतम् ।
क्रियते किं तथा भक्तिव्यवहारो किं न भूयताम् ॥४१॥

यस्याखिलस्य वृक्षस्य वृक्ष एव परंतु सः ।
शाखोपशाखारूपेण विस्तारेण द्वितीयवान् ।।४२।।
गृहीतेऽप्यगृहीतेषु मुद्गैर्मुद्गेष्वहो यथा ।
न चित्रं हि तथैवात्र देवत्वेन कृतं द्वयो : ।।४३।।
अक्षता देवता सैव नार्चिताप्यक्षतासु वै ।
इदानीमक्षपाताभिः सा पूज्या भवते किमु ।।४४।।
हे दीप्तिकलिके दीप्तिवस्त्राणि त्वं प्रवेशथाः ।
इति चोक्तं वचस्तर्हि नग्ना तिष्ठति सा किमु ।।४५।।
चंद्रत्वं चंद्रिकासीति नोक्तं यद्यपि केनचित् ।
तथापि ताः कलाः सर्वाः स एवास्ते न संशयः ।।४६।।
अग्नित्वमग्निदेहे तु सर्वत्रैव विनिश्चितम् ।
किमर्थमेतद्युगलं न दानं दानमेव च ।।४७।।
तस्माद्भजेदयं यर्हि तर्हि भक्तोऽन्यथा न किम् ।
इत्थंभूतोप्यसावास्ते शिव एव स्वभावतः ।।४८।।
भक्त्यभक्त्योरथैकत्र जातं भोजनभाजनम् ।
शमित्वा वर्तयः कर्माकर्मणोरुभयोः सदा ।।४९।।
तस्मादुपनिषद्भागा निंदाभूता भवंति वै ।
अथवा तस्य निंदैव विशदस्तोत्ररूपिणी ।।५०।।
नोचेन्निदास्तुतिद्वंद्वं मौनार्थमपि गच्छति ।
मौनं मौने तथा शब्दैरुक्तवत्यपि वर्तते ।।५१।।
अमार्गेऽपि पदे न्यस्ते शिवयात्रा भवेद्ध्रुवम् ।
शिवं प्रति गतोप्यद्धा नैव कुत्राप्यगादसौ ।।५२।।
चलनाचलनद्वंद्वं मिलित्वैकमभून्मिथः ।
इदमीदृक्कौतुकं वै स्थानेऽस्मिन्वर्तंतेराम् ।।५३।।
यह्याकस्मिकदृष्टेऽपि शिवदर्शनसंभ्रमः ।
भुज्यते येन केनापि कस्मिंश्चित्समयोऽपि वा ।।५४।।
दृश्यमाने शिवेऽस्याग्रे परं दृष्टं न किंचन ।
यस्मात्सादृश्यभावोऽभूदुभयोर्देवभक्तयोः ।।५५।।
कंदुकः स्वयमामुक्तः स्वयमेवोत्प्लवेत्तथा ।

स्वयं प्रतिहतश्चापि गृहीतो यत्र वा स्वयम् ॥५६॥
ईदृशी कंदुकक्रीडा दृश्यते यदि चेत्कदा ।
तर्ह्यनया प्रबुद्धस्य सादृश्यं ब्रूमहे वयम् ॥५७॥
कर्महस्तो न संसक्तो नापि ज्ञानप्रवेशनम् ।
इत्थमेवोपास्तिरियं भवत्यंगेन सर्वदा ॥५८॥
नोद्भवेन्न शमेद्वापि स्वांगेनांगे हि शब्दति ।
सुखं केवलमस्येदं सुखोपशमनं यथा ॥५९॥
किंचिदेकमिदं मर्म भक्तेर्गूढमकृत्रिमम् ।
योगज्ञानैकविश्रामभूमिकेयं विराजते ॥६०॥
अंगेन खलु संजाताः परं ये नामरूपयोः ।
भेदास्तेप्यनयोर्विष्णुहरयोर्लीनतां गताः ॥६१॥
अहोऽर्धनारीपुरुषौ गिलनोद्गिलने यथा ।
कुर्वंतौ ग्रहणं जातं सर्वग्रासेन चैकदा ॥६२॥
खादित्वा वाच्यजातं च पीत्वा वाचकतामपि ।
स्थिता निद्रावशा भूत्वा परावागत्र सर्वदा ॥६३॥
प्रभो शिव शिव स्वामिन्नियत्यानंदभूमिका ।
गृह्यते दीयतेऽस्माभिरेकैरेवं कथं कृतम् ॥६४॥
विनिद्रं बोधितं निद्रायुक्तं निद्रावशीकृतम् ।
अस्मानस्मत्त्वमानीतं तस्माच्चित्रमिदं तव ॥६५॥
वयं तवैव हि परं प्रीत्या यन्मामका इति ।
ब्रूषे तत्पुनरुक्तं वै प्रभोस्तव विराजते ॥६६॥
कस्य किंचिन्न गृह्णासि तथा स्वीयं ददासि न ।
किं जानाति कथं स्वीयं गौरवं कारयस्यहो ॥६७॥
गुरुत्वात्सुंदरो यावांस्तावानेव लघूनपि ।
तारयित्वा गुरुलघु वेत्ति यस्तव सेवकः ॥६८॥
दत्त्वा शिष्यान्विभागान्वै ददात्यद्वैतनिश्चयः ।
स्फुटे तर्हि किमर्थं ते शास्त्राण्यायांति वंदिताम् ॥६९॥
बहु किं दानदातृत्वमिति योऽयं प्रपंचकः ।
तं व्ययीकृत्य भवसे सखा तोषेण तेन वै ॥७०॥

दशमोऽध्यायः

(ग्रंथपरिहारः)

श्रीमन्निवृत्तिराजन् यत्त्वया करतले मम ।
सुखीकृतं तत्तु मया सुखं भोज्यं हि मौनतः ॥१॥
परंत्वीशेन सूर्यस्य हस्ते या दीप्तिसंहतिः ।
दत्ता तया जगत्सर्वमंतर्वर्तीकृतं ध्रुवम् ॥२॥
विधोर्यदमृतं दत्तं सर्वं तस्यैव तत्किमु ।
अथवा सिंधुभिर्दत्तं मेघानामेव किं जलम् ॥३॥
दीपकेऽस्ति प्रकाशो यः स गृहस्यैव भूषणम् ।
गगने योऽवकाशोऽस्ति विश्वस्यैवाखिलस्य सः ॥४॥
अगाधान्युच्चलंतीति विधोः शक्तिर्न सा किमु ।
वसंतः कुरुते तर्हि दानदाः स्युः महीरुहाः ॥५॥
तस्मादिदमसंवार्यमौदार्यं खलु दैविकम् ।
त्वदौदार्यं विना स्वामिन्स्वातंत्र्यमिदं न मे ॥६॥
एतावानिति किं दास्ये परिहारं पुनः पुनः ।
प्रभुप्रभावविन्यासस्यांतरायेण मूढवत् ॥७॥
अस्माभिरुक्तं यत्किंचित्स्वस्मिन्नेवास्ति तस्फुटम् ।
स्वप्रकाशाय शब्देन किं प्रकाशितुमाप्यते ॥८॥
कदाचिदथवा मौनमस्माभिः स्यात्कृतं यदि ।
तर्हि नैव भवेत्किंतु जनेऽस्मिन्जनदर्शनम् ॥९॥
जनदृश्यो जनस्तर्हि द्रष्टैव दृश्यरूपभाक् ।
न कृतोऽप्यस्ति सिद्धान्तः स्वतः सिद्धो ह्ययं ध्रुवम् ॥१०॥
नास्मात्परतरं संविद्रहस्यं किंचिदस्ति वै ।
तथैवेदं तदादावप्यास्ते एव विनिश्चितम् ॥११॥
तर्हि न ग्रंथविस्तारो घटेदिति वदाम चेत् ।
तर्हि सिद्धानुवादं वै प्रीत्या कर्तुं लभामहे ॥१२॥

तदेव प्रीतिमच्छश्वत्परं भोगेन वा रुचिः ।
तस्मात्सिद्धानुवादोऽसौ सुतरामुचितो हि नः ॥१३॥
नैवमस्ति मयेदं तत् गौप्यमुक्त्वा स्फुटीकृतम् ।
मया न दर्शितं तर्ह्यप्यास्ते प्रकटमेव तत् ॥१४॥
पूर्णाहंतायुताः स्वैरं वयमस्मासु घट्टिताः ।
लुप्ताः प्रकटिता वापि कस्येदानीं भवामहे ॥१५॥
स्वात्मानमर्प्यंते किंतु कृतं स्वेन निरूपणम् ।
तूष्णीत्वे नाथ वा तद्वन्नष्टं स्यादित्थमस्ति किम् ॥१६॥
तस्मात्सरस्वतीयं मे मौनस्यापि हि मौनताम् ।
कुरुते मकरी यद्वन् मौनं पानीयरेखिता ॥१७॥
एवं दशोपनिषदैरग्रे स्वीयपदानि नो ।
चलंतीति विलोक्यात्र बोधेन सह मज्जितम् ॥१८॥
ज्ञानदेवो वदत्येतत् श्रीमदनुभवामृतम् ।
संसेव्यं सर्वदा जीवन्मुक्ता एव भवंत्विति ॥१९॥
ध्रुवं विलासिनी मुक्तिः केवलानुभवामृतम् ।
परं परामृतं चापि वर्धयेत्सुधयानया ॥२०॥
नित्यं चंद्र स एवास्ते राकायामन्य एव सः ।
कस्मादिदमहं वक्तुं लभामि रविसन्निधौ ॥२१॥
यदा तारुण्यवृद्धिः स्यात् तदा स्वांगे न माति तत् ।
यर्हि तत्रैव तारुण्यं सर्वदास्ते निगूढवत् ॥२२॥
वसंतागमने स्वीयैः फलपुष्पैर्महीरुहः ।
अंतरिक्षगताभिः स्वशाखाभिर्विलसंति वै ॥२३॥
तस्माद्युक्तमिदं स्वानुभवामृततया मया ।
स्वानुभूतिगुणेनाढ्यं श्रीगुरोः परिवेषितम् ॥२४॥
मुक्तो मुमुक्षुर्बद्धश्च भेदास्तावदिमे ध्रुवम् ।
स्वानुभूतिसुधास्वादो विरुद्धो यावदेव हि ॥२५॥
गंगायां स्नातुमायाता आपो गंगात्वमागताः ।
यथा वा तिमिराण्यायुः सूर्यसंगेन सूर्यताम् ॥२६॥
नास्ति स्पर्शमणेर्यावन्निष्कर्षस्तावदेव हि ।

शुद्धाशुद्धमिदं वाच्यं तल्लाभे शुद्धमेव तत् ॥२७॥
गोसमाजस्थले यद्वद् गोभाराः संमिलन्ति वै ।
सलिलानां समूहानां सागरेऽन्तर्हिता यथा ॥२८॥
तथा तस्मिन्नक्षरेऽपि विलीयन्ते जनाः खलु ।
बहुना किं शिवेनैव येषां साम्यं भवेद् ध्रुवम् ॥२९॥
अकारादिषु वर्णेषु पंचाशन्मातृका यथा ।
समीलंति तथा नास्ति द्वितीयं च चराचरे ॥३०॥
ज्ञानदेवो वदत्यस्मादिदं स्वानुभवामृतम् ।
विबुधैर्भुज्यतां प्रीत्या विश्वानंदकरं परम् ॥३१॥

इति श्रीज्ञानदेवेन कृते प्राकृतभाषया ।
बुधानंदकरे ग्रंथे नाम्ना स्वानुभवामृते ॥१॥
श्रीमत्प्रह्लादनामा यः पंढरीक्षेत्रसंस्थितः ।
विप्रवाक्यानुरोधेन कृतवान् श्लोकसंचयः ॥२॥
प्रीयतां विठ्ठलस्तेन पुंडरीकवरप्रदः ।
सर्वं गतागतं चापि शोधनीयं बुधैः सदा ॥३॥
कश्चिद्विप्रः समस्तश्रुतिहृदयविदाम् अग्रगण्यः प्रशान्तः ।
क्षेत्रं श्रीपांडुरंगाभिधमलमगमद् ग्रंथमेनं बुभुत्सुः ॥
तेनैतद् ग्रंथवेत्ता सकलगुणनिधिः सज्जनैर्गीतकीर्तिः ।
प्रह्लादः प्रार्थितः सन्सुगममनुपदं श्लोकमेकं चकार ॥४॥

APPENDIX C

I. RELATION OF SELF WITH MIND AND BODY

Commenting upon the word "Chetana" in the Bhagavadgita XIII, 6. Jnanadeva says —

"The existence of Spirit (Chaitanya), which is not attached and only a perceiver in the body, is called 'Chetana' (life). It is standing awake from the nails of the feet to the hair of the head. It does not change during the three states (i.e. wakefulness, dream and sleep). It is like a spring to the garden of Prakriti (Primeval matter) and is the cause of blossoming the flowers of mind and intellect. It operates equally in the animate as well as inanimate portions. Though unaware of his army a king gets victory against his opponents by his mere command. Rising of the full Moon causes tides in the distant sea-waters. The piece of iron moves in the presence of a magnet. A female tortoise nourishes her young ones merely by her casting her look instead of sucking them at her breast. In a similar manner, The Self inside, causes the movements of the body by Its simple presence.

—Jnaneshwari, XIII-134-141

The instance of a female tortoise is very significant. It shows that the relation of the Self with mind and body is not merely that of a disinterested spectator but that of a parental affection.

II. GOD AND THE WORLD

The presence of God is not concealed by the presence of the World. God Krishna says to Arjuna—

"Therefore, I am the father, Prakriti is the mother and the world is the offspring. Let your mind be not distracted by perceiving so many bodies because elements like mind and intelligence are the same in all of them. Are there not different limbs on the same body? So the world is one though it is full of diversity. Different branches, high and low, sprout from the same tree. I am related to the world just as the clay is related to a pot or the cotton to a piece of cloth. The pot is the son of clay! A piece of cloth is the grandson of the cotton! Waves are the offspring of the ocean. In the same manner I am related to the animate and inanimate world. Fire and its flames are the same. In fact I am all and hence it is futile to talk even about any relation.

If it is said that I am concealed by the existence of the world then who it is that blossoms in the form of the world? Can a Manika (RED JEWEL) be concealed by its own lustre? Does a chip of gold loses its goldness if turned into an ornament? Does a lotus loses itself when it blossoms into so many petals? When a seed of grain is sown and grows into an ear of corn, is it distroyed or appears in its enhanced glory? So there is no need of drawing the curtain of the world away in order to have My glimpse, because I am the whole panorama."

— *Jnaneshwari, XIV-117-128*

III. THE UNDEVIATING DEVOTION

To understand God as He really is, is the sign of true devotion.

"The person who serves Me with unswerving devotion is able to control the three Gunas (i.e. the qualities of Sattva — understanding, Rajas — creative endeavour, Tamas — inertia). Here it should be clearly understood — Who am I? What is Bhakti (devotion)? What is Avyabhichar (undeviating)? So listen, oh Parth! I am like this. The lustre of a jewel is the jewel itself. Fluidity is the water. Space is the sky. Fire is the flame. The bunch of petals is the lotus. A tree is its foliage and fruit. The aggregate of ice is the Himalaya. Milk coagulated is the curds. In the same way I am all what is called the world. It is not necessary to peal the disk of the Moon to have its vision. Ghee though frozen is the ghee itself. A pot is the clay though not broken to pieces. So It is not the case that I should be found out after annihilating the world, it is I who is everything. To understand Me in this way is Avyabhichari Bhakti (undeviating devotion). To see the difference is deviation.

Therefore, giving up the conception of difference, a person should know Me alongwith himself. He should not regard himself as different from Me as a circular tiny portion of gold is not different from the whole block of gold. He should understand well how a ray of light though proceeds from its origin (i.e. that light) is continuous with it. Like atoms on the surface of the earth or particles of ice in the Himalaya mountain, all the 'Egoes' (Conscious thinking subjects) dwell in Me. A ripple smali or great is not different from water. So he should know himself as not different from Me. Such insight is called Bhakti. This is the supreme knowledge. The essence of Yoga is the same.

—*Jnaneshwari XIV-372-379*

IV. THE NAME OF GOD

Singing God's Name is the Royal Road to God-realization.

(अष्टांग योगे न शीणीजे etc)

"Do not exhaust yourself by the exertions of eightfold Yoga. Do not take yourself to Yama (Forbearance) and Niyama (Observances). Sing the Name of God. Listen to it while singing and admiring. Let your mind and body vibrate to the tune of that song. Cross this ocean of life with ease and mirth. Dear Friend, Take only to that means — The means of Name by which you will be united with God Vitthal."

— Sakal-Sant-Gatha P. 51

(तत्वमस्यादि महावाक्य उपदेशु ।
नामाच्या अर्थांश नाहीं तेथे ॥ etc)

God's Name is greater than the Sacred Scripture's advice of 'Tat Twamasi'— That Thou Art.

Not even a half of the worth of The Name is there in the great utterance of the Scriptures 'That Thou Art'. I have found Thee near at hand by singing Thy Name. Now I shall not lose sight of Thee even for a moment, Oh! Life of my life! The heroic Vaishnavas loudly proclaim Thy Name and the messengers of Death are taking to their heels.

Therefore, Name that leads to a particular Samadhi (a trance of Divine Love) is in a way a spiritual exercise of Nirguna (Absolute Reality). You will understand this if you try to know the real nature of The Self-luminous Absolute. In this way I have caught hold of such a lovely vision in my heart. Now how can be another birth possible?

I have realized Him who is unknowable to all scriptures. (or beyond the reach of all the other spiritual endeavours). I have caught Him in my heart with steadfast cognition. While contemplating God Vitthal all sorrows vanished.

—Ibid—P. 52.

In the above passage Jnanadeva makes an acute and most significant analysis of the spiritual exercise and experience of lovingly uttering or remembering God's Name. He says that singing God's name is also the exercise for experiencing the Nirguna or the Absolute. We have already seen that Jnanadeva identifies God with the Absolute, or Saguna with Nirguna. Sometimes he conveys the same conception by saying that Saguna and Nirguna are both aspects of the same God. Now what is Saguna and what is Nirguna? God knowing Himself is Nirguna while God loving Himself is Saguna. The way of singing God's Name leads to Saguna. — to God loving Himself. God knowing Himself, who is no other than The Self-Luminous Reality, is identical with God loving Himself. So the path of singing God's Name can be termed the exercise of Nirguna in the light of the conception of the Self-Luminous Reality that is also the Self-Loving Reality.

Everything without God's loving contemplation is worthless.

(विठ्ठलु नाहीं जये शरीरीं etc)

Oh, why they are born upon this earth whose hearts do not find room for Vitthal? A city without Vitthal is like a dreary forest. Listen to me. The land without Vitthal is like a cemetery. The tongue without Vitthal is like the sky without Sun or Moon. All secrets, all rituals, all theoretical discussions that are devoid of Vitthal are futile exertions. At Pandhari there stands the very incarnation of Existence, Knowledge, and Bliss overflowing with Love. Placing His arms on His waist, He is waiting for devotees. There is no real satisfaction and fulfilment of the longing of love without Vitthal. My spiritual Master Shri Nivrittinath has given it to me. Blessed am I to receive that love. Shri Vitthal has brought me to such a state.

V. THE GLORY OF GOD

God Vitthal of Pandharpur is symbol of Love Divine. He is dear to Jnanadeva's heart. Jnanadeva describes His wonderful glory.

Oh, How This God who has no root, no trunk, no foliage nor any leaf, has come to my abode.

He is standing as Nirguna and shining as Saguna. He is giving out the lustre of Jiva (Individual Self) and Shiva (Universal Self).

His ways and His plays are incomprehensible. He is enjoying His festival spontaneously.

Jnanadeva says — I cannot understand the greatness of This God who is happily residing animate as well as inanimate objects.

—*Sakal-Sant-Gatha, P. 274*

(*Note the description of Saguna and Nirguna*)

(मूळ ना ढाळ शाखा ना पल्लव । तो हा कैसा देव आला घरा ॥
निर्गुणपणें उभा सगुणगें शोभा । जीव शिव प्रभा दाविताहे ॥
नकळे याची गती नकळे याची लीला । आपेआप सोहळा भोगीताहे ॥
ज्ञानदेव म्हणे न कळे याची थोरी । आपण चराचरीं नांदताहे ॥)

VI. GOD-DEVOTION — THE CENTRAL VIRTUE

Jnanadeva regards Bhakti as the central virtue. It is the supreme value. Life without it is empty and worthless.

"Fie upon that life which is devoid of My Bhakti. Are there not so many stones scattered upon the ground? Though a Nimb tree bears abundant fruits crows only will feast upon them. In the same way Though a person without Bhakti is prosperous, he becomes abode of all vices."

—*Jnaneshwari, I-436-37*

On the other hand Bhakti nourishes all moral qualities. Because a Bhakta loves God he loves all His creatures. Love breeds in him the qualities of courage, calmness, and equanimity.

"The devotee has no ill-feeling towards any being. Like Chaitanya (Spirit) he has no consciousness of mine and thine. The Earth does not know anything like welcoming worthy people and driving away unworthy. The compassionate Prana (Vital Breath) does not say that it will reside in the body of a king and renounce the body of a beggar. Water has no conception of satisfying only the thirst of a cow and of killing a tiger by turning itself into a venom. In the same manner the Bhakta is the friend of all beings. He is the very foundation of compassion."

Ibid-XII-145-48

"There is no dint of partiality in him. He behaves equally with his friend and foe. A lamp does not know of spreading light in its own house and darkness in that of the other. A tree gives its shade to one who has planted it and also to one who strikes it asunder. A sugar-cane is not sweet only to him who has cultivated it and bitter to him who crushes it. In the same way a devotee looks equally upon his enemy as well as upon his companion."

Ibid-XII-197-200

VII AMṚTĀNUBHAVA AND SPANDAKĀRIKĀ

As stated in Chapter VIII, Jñānadeva was influenced by Kashmir Śaivism in his philosophical outlook of Cidvilāsa or Sphūrtivāda. Sphūrti is identical with Spanda in Kashmir Śaivism. Spanda is also designated as Sphurattā of Parama Śiva. The most important work of Śaivism, next to Śiva-Sūtras, is Spanda-Kārikā which is attributed to Vasugupta himself by some and to his disciple Kallata by others.

Dr. S.N. Dasgupta has given a summary of the philosophical outlook of Kashmir School of Śaivism. He says :

"One of the most interesting systems of idealism is that of Kashmir School of Śaivism as described in the Śivasūtras and the works of Ksemarāja, Abhinavagupta and others. According to these systems pure consciousness is ultimate Reality which is self-spontaneous and it is this self-spontaneity of itself that is called Māyā. It is this self-spontaneous pure consciousness that manifests itself as the inner psychological categories and the objective presentations that form the data of objective perception. The world-creation is not thus a creation of the indescribable māyā-stuff which has for its ground the changeless Brahman, but it is the pure consciousness which, while remaining unchanged itself, makes appearances on itself through its powers, which though not different from it yet show themselves as it were different from it. So the world appearance is not false, only it is to be remembered that it is but the manifestation of one pure consciousness. It is by limiting its one infinite consciousness that it appears as individual perceivers.

This limitation, again, is not something different from the nature of this pure consciousness, but only a mode of it".

(*Indian Idealism*, pp. 193-194)

Jñānadeva also thinks that the cause of the expansion or contraction is no other than the Supreme Reality—God Himself (*Amt.* 7.257).

Some similarities of important conceptions in both "Spanda-Kārikā" and "Amṛtānubhava" are worth noting.

(1) The concept of निमेष and उन्मेष

The first verse of Spanda-Kārikā runs thus :

यस्योन्मेषनिमेषाभ्यां जगतः प्रलयोदयौ ।

तं शक्तिचक्रविभवप्रभवं शंकरं स्तुमः ।।१.१।।

The Parama Śiva is the Supreme Reality. He is described in this verse as the source of all the powers and the creation and dissolution of the world is due to the opening and closing of His eyelids. That means they are due to His own संकल्प or sweet will.

निमेष and उन्मेष literally mean closing and opening of the eye-lids.

A similar conception is found in Amṛtānubhava :

दोन्ही विशेष गिळी । ना निविष्टाते उगळी ।

उघडी झापी एके डोळी । वस्तु की हे ।।७.१८३।।

पातया पाते मिळे । की दृष्टत्वे सैंध पघळे ।

तिये उन्मीलिता मावळे । नवलावो हा ।।७.१८४।।

The swallowing of the two particulars i.e. the seer and the seen and emitting their opposites is like the opening and closing of the eyelids of God, the Supreme Substance.

How wonderful it is that as soon as His eyelids close the Ātman assumes the form of a seer which vanishes as soon as His eyelids open! This means that God manifests the world or remains in his own form of Eternal Consciousness at his sweet will.

(2) The concept of शिवशक्तिसमावेशन

शिवशक्तिसमावेशन means merging of the individual self in Śiva and Śakti. In the first verse quoted above the author of Spanda-Kārikā pays his homage to God Śaṅkara by lauding Him. स्तुमः means we laud. The sense of this lauding is explained by Kṣemarāja (Commentator) thus:

तं विश्वोत्कर्षित्वेन परामृशन्तः तत्क्लृप्तकल्पितप्रमातृपदनिमज्जनेन समाविशामः ।

Here the sense of lauding is that by considering Him as excelling the entire cosmos we enter into His being by obliterating the state of assumed agency brought about by Himself, i.e. by merging our limited self in Him, which also is the form assumed by Lord Śaṅkara.

The first chapter in the Amṛtānubhava is named शिवशक्ति-समावेश and at the end of it Jñānadeva pays his homage to Śiva and Śakti in the same way.

म्हणोनि भूतेश भवानी । वंदिली न करोनि सिनानी ।
मी रिघालो नमनी । ते हे ऐसे ।।१.६० ।।
मीठे सिंधुत्वाचा लाभु । मांडूनि मीठपणाचा लोभु ।
तेवी अहं देउनी मी शंभु । शांभवी झालो ।।१.६३ ।।
शिवशक्ति समावेशे । नमनम्या केले ऐसे ।
रंभागर्भ आकाशे । रिघाला जैसा ।।१.६४ ।।

Therefore without differentiating Śiva and Śakti from myself I proceed to pay homage to both of them in this manner.

The salt took the advantage of becoming ocean by giving up its attachment to saltness; similarly I became one with Śiva and Śakti by renouncing my ego.

Thus I have paid my homage by entering my self, i.e. merging myself in Śiva and Śakti just like the empty space inside a plantain tree would merge itself in the outer one.

(3) The concept of the close embracing of Śiva & Śakti

The Spanda Śakti differentiates herself in minor Śaktis.

The original Śakti and all the other Śaktis are described as embracing Śiva and enjoying the sport of the creation of the world.

Ksemarāja commenting on the first verse of Spanda-Kārikā says—

एता हि देव्यः श्रीमन्मंथानभैरवं चक्रेश्वरम् आलिंग्य सर्वदा एव जगत्सर्गादि-
क्रीडां संपादयन्ति इति आम्नायः ।

(These divinities embracing the exalted Manthāna Bhairava who is the lord of the aggregate of these divinities bring about the play of the manifestation etc. of the universe. This is what the sacred tradition says.) चक्र means the aggregate of different powers. चक्रेश्वर is the Lord of these. मन्थानभैरव is the supreme Lord who is the resting place of all.

स्पन्दशक्ति is the original supreme Śakti of शिव. She is not only inseparable from Śiva but is the very heart of Śiva and hence designated as His हृदय.

Jñānadeva has described God and Goddess (देव and देवी) as parents of the universe (Amt 1.1). Both are the very life of each other (जिये दोघे जीवप्राण । जिया दोघा ।। १.१२). They embrace so closely that they merge themselves in each other (जया दोघांच्या आलिंगनी । विरोनि गेली दोनी ।। १.४७). The Divine couple give birth to the child in the form of universe (जे बाल जगाये वढे । वियाली ।।१.६).

(4) The concept of सुप्रबुद्ध or प्रबुद्ध

In Spanda-Kārikā the man who has attained full enlightenment is called *suprabuddha* (सुप्रबुद्ध). अप्रबुद्ध is ignorant and प्रबुद्ध is partially enlightened. But the word प्रबुद्ध is also used in the sense of सुप्रबुद्ध. He is described as realizing his identity with God Śiva in all the states of waking, dream and deep sleep:

तस्योपलब्धिः सततं त्रिपदाव्यभिचारिणी ।
नित्यं स्यात्सुप्रबुद्धस्य... ।।१.१७।।

(The fully enlightened has always undeviating knowledge in all three states.)

He experiences that there is no state which is not Śiva and that there is no difference between the experient and the object of experience:

तस्मात्सर्वार्थचिन्तासु न सावस्था न या शिवः ।

भोक्तैव भोग्यभावेन सदा सर्वत्र संस्थितः ॥२.४॥

(Whether in the word, object or thought there is no state which is not Śiva. It is the experient himself who always and everywhere abides in the form of the experienced i.e. it is the Divine Himself who is the essential Experient and it is He who abides in the form of the universe as His field of experience.)

He sees all the universe as the sport of Śiva:

इति वा यस्य संवित्तिः क्रीडात्वेनाखिलं जगत् ॥२.५॥

Jñānadeva also designates the person of full enlightenment as प्रबुद्ध and his way of life as प्रबुद्धाची सरली in the 9th chapter of Amṛtānubhava—तरी बोलिजे सरली। प्रबुद्धाची (९.५७). प्रबुद्ध of Jñānadeva is the same as in Spanda-Kārikā, as we shall see from the following description.

No difference is left for him between भोक्ता and भोग्य, subject and object. Jñānadeva gives poetic description of such a state. In that state fragrance assumes the form of the smelling organ, sweet tunes assume the form of ears and eyes that of a mirror (9.1-7).

आता आमोद सुनासजाले । श्रुतीस श्रवण रिघाले ।

आरिसे उठिले । लोचनासी ॥९.१॥

तैसे भोग्य आणि भोक्ता । दिसे आणि देखता ।

हे संरले अफुटा । अद्वैतामाजि ॥९.६॥

Though he might be engaged in various activities he is inactive all the while.

व्यापाराचे गाडे । मोडताही अपाडे ।

अक्रियेचे न मोडे । पाउल केही ॥९.२०॥

He may wander at any place. It is his pilgrimage to Śiva.

घालिता अव्हासवा पाये । शिवयात्रा होत जाये ॥७.५२॥

This is because he experiences no place which is without Śiva. Every space is filled with God and the temple of God itself is merged in God.

देवाचिया दाटणी । देउला झाली आटणी ॥९.३६॥

The special feature of Jñānadeva's प्रबुद्ध is that though he attains full enlightenment and realizes his identity with God, he can still find room for loving devotion even after this in his अद्वैत condition. Jñānadeva's remark is worth noting. He says—

देव देऊळ परिवारु । कीजे कोरूनि डोंगरु ।
तैसा भक्तीचा वेव्हारू । कां न व्हावा ? ॥९.४१॥

The image of God, the temple and God's attendants are carved in the same rock of a mountain e.g. the rock-cut Kailāsa Temple at Elura. In the same way why should there not be the performance of Bhakti in the state of अद्वैत (9.41)?

Jñānadeva points out that if this प्रबुद्ध desires to enjoy the relation of master and servant in this state of identity, then God Himself divides Himself into God and His devotee along with the various instruments of worship!

ऐसाही स्वामी भृत्युसंबंधा । लागी उठली श्रद्धा ।
ते देवोचि नुसधा । कामविजे ॥९.३८॥
अवधियाचि उपचारा । जपध्यान निर्धारा ।
नाही आन ससारा । देवे वाचुनी ॥९.३९॥

Jñānadeva is the advocate of such supreme devotion. It is ज्ञानोत्तर or पराभक्ति. It is the भक्ति of सिद्ध. The भक्ति of a साधक or a spiritual aspirant is अपराभक्ति—devotion of a lower level. Bhagavadgītā mentions पराभक्ति: "मद्भक्तिं लभते पराम्" (18.54). It is the fruit of the highest knowledge. The Bhakti of lower level is transformed into that of the higher level. अपराभक्ति is transformed into पराभक्ति which even a जीवन्मुक्त should enjoy. So Jñānadeva says—

ज्ञानदेव म्हणे श्रीमंत । हे अनुभवामृत निखिल ।
सेवुनि जीवन्मुक्त । हेचि होतु ॥१०.१६॥

Even the emancipated one should drink the draughts of this pure and sweet ambrosia of the highest spiritual experience of पराभक्ति.

APPENDIX D

I. PLAY OF CHINMATRA (चिन्मात्र)

In the chapter IX of Amritanubhava Jnanadev describes the movement of भोग्य-भोक्ता (The object of enjoyment and the enjoyer.) दृश्य-दृष्टा (The object of sight and the seer) in the unbroken Whole of Reality. The original ovi is

तैसे भोग्य आणि भोक्ता। दिसे आणि देखता॥
ते सरलें अद्वैता। अफुटामाजी॥६॥

Here सरले means it becomes nil or it spreads out. Another reading of the word is संसरले which means spreads out. Jnanadev is not an illusionist. He does not think the world of भोग्य and भोक्ता as an illusion. He thinks the whole world is चिद्विलास or the play of Absolute Reality. Hence the reading संसरले is appropriate and सरले has also the meaning of spreading out.

Shiv Kalyan in his commentary explains the situation rightly. He says

स्फुरणमात्र वस्तु जें कांही। तें फुटे ऐसें जड नाहीं।
मग भोग्य तेथें काई। आणि भोक्ता कवणु॥
आतां जें दिसे भोग्यभोक्तेपण। किंवा दृश्य आणि देखता जाण।
ते चिन्मात्र न फुटोन। विलासत असे॥

Jnanadev himself has cleared this problem of भोग्य and भोक्ता and their nature in the next ovi, where he gives the instance of a shevanti flower blooming into thousand petals.

The shevanti flower which does bloom though there appear a thousand petals remains itself one only. The flower does not become thousand flowers. In this way भोग्य and भोक्ता though appear two, they are only the unbroken Whole of Reality, what appears to is its playfulness.

II. SUPREMACY OF PREM BHAKTI (LOVING DEVOTION)

There are many kinds of Bhakti, of which Akritrim Bhakti is regarded as superior, Akritrim Bhakti is Sahaj Bhakti (सहजभक्ति) or Natural devotion. The state of Jivanmukti (जीवन्मुक्ति) is also similar to this Bhakti. Here the word Bhakti means which is not विभक्त (separation) where God and devotee become one and there is the enjoyment of oneness or the so-called ब्रह्मानंद. There is no question of Prem, or Love of God. Jnanadev has extolled such Bhakti but ultimately his pronouncement on the problem of Bhakti is that of all kinds of Bhakties, the supermost Bhakti is Prem Bhakti. He calls it as the Fifth purusharth while मोक्ष as the fourth one. He says in his "Jnaneshwari".

चहु पुरुषार्थाशीरी भक्ति जैसी

Hence this Prem Bhakti becomes superior than the state of जीवन्मुक्ति. In all Bhakties mentioned above like Sahaj Bhakti, Akritrim Bhakti or Jeevan Mukti there is the experience of joy of identity with nirgun Brahma, but in the Prem Bhakti there is the experience of God's supreme love, which is not found in Brahmananda. Now the Sahaj Bhakti is also called Advait Bhakti because the experience of Brahmananda is found in the Advait Bhakti, Jnanadev in the IX chapter of Amritanubhava has said that the experience of Prem Bhakti and its outward expressions can be possible in Advait Bhakti. He gives an instance of rock in the mountain where in the same rock there can be carved a God is devotee and instrument worship, but the rock is the same, it does not become three in number so in the Advait stage these three God, worship and the means of worship are possible and there is only oneness and not separate things.

देव देऊळ परिवारु। कीजे कोरुनि डोंगरु॥
तैसा भक्तीचा वेव्हारु। कां न व्हावा॥४१॥

Here we should understand the situation of the two Bhakties. A Jeevan Mukt generally doesn't accept Prem Bhakti, but fortunately he comes in contact with a great Prem Bhakt (Loving devotees) and by contact with him he also experiences the draught of Prem Bhakti. He thirsts for such Prem Bhakti, and he is transformed into a Prem Bhakt.

In "Shrimad Bhagawat Puran" we have a verse where a Jeevan Mukt is tempted by Prem Bhakti.

आत्मारामाश्च मुनयो निर्ग्रन्था अप्युरुक्रमे।
कुर्वन्तहैतुकीं भक्तिमित्थंभूतगुणो हरिः॥

(श्रीमद् भागवत १।७।१०)

It means that even Jeevan Mukta sages like to sing the glory of Lord God.

Jnanadev also in one of his abhangas says,

ज्ञान गिळोनी गावा गोविंदा गा।

One should swallow even the joy of supreme knowledge or Mukti and sing Govind. In the Xth chapter of Amritanubhava while concluding the subject he has said

मुक्ती किर वेल्हाळ। अनुभवामृत निखिळ॥
परी अमृताही उठी लाळ। अमृतें येणें॥२०॥

This means though Mukti is nice this Anubhavamrit is very pure i.e. Pure Prem Bhakti which even Mukti when she tastes it, she also is desirous of tasting it.

III. MEETING OF GOD-LOVERS

Jnanadev has described beautifully the meeting of loving devotees in the Xth chapter of "Jnaneshwari".

He says that in their heart they have become one with God. He has become their life. By intense Love of God they have become mad and forget life and death. While communicating the sweetest happiness to each other they dance without shamefulness or without consciousness of any other things as two lakes which are in close proximity to each other send their waves into one and another as mingling waves form as it were a crest house for them. Similarly the joy of the two lovers of God mix with each other. And which becomes ornaments for each other. As the sun may wave lights before the sun or as the Moon may embrace the moon or as in full equality one stream may mix with another. Similarly the equal love of these saints makes a happy confluence on the top of which rise the sattvik emotions. Then by the power of their great happiness they run out of themselves and being filled with God then begin to proclaim to the whole world, which has passed between pupil and teacher in their privacy. These saints now proclaim to the whole world like rumbling cloud. As when the unblown Lotus-Flower begins to blowout, it cannot contain within itself its own fragrance and therefore distributes its virtue to the king and pauper alike, in that way they proclaim God to the whole world and in the joy of proclamation they forget the fact of proclaiming and in that happy forgetfulness, they sink their body and mind (X, 119-128).

BIBLIOGRAPHY

१. श्री ज्ञानदेवकृत अमृतानुभव व त्यावरील श्री शिवकल्याणकृत नित्यानंदैक्यदीपिका ... सं. अ. मो. कुंटे, प्र. निर्णयसागर प्रेस स. १८८८.

२. श्री अमृतानुभव, प्रल्हादपंत बडवे यांची संस्कृत समश्लोकी व कै. गर्दे यांची समआर्या सं. कै. खं. कृ. गर्दे प्र. के. बी. ढवळे मुंबई, मुंबई वैभव प्रेस १९२९.

३. श्री ज्ञानेश्वर विरचितामृतानुभवः ... श्रीमत्परमहंस श्रीजीवन्मुक्त-यतिवरदत्तगीर्वाणालंकरणः, सुबोधिन्याख्यया व्याख्यया समेतः मुंबई वैभव प्रेस, १९२१.

४. सटीक अमृतानुभव ... हंसराजस्वामीकृत समओवी ... प्र. का. वा. खांडेकर, मु. गणपत कृष्णाजी छापखाना स. १८९५

५. निरंजन रघुनाथांचे समग्र ग्रंथ...यांत निरंजन माधवकृत अमृतानुभवावरील अनुभवामृत....पदबोधिनी टीका आहे. सं. प्र. य. व्यं. कोल्हटकर बी. ए., एल्एल्. बी. स. १९३५.

६. अनुभवामृत...तात्पर्यबोधिनी टीकेसह. ले. वे. शा. सं. बाळशास्त्री अण्णाबुवा हुपरीकर, प्र. आबाजी रामचंद्र सावंत, श्री. रामतत्व छापखाना, बेळगांव, सन १८९८.

७. अमृतानुभव...अनुवादक वि. न. जोग, निर्णयसागर, मुंबई, स. १९०५.

८. अमृतानुभव...सार्थ व सटीक, नानामहाराज जोशी साखरे यांचे चिरंजीव विनायकबुवा, प्र. त्रिं. ह. आवटे, इंदिरा छापखाना स. १९०५.

९. अमृतानुभव...अमृतवाहिनी नामक टीकेसहित ले. आत्माराम कृष्ण केणे उर्फ ज्ञानेश्वरीबुवा श्रीगोंदेकर यांच्या टिपणावरून रा. ब. डोंगरे प्र. ज्ञा. आ. केणे, श्रीगोंदे, मु. गणेश प्रिंटिंग वर्क्स, पुणें स. १९२८.

१०. अनुभवामृत रहस्य, राजारामबुवा ब्रह्मचारी कृत, प्र. के. रा. गोंधळेकर, पुणें, स.१९१७.

११. अनुभवामृत...दीपिका, कोश, पाठभेद, अन्वय, अर्थ, विवरण यासह ले. व. प्र. सी. सुबंध पुणें मु. इंदिरा छापखाना, पुणें, स. १९३०.

१२. अमृतानुभव ... सार्थ व साकीबद्ध अनुवादासह, बा. मा. जोशी मु. प्र. अ. भट, यशवंत प्रेस, पुणें, आ. २ री. स. १९२४.

१३. अमृतानुभव भावार्थ मंजरी ... श्रीसंत कवी दासगणु कृत प्र. वि. य. मराठे, नांदेड मु. मनोरंजन प्रेस मुंबई, स. १९२९.

14. Amritanubhava or Elixir of life Tr. by A. V. Khasnis, B.A.,LL.B., Printed at Radha Printing Works, Bijapur M.S.S. (1935).

II

१. ज्ञानदेव कृत भावार्थ दीपिका ज्ञानदेवी ... सं. रा. वि. माडगांवकर, मुंबई, तत्त्वविवेचक प्रेस, स. १९०७.

२. श्री ज्ञानेश्वरी ... सं. अ. मो. कुंटे, प्र. व. मु. निर्णयसागर प्रेस, मुंबई, पंचमावृत्ति स. १९१५.

३. ज्ञानेश्वरी ... सार्थ ... वि. ना. साखरे, प्र. त्र्यं. ह. आवटे, इंदिरा छापखाना, पुणें आवृत्ति ३ री, स. १९२२.

४. ज्ञानेश्वरी ... सार्थ ... ले. व. प्र. ह, भ. प. बंकटस्वामी, मु. गणेश प्रिंटिंग वर्क्स, पुणें स. १९२७.

५. ज्ञानेश्वरी ... सं. वि. का. राजवाडे, प्र. सत्कार्योत्तेजक सभा धुळें, मु. आत्माराम छापखाना, धुळें, स. १९०९.

६. श्री ज्ञानदेवी, अ. १ ला ... सं. डॉ. रा. ग. हर्षे, मु. राजमुद्रणालय, फलटन, स. १९४७.

७. सार्थ ज्ञानेश्वरी .... बा. अ. भिडे, मुंबई वैभव प्रेस, स. १९३४

८. सार्थ ज्ञानेश्वरी ... प्रिं. शं. वा. दांडेकर, प्रसाद प्रकाशन, पुणें स. १९५३.

९. संस्कृत ज्ञानेश्वरी (अ. १–६) म. पां. ओक, पुणें, स. १९२९.

१०. गीर्वाण ज्ञानेश्वरी (अ. ७–१२) अ. वि. खासनीस, प्र. ओरिएंटल बुक एजन्सी, पुणें १९३१.

११. श्री ज्ञानेश्वरी टीका—ग. कृ. आगाशे, मिरज १९३३.

१२. ज्ञानेश्वरी मार्गदर्शिका सूचि, कृष्णानंद, पुणें १९४३.

१३. हरीपाठ व चांगदेव पासष्टी ... अर्थासह ले. ह. भ. प. विष्णुबुवा जोग प्र. ल. रा. पांगारकर, मु. हनुमान छापखाना, पुणें आ. ३ री स. १९१९.

१४. प्रेमामृत—(हरिपाठ विवरण)–मो. सुं. संझगिरी, बी. ए., मुंबई.

१५. हरिपाठ-रहस्य—श्री बाबाजी महाराज, १९५४, पुणें.

१६. हरिपाठ विवरण–श्री धुंडामहाराज देगलूरकर, औरंगाबाद, १९५५.

१७. पासष्टी ... प्रदीप....सं. व. प्र. प्र. सी. सुबंध मु. मुंबई वैभव प्रेस, १९३६.

१८. श्री पासष्टी भावार्थ दीपिका .... दासगणु महाराज कृत प्र. वि. ल. सुबंध, मनोरंजन प्रेस, मुंबई स. १९३१.

१९. ज्ञानदेवाची गाथा ... सं. ह. भ. प. विष्णुबुवा जोग, प्र. त्रि. ह. आवटे, इंदिरा छापखाना, पुणें स. १९०७.

२०. ज्ञानेश्वर वचनामृत ... डॉ. रा. द. रानडे, एम्. ए., डी. लिट्. गणेश प्रिंटिंग वर्क्स व आर्यभूषण प्रेस, पुणें, स. १९३३.

२१. ज्ञानदेवाची भजनें ... सं. विनोबा ... प्र. ग्राम-सेवा-मंडळ, वर्धा, स. १९५२.

२२. संतवचनामृत ... डॉ. रा. द. रानडे (स. १९३३).

२३. श्री सकल संत-गाथा...सं. गो. शं. राहिरकर, भा. पं. बहिरट, एम्. ए. व भोगीलाल कंपनी, बी. ए., एल्. एल्. बी., प्रेमबोध प्रकाशन, पुणें, १९५५.

24. Dnyaneshwari (English Translation) by R. K. Bhagawat, Poona 1954.

२५. चांगदेव पासष्टी–सं. पांडुरंग शर्मा, पुणें, १९५५.

III

१. प्रिं. शं. वा. दांडेकर, एम्. ए. ... श्रीज्ञानदेव चरित्र ग्रंथ व तत्त्वज्ञान, मु. गणेश प्रिंटिंग वर्क्स, पुणें स. १९३२.

२. प्रिं. शं. वा. दांडेकर, एम्. ए. ... वारकरी पंथाचा इतिहास, मु. इंदिरा छापखाना, पुणें स. १९२७.

३. श्री. बाळशास्त्री हुपरीकर ... विद्यारण्य व ज्ञानेश्वर प्र. वि. गो. विजापूरकर एम्. ए., समर्थ प्रसाद छापखाना, स. १९०२.

४. श्री. बाळशास्त्री हुपरीकर... शंकराचार्य व ज्ञानेश्वर, प्र. वि. गो. विजापूरकर, एम्. ए., समर्थ प्रसाद छापखाना, स. १९०२.

५. डॉ. शं. दा. पेंडसे, एम्. ए., पी. एच्. डी.... श्रीज्ञानेश्वरांचे तत्त्वज्ञान, प्र. के. भी. ढवळे, मुंबई, सन १९४१.

६. श्री. बा. म. हंस...ज्ञानदेव...सं. प्रा. ऊर्ध्वरेषे पुनर्मुद्रण, १९४२.

७. श्री. भारद्वाज...ज्ञानदेव व ज्ञानेश्वर...प्र. गं. म. दाभोळकर, चित्रशाळा प्रेस, पुणें, स. १९३१.

८. प्रो. मा. दा. आळतेकर, श्री. ज्ञानदेव, मुंबई, १९४०.

९. श्री. वा. का. कामत, ... ज्ञानेश्वरी हृदय .... प्र. कृ. ह. चिंचोरे बी. ए., मु. मधुकर प्रिंटिंग प्रेस, बेळगांव, आ. ३ री. स. १९३८.

१०. श्री. न. चिं. केळकर... ज्ञानेश्वरी सर्वस्व, प्र. म. म. केळकर, पुणें स. १९४६.

११. श्री. ल. रा. पांगारकर ... ज्ञानदेव चरित्र व ग्रंथ विवेचन, प्र. ढवळे, मुंबई, स. १९५४.

१२. डॉ. शं. गो. तुळपुळे... पांच संतकवी...आनंद मुद्रणालय, पुणें १९४८.

१३. श्री. ल. रा. पांगारकर ... मराठी वाङ्मयाचा इतिहास ... खंड १ ला, ज्ञानेश्वर नामदेवांचा काल...मुंबई वैभव प्रेस, स. १९३२.

१४. श्री. वि. ल. भावे ... महाराष्ट्रसारस्वत ... प्र. भारत इतिहास संशोधक मंडळ, पुणें, स. १९१९. (चतुर्थावृत्ति पुरवणीसह स. १९५२).

१५. ज्ञानेश्वर दर्शन भाग १ व २, प्र. ज्ञानेश्वर मंडळ नगर स. १९३४.

१६. प्रा. गं. बा. सरदार, एम्. ए. ... संतवाङ्मयाची सामाजिक फलश्रुती, प्र. म. सा. परिषद, पुणें, स. १९५०.

१७. प्रा. र. न. फाटक...श्रीज्ञानेश्वर, वाङ्मय आणि कार्य....प्र. वा. पु. भागवत, मुंबई, १९५२.

१८. डॉ. शं. दा. पेंडसे...ज्ञानेश्वरीचा अभ्यास, प्र. शिक्षण प्रसारक मंडळी, पुणें, स. १९५४.

१९. प्रिं. शं. वा. दांडेकर...श्री ज्ञानदेवांचें जीवन विषयक तत्त्वज्ञान, प्र. नागपूर विद्यापीठ स. १९५५.

२०. पांच संप्रदाय...पं. रा. मोकाशी, एम्. ए., प्र. प्रसाद प्रकाशन, पुणें, स. १९५४.

२१. संतवाणीचा अमृतकलश...भा. पं. बहिरट, एम्. ए., पंढरपूर संशोधक मंडळ, स. १९५५.

22. Prof. R. D. Ranade—Mysticism in Maharashtra.
,, ,, —Pathway to God, 1954.

23. Edwards — Jnanadeva, the Outcast Brahmin, Poona 1941.

२४. प्रो. शं. गो. वाळिंवे....ज्ञानेश्वर चरित्र आणि ज्ञानेश्वरी चर्चा, प्र. मयूर एजन्सी, १९५०.

२५. श्रीज्ञानेश्वर माउलीची ज्ञानोत्तर प्रेमभक्ति, ना. वा. काळे, नागझरी, १९५३.

२६. प्र. श्री. ना. बनहट्टी–वाङ्मय विमर्श, चित्रशाळा पुणें, १९५५.

IV

1. Dr. R. G. Bhandarkar — Vaishnavism, Shaivism and Minor Religious systems.
2. Dr. S. N. Dassgupta — Indian Idealism.
,, ,, — History of Indian Philosophy Vol. I-IV
4. Dr. K. M. Sen — Medieval Mysticism of India.
5. Deusson — Philosophy of Upanishadas.
6. J. C. Chatarji, B. A. — Kashmir Shaivism.
7. Dr. B. L. Attreya — Yoga-Vasisth and Its Philosophy.
8. Prof. Shrinivasachari — The Philosophy of Vishistadvait.
9. Dr. B. N. Krishnamurti — Madhwa's Theistic Realism.
10. Dr. P. T. Raju — Thought and Reality.
11. Dr. Sarkar M. N. — Vedantism.
12. Max Mullar — Six systems of Indian Philosophy.

13. Dr. R. Metz — A Hundred years of British Philosophy.
14. Bergson — Two sources of Morality and Religion.
15. Pringle — Pattison — Idea of God.
16. Bakewell — Source Book of Ancient Philosophy.
17. Prof. Hiriyanna — Outlines of Indian Philosophy.
18. P. Nagaraj Rao M. A. — Schools of Vedant.
19. Bradley — Appearance and Reality.
20. Saraswati Bhavan Studies Vol. II.
21. Naradabhakti Sutram, Ed. L. R. Pangarkar, (1927).
22. Shandilya Sutra with the commentary of Swapneshwar, Pub. Panini office, Allahabad (1925).
23. Shuddhadvait Martand — by Goswami Giridhar (Chowkhambai series).
24. Yatindramatadipika of Shrinivas (Anandashram,) with the commentary of M. M. Abhyandar.
25. Vedantparijata — Saurabha of Nimbark (Chowkhamba Samskrit series).
26. Upadhikhandan of Madhwacharya with the commentary of Jaytirth, Kumbhakonam (1927).
27. Gorakhanatha — Siddhasiddhanta Paddhati.
28. Brahma Sutra — Shankar Bhashya. (Nirnaya sagar) .
29. Bramha Sutra Ramanuja Bhashya. With shrutaprakashika (Nirnayasagar Press).
30. Shivasutras with Vimarihini (Kashmir series) 1911.

V

(Articles)

1. Dr. Jadunath Sinha — "Bhagwat Religion, The cult of Bhakti" In The Cultural Heritage of India Vol.

II Published by Shri Ramakrishna Centinery Committee, Belur.

2. Prof. A. K. Banerjee "The Shiva-Shakti cult of Yogi Guru Gorakhanatha", Prabudha Bharat (Oct. and Nov. 1943)

3. Subandha P. S. — Namdeva Magazine Sept. 1943.

4. Dr. D. G. Londhe — "Philosophy of Dnyanadeva", in the proceedings of the Second session of The Indian Philosophical Congress (1926).

5. Prof. S. V. Dandekar — Tatwajnanmandir Traimasik, XIX — 1, 2, 3.

6. Shri Pandurang Sharma — Chitramayajagat, August 1921 — June 1923.

7. Mr. Kanole — Bharat Itihas Samshodhak Mandal Traimasik Ashadha 1874.

8. Dr. Grierson — "Bhakti Marga", Encyclopaedia of Religion and Ethics.

VI

(Manuscripts.)

1. Bhayyakaka Kibe — Jyotsna — a commentary on Amt. in Marathi Prose.

2. Vireshwar — A Commentary on Amt.

3. Harihar (?) — "Rashtra Bhashya" — Com. on Amt. partly in Sanskrit and partly in Marathi.

SUPPLEMENTARY BIBLIOGRAPHY

(1) अनुभवामृत—सं० डॉ० वा० दा० गोखले

प्र० नीलकंठ प्रकाशन, पुणे (1967)

Nearby 200 manuscripts are collated and various different readings noted.

(2) सार्थ अनुभवामृत व चांगदेव पासष्टी

प्रा० शं० वा० दांडेकर

सं० व प्र० सुपडु महाजन, वारकरी शिक्षण संस्था, आलंदी (1978)

Notes of Prof. Dandekar were taken down by Shri Mahajan & published. Prof. Dandekar defends स्फुर्तिवाद of Jñānadeva. He says that it was originally put forth by Kashmir Śaivism. Jñānadeva has refuted in Amṛtānubhava various objections brought against it.

(3) अमृतानुभव—प्रा० विं० दा० करंदीकर

(प्र० मौज प्रकाशन, मुंबई)

This is a versification of Amṛtānubhava in current Marathi, with a fine introduction appreciating Jñānadeva's गूढाद्वैत as well as his poetic excellence.

(4) अनुभवामृत—राष्ट्रभाष्य

(सं० भा० पं० बहिरट, म०म० पोतदार, पं० बालाचार्य खुपेरकर)

(प्र० संतवाङ्मय मंडल, पंढरपूर) (1966)

This is a commentary on अनुभवामृत by Harihar (died 1819 A.D.) which is partly in Sanskrit and partly in old Marathi. हरिहर was a great scholar and criticises the concept of माया.

(5) श्रीचांगदेव—पञ्चषष्टि:

सटीक संस्कृतानुवाद : by Shri L.V. Deshpande

(प्र० मनोहर ग्रंथमाला, पुणे) (1972)

(6) ज्ञानदेव व प्लेटो—प्रि० शं० वा० दांडेकर
(प्र० शिक्षण प्रसारक मंडली, पुणे) (1967)

(7) ज्ञानेश्वरांची जीवननिष्ठा—प्रा० गं० बा० सरदार
(प्र० शिक्षण प्रसारक मंडली, पुणे) (1971)

(8) श्री शैवागम व ज्ञानेश्वर—पं० बालाचार्य खुपेरकर
(प्र० शि० प्र० मंडली, पुणे) (1960)

(9) Dnyandeva—Prof. S.V. Dandekar (Pub. Maharashtra Information Centre, New Delhi) (1969).

(10) Jñānadeva—Shri P.Y. Deshpande (Pub. Sahitya Academy, New Delhi) (1973)

(11) Jñānadeshwari
(English Translation by Shri Pradhan)
(Pub. George Allen & Unwin Ltd. London) (1972)

(12) ज्ञानेश्वर प्रणीत भक्तियोग—प्रा० स० र० गाडगील
(प्र० दास्ताने रामचंद्र कंपनी, पुणे) (1980)

(13) भक्ति साधना—भा० पं० बहिरट
(प्र० मॅजेस्टिक बुकस्टाल, मुंबई 4) (1981)

(14) वारकरी संप्रदाय—उदय व विकास—भा० पं० बहिरट व प० ज्ञा० भालेराव
(व्हीनस प्रकाशन, पुणे) (1972)

(15) ज्ञानेश्वरांचे तत्वज्ञान—प्रा० पद्मा कुलकर्णी
(Academy of Philosophy & Religion, Belgaum) (1978)

INDEX

K

L

M